KB's History Of In Your House

By Thomas Hall

A look back at a WWF pay per view series that spanned nearly four years, running from the New Generation into the heart of the Attitude Era with a string of both masterpieces and absolutely terrible matches along the way. We'll be looking back through each of the twenty eight entries in the series with each show broken down match by match and segment by segment. Included will be history, analysis, play by play and ratings of every match on every show.

Introduction

Pay per views (PPVs) are something I'm sure you're all familiar with. They're the mega shows that the weekly TV shows build up to and most of the major matches happen at these events. Today the PPV market has been changed due to the introduction of streaming, mainly through the WWE Network. That wasn't always the case though and it used to be quite expensive.

When pay per view first started, you could count the number of events in a year on a single hand. Wrestling on pay per view was introduced in 1985 and it wasn't until 1987 that more than one WWF event aired in a calendar year. Compare that to today, when you can barely go a full month without a pay per view and occasionally have more than one a month, especially if a company other than WWE gets involved.

So when did everything start changing? As is usually the case, it came in the 1990s. WCW's Eric Bischoff came up with a simple idea: if the fans will buy four PPVs a year, maybe they'll buy seven a year. Eric was proven correct, so the number of PPVs kept increasing until we reached the stable number of one a month. However, this became very expensive as the shows sold for $30 apiece, meaning getting every PPV from one company would cost over $200 a year. For many fans, that was simply out of the questions, especially for younger fans who didn't have jobs yet.

However there was hope on the horizon in 1995. At the time, the WWF only held five PPVs a year: the traditional Big Four (Royal Rumble, Wrestlemania, Summerslam and Survivor Series) plus King of the Ring. The decision was made to add more PPVs to the lineup, but these would be different than the usual shows. The solution was the focus of this book: the In Your House series.

These shows wouldn't be the typical shows for three reasons. First of all, they would only run two hours as opposed to the usual three. Second, the main events would be at a lower level of importance than the major shows. However there was a major trade off for these two downgrades: the first five of them would sell for the far lower cost of $15, with the sixth seeing a price raise to a still significantly lower than usual $20. It was a very smart move as the shows did solid numbers (by comparison to the major shows) due to the lower costs.

That brings us to why you're reading this. We're going to be looking at all 28 In Your House PPVs and breaking down each match, segment and show as a whole to see what worked, what didn't work and how the stories progressed. I'll also be including interludes between the shows to explain events that happened at the other non-In Your House PPVs. These shows ran from June of 1995 until April of 1999 so there's a lot of ground to cover. Let's get to it.

I'll be grading each match (Assuming it lasts over three minutes. I really don't find it fair to rate a match if it doesn't last that long as how good or bad can it be in so little time?) on a scale of A+ to F- just like you probably saw in school. Most of the matches are long enough to rate and while some are worse than others, there's always something to talk about in each one.

Keep in mind that these are nearly twenty years old but I'll try to not look too far into the future, unless there is something that jumps of the page. I'll also try to reference things that were happening around the time for the sake of some clarification and context. For the most part I'm sure you can figure out what's going on, but there may be a thing or two going on at the time that could change your perception of what happened on the show.

Also note that there were some dark matches taped after most of the earlier events. Most of them are available to see elsewhere, but since they were not part of the official pay per view, I won't be including them. Most of them were little more than a way to pad out the show as charging full ticket prices for a two hour show would have been a really bad idea.

Finally I'm going to assume you know who most of the bigger names are as well as their finishing moves. I really don't think you need a lesson on who people like Bret Hart or Diesel are or what the Stone Cold Stunner or Sweet Chin Music are and it would be a waste of your time to explain them in more than very basic detail.

Crawling In The Dark

We'll start with a bit of background for the first show. It's June of 1995 and the WWF is running on Diesel Power. The 7'0 monster possibly more famous as Kevin Nash has been WWF Champion since November and no one has been able to stop him. His title is on the line at our first show as he defends against another giant named Sid. Sid was Shawn Michaels' bodyguard after Shawn had fired none other than Diesel himself. Diesel retained his title against Shawn at Wrestlemania XI back in April and Sid attacked Shawn the following night, saying he could fight on his own.

The other major match we have is Bret Hart vs. Japanese star Hakushi in a fondly remember encounter. Bret is arguably the biggest star in the company but had (falsely) been accused of making discouraging remarks about Japanese fans. Hakushi is here to defend the honor of his homeland and prove that Japan is greater than Bret's home country of Canada. Bret will also be facing his long time rival Jerry Lawler later on in the night.

In Your House #1
Date: May 14, 1995
Location: Onondaga War Memorial, Syracuse, New York
Attendance: 7,000
Commentators: Vince McMahon, Doc Hendrix

Other than the matches mentioned, the main story tonight is the WWF giving away an actual house down in Florida to play up the In Your House name. This was a major idea that was heavily promoted on WWF television leading up to the show. It was a nice marketing idea as it gave some adults a reason to care about the show and possibly buy it for their kids. Let's get to it.

The opening video talks about the clash of the giants as well as several other matches on the card.

It's Mother's Day, meaning the announcers are going to talk about moms a lot tonight.

The set is exactly what you would expect: a big house with the wrestlers walking through the garage to get to the ring.

Bret Hart vs. Hakushi

Hakushi has his manager Shinja (rocking a white suit) with him. Bret is in the back and says he's going to prove how great he is and that he's dedicated this match to his mother. How nice of him. Hakushi is a very unique looking wrestler as he has Japanese characters all over himself, giving him a nickname of the walking Japanese menu. Bret grabs a headlock to start but Hakushi easily escapes to a standoff. Now Bret tries the arm, only to be pulled to the mat by the hair.

The geographically confused fans chant USA as Hakushi takes Bret down with a flying headbutt for two. It's off to an armbar as this is still firmly in first gear. The stupid USA chant begins again, or maybe they're all fans of the referee? Now it's Bret on the arm before easily armdragging Hakushi down again, this time to the floor for a breather. Back in and Bret pounds away as things start to pick up again. Hakushi comes back with a kick to the face and what would eventually be called a Vader Bomb for a near fall.

Jerry Lawler is watching gleefully in the back as he still gets to face Bret later in the night. Hakushi stomps Bret down in the corner and hits what we would call a Bronco Buster before stopping to pose. Back up and Hakushi blocks an O'Connor Roll, sending Bret to the floor so he can be stomped even more by Shinja. Another Shinja distraction allows Hakushi to choke even more as the crowd is getting into this. Bret's comeback is easily stopped by a tilt-a-whirl backbreaker, setting up a swan dive headbutt from Hakushi for two. Hakushi's springboard splash misses completely and Bret is back on his feet.

Bret comes back with the Five Moves of Doom (Russian legsweep, backbreaker, middle rope elbow, atomic drop, Sharpshooter, pick an order for the first four) but he has to stop and deal with Shinja again. Bret pounds away on Hakushi but gets tripped by Shinja AGAIN, finally causing him to dive through the ropes and pound away, hopefully not ruining the suit (that would be a shame).

Back in and Hart reverses a suplex into one of his own, sending both guys out to the floor in a nice crash. Shinja's distraction allows Hakushi to get back up and hit a top rope Asai moonsault to take both guys down again. Hart's ankle might have been

5

twisted in the process. Bret is pulled back in but has his rollup countered into an attempted German suplex, only to counter that into a victory roll to finally put Hakushi away at 14:39.

Rating: B. Really solid match here and a great way to open up the show as well as the series. Hakushi wasn't really much of note after this but that's what Bret was best at: getting the most out of anyone he worked with. Really fun match here which had the time to get going and build into what it needed to be.

Post match, Bret twists his knee getting to the floor. I'm sure that's completely legitimate.

A way too excited woman looks at the entries in the sweepstakes for the house. We even get a video of the truck bringing the entries here earlier today.

Jeff Jarrett/Roadie vs. Razor Ramon

Handicap match here after Roadie (more famous as the Road Dogg) helped Jarrett take Razor's Intercontinental Title at the Royal Rumble. Razor's normal partner the 1-2-3 Kid is out with an injury and calls in to say he's watching the match. In the back, Razor also dedicates this match to his mom. Vince yells about Roadie and Jarrett both being in the ring to start, prompting Hayes to say that Vince doesn't make the rules around here in a funny line.

Jarrett starts for the team and is promptly punched down and then slapped in the face. Roadie is lurking around the floor before getting back up on the apron. Back in and Jeff misses a dropkick before being clotheslined hard out to the floor. Roadie gets in a cheap shot to take Razor down from behind, allowing Jarrett to connect with an enziguri to take over. Not that it matters though as Ramon catches Jeff's crossbody in the fall away slam for two.

Roadie comes in for his first match and scores with a quick clothesline and a snapmare to put him down. Back to Jarrett who gets a quick two off a sunset flip before Razor gets the same off a small package. Not exactly thrilling stuff so far but they're not boring the people to death. After more basic stuff from Roadie it's back to Jeff, only to have him jump right into a punch to the ribs. Razor is backdropped out to the floor and there goes his bad knee again. Roadie adds a middle rope clothesline and Ramon is in big trouble.

Back in and Ramon is dazed but still manages to roll through a top rope crossbody from Jeff into a two count, only to be taken right back down with a neckbreaker. Jeff's running hip attack only hits ropes but Razor collides with him, putting both guys down again. Ramon has the word Kid written on his boots. Back up again and Razor hits a belly to back suplex, putting both guys down one more time.

Jeff is able to make the tag before Razor can get up and it's Roadie hitting a middle rope knee drop for two. We hit the chinlock for a bit before Razor fights up and jawbreaks his way to freedom, putting both guys down for the third time in five minutes. Razor suplexes both guys down but Jeff goes to the bad knee to slow him up. The Figure Four is kicked away though, sending Jeff into Roadie and a quick Razor's Edge takes Jeff out for the pin at 12:36.

Rating: C. Not bad here but it could have been the same match in about half the time. On top of that the knee injury really didn't play much of a role in the match after the announcers talked so much about how bad Razor's knee was. This feud wouldn't last much longer but it worked pretty well for both Jarrett and Ramon.

Post match the heels go after the knee but Portuguese wrestler Aldo Montoya tries to make the save. That goes nowhere so here's an unnamed man from the crowd for the real save, only to have him be taken away by police.

Jerry Lawler wants to face Bret right now but WWF President Jack Tunney says no.

Video on Sid dominating his way to the title match tonight.

King of the Ring Qualifying Match: Mabel vs. Adam Bomb

Bomb is about 6'4 and over 300lb but Mabel towers over him at 6'10 and 508lb. Mabel has recently turned heel so he jumps Bomb before the bell rings. A splash in the corner has Bomb in trouble but he comes back with right hands to send Mabel to the floor. Adam dives out onto Mabel and pounds away before sending him back inside for a pair of top rope clotheslines, getting two each. Not that it matters much though as Mabel catches Adam's crossbody and falls down on him (think Mark Henry's World's Strongest Slam) for the pin at 1:54. Mabel was his usual worthless self here.

Razor introduces the man that saved him as Caribbean wrestling legend Savio Vega.

Tag Team Titles: Smoking Gunns vs. Yokozuna/Owen Hart

Hart and Yokozuna are defending after Yokozuna returned as Owen's mystery partner at Wrestlemania, where they took the belts from the Gunns (Billy and Bart). They're also managed by Mr. Fuji and Jim Cornette. Before the match, Lawler is out here again but still can't get his match with Bret at the moment. Billy tries to grab a headlock on the 600lb+ Yokozuna and it works as well as you would expect it to. A pair of dropkicks work a bit better but Yoko headbutts Bart down before bringing in Owen.

The Gunns can handle a guy Owen's size and take him down with a nice dropkick/suplex combination, only to go after Yoko again for some reason. Hart comes back with an enziguri to take Billy down before it's back to Yoko for a big clothesline. We hit the nerve hold on Billy before Owen gets two off a neckbreaker.

A great looking enziguri puts Billy on the outside but he avoids a charge, sending Yoko into the post. Owen misses a charge of his own and there's the somewhat hot tag off to Bart. A suplex puts Hart down and the Gunns hit a belly to back/neckbreaker combo for another two before Bart misses a dive and lands on the floor. Yoko drops a leg to crush him ever further before throwing him back in to Owen for the retaining pin at 5:44.

Rating: D+. The match wasn't anything great but with less than six minutes there's only so much they could have done. The problem with Yokozuna is there's only so much anyone can do against him and it makes it hard to work around him. Not a horrible match due to Owen but it still wasn't anything of note.

Diesel is sad because his mom died right after Christmas so he wishes all the other Mother's a good day. He's sore from an attack by Henry Godwinn but says he's 100%. Diesel is also glad that Shawn Michaels will be watching at ringside.

8

Here's Jerry Lawler in the ring with his.....mother, who looks to be about 24 years old. She wants to see Lawler, who is in his mid 40s here, beat Bret and then challenge Bret's mom to a fight.

We cut to the back to see Bret almost dancing because, in classic Hart fashion, he faked the injury.

Jerry Lawler vs. Bret Hart

Jerry didn't see the interview so Bret limps to the ring again, only to climb in with ease. Lawler tries to run but gets caught in the corner where Bret pounds away. Bret takes him down with a slam and some legdrops followed by a BIG backdrop. It's all Hart so far but Lawler comes back with a quick piledriver (his finisher) but Bret is up in just a few seconds. He pounds way on Jerry in the corner again before piledriving Lawler down for one.

Jerry comes back with a slam of his own while going up top, only to jump into Bret's fist to the ribs. Bret pounds away but here's Shinja to distract Hart for about the 12th time tonight. The referee is knocked into the ropes and gets his ankle tied up in the ropes as Bret hits the Russian legsweep. Hakushi comes in and takes out Bret with a kick to the head and two top rope headbutts, giving Lawler the easy pin at 5:01.

Rating: D+. Again, this didn't have the time to go anywhere as the last two matches haven't even combined to go 11 minutes. Lawler vs. Hart was a feud that went on for over two years and would culminate soon enough, though this wasn't the best entry in their series. It did further both itself and Bret vs. Hakushi though, so well done on the double booking.

Post match Bret gets up but Lawler escapes with his "mom".

Sid very slowly says he'll win the title and that he rules the world.

We look at the sweepstakes house in Orlando. Interviewer Todd Pettengill finds some rakes in the garage so he and the annoying interview can mix up the entries before drawing out the winner whom they call with the results. Thankfully this only takes about five minutes.

The announcers talk about the main event for a bit.

WWF Title: Sycho Sid vs. Diesel

Diesel is defending of course and Sid has Ted DiBiase as his manager. The idea here is they both use powerbombs as their finishers, which should tell you a lot about this match. Diesel fires off forearms to start and hits some running clotheslines in the corner to stagger Sid. An elbow to the jaw puts Sid on the floor and it's time for a breather. Back in and three straight clotheslines get two on Sid as this is all Diesel so far. Sid pulls Diesel to the outside and knocks him down to take over for the first time.

Diesel is sent into the apron and post as the match slows way down with the challenger in control. A running boot to the side of the head has Diesel in even more trouble before they head back inside for clubbing forearms to Diesel's back. Sid stops to pose, meaning he didn't pay attention to the opening match. More shots to the back have Diesel in even more trouble and we hit a camel clutch. After about a minute and a half in the hold Diesel fights out, only to have Sid cannonball down onto his back for two.

Back to the camel clutch with Sid leaning forward, as in the exact opposite of what he's supposed to be doing. At least pull your arms back man. Diesel starts breaking it, presumably out of boredom, and avoids a second cannonball attempt. Not that it matters though as Sid chokeslams him down and hits a quick powerbomb but poses instead of covering. DiBiase freaks out until Diesel is up at about two and one tenth. Diesel avoids a charge into the corner and drops Sid face first onto the buckle. There are the big boot and the Jackknife powerbomb but DiBiase's other man Tatanka comes in for the DQ at 11:31.

Rating: D. There's a reason you rarely see matches with the same style going for a long time: they're not very good. The styles clash is too much to overcome and when it's such a basic style like these two have, it doesn't work well at all. Two similar styles can work, but you better be awesome at that style. Sid isn't particularly good at anything in the ring and this was a prime example.

Post match Sid, Tatanka and DiBiase triple team Diesel until Bam Bam Bigelow, who DiBiase fired a month earlier, makes the save. Wasn't Shawn supposed to be watching live?

Overall Rating: D+. The opening match was solid stuff but after that everything flew by until the horrible main event. This was a bad time for the company as Diesel wasn't very interesting on top of the card but he could have good matches with the right opponents. Sid was so far from the right opponent that he was left, making for a bad match. Not much to see here but things would get a lot better. Also, the show only ran for 96 minutes, which just isn't enough to go anywhere.

Not a lot would change over the next two months. The main event of King of the Ring (the show between the first two In Your Houses) saw Diesel and Bigelow defeating Tatanka and Sid while Mabel won the King of the Ring tournament. Shawn Michaels has also made his return and set his sights on Jeff Jarrett and the Intercontinental Title. The main event for our second show is Diesel vs. Sid II, this time in a lumberjack match.

In Your House #2: The Lumberjacks
Date: July 23, 1995
Location: Nashville Municipal Auditorium, Nashville, Tennessee
Attendance: 6,482
Commentators: Vince McMahon, Jerry Lawler

This is more or less the sequel to In Your House #1, which is odd given there being an entirely separate PPV in between. Almost all of the matches are continuations of feuds from the first show with only one or two being added from King of the Ring. Sid vs. Diesel almost has to be better than the first time around. Literally, it can't be as bad as it was the first time. Let's get to it.

The opening video has a country music video theme.

Vince talks about gold and platinum crushing people's souls in Nashville.

Roadie vs. 1-2-3 Kid

Kid jumps Roadie in the aisle and we're off and running. Back in and Roadie tries to speed things up but lands face first on the mat instead. Kid comes out of the corner with a headscissors to send Roadie to the outside and there's a slingshot kick to the face to put him down again. They get back inside again with Roadie catching a charging Kid in a powerslam. Jeff Jarrett is getting ready for his concert later instead of watching his friend's match.

Roadie hits a Cactus Clothesline to put both guys on the floor before sending Kid face first into the post. A backdrop gets two as Jarrett is talking to his backup singers. Kid fights up from a chinlock and avoids a top rope splash to put Roadie down. A spinwheel kick gets two for the Kid and his top rope splash connects for two more. Kid's hurricanrana is caught in a powerbomb for two. Kid goes up and gets crotched, allowing

Roadie to hit a sloppy piledriver off the middle rope (which could have gone very badly) for the pin at 7:26.

Rating: D+. This didn't do it for me at all as it wasn't very fast paced and most of the match was spent doing basic stuff. Roadie was nothing special in the ring as no one cared about him yet and he hadn't figured out how to show off his charisma. He actually quit the day after this show due to unknown reasons before coming back a few months later. The ending looked better than anything else they could have done though.

Ted DiBiase and the Million Dollar Team says they're ready to help Sid get the title tonight.

Men on a Mission vs. Razor Ramon/Savio Vega

Men on a Mission is King Mabel and Sir Mo, with the latter being one of the most worthless people to ever step inside a ring. Mabel beat Vega to win the King of the Ring with Ramon in Vega's corner. Razor has heavily taped ribs which has kept him out of action for about six weeks but he takes the tape off and throws it at Mabel. Mo starts with Ramon and gets a toothpick in his face for good measure. Razor ducks a clothesline and catches Mo in a fall away slam to show how good his ribs are.

It's off to Savio for some chops and a clothesline takes Mo down again. Mo gets away long enough for the tag to the big king but Savio speeds away at first. It doesn't last long though as Mabel catches him in a Boss Man Slam for a close two. Mabel: "GET UP BOY AND KNEEL TO THE KING!" The big man actually hits an enziguri for two on Savio but the match slows from there as Mabel can't keep up the pace.

Back to Mo who gets two off a suplex before it's off to Mabel for a slam and a nerve hold. Vega actually tries a slam but the 220lb man can't slam a guy over twice that size. Mabel snaps Savio's neck across the top rope before Mo chokes away a bit more. Mabel drops a big leg on Savio's neck but Mo misses a horrible looking moonsault.

The hot tag brings in Razor to clean house and a belly to back superplex gets two on Mo but Sir gets in a shot to the ribs to stop Razor cold. Mabel comes in and goes up, only to be slammed down to really fire up the crowd. Mo cheats again but Mabel

13

misses an elbow drop, giving Razor two. Vega and Mo fight to the floor and Mabel crushes Razor in the corner. A belly to belly suplex gets the pin for the King at 10:09.

Rating: D+. Mabel was built up as a monster, looked like a monster and fought like a monster. There was just one problem with him: he wasn't any good. It's as simple as that. The size was all he had going for him, yet he he was pushed for months and months as a top heel. Is there any wonder why this was such a horrid time for the company?

There's a rumor that Ted DiBiase has bought off at least one of Diesel's lumberjacks but they all deny it.

We go to the Roadie (called Road Dogg here by Vince) for Jeff Jarrett's intro. The idea was Jeff had sworn he could sing for months now but finally has to back it up. After talking for awhile, Jeff sings With My Baby Tonight, though the voice sounds a bit like a certain Dogg that we've heard many times over the years. As I mentioned Roadie and Jarrett both left the next day, which stopped the reveal of Jeff lip syncing to Roadie's voice. The fans seem split but almost no one is thrilled.

Henry Godwinn vs. Bam Bam Bigelow

Henry, a big hog farmer (1995 was weird) is an associate of DiBiase but not a full member of the Million Dollar Team. Bigelow runs him over to start and catches him in a belly to back suplex to take over. Another belly to back sets up a shoulder block to send Henry out to the floor. Back in and a DDT drops Godwinn again but he low bridges Bigelow to the floor. You can easily see the lack of effort or interest from either guy here.

Henry slams Bigelow on the floor before a clothesline gets two for Godwinn back inside. We hit the chinlock for a bit before Henry grabs the slop bucket. That goes nowhere so here's even more choking as the match just keeps going. A slam gets two on Bam Bam but he comes back with some slow motion headbutts. Bigelow misses a top rope headbutt but avoids a middle rope knee drop before quickly pinning Henry at 5:33. I'm pretty sure that was a legitimate injury, leading to the fast pin.

Rating: F. If they don't care, why in the world should I either? It was clear that neither guy had any interest in the match and it was very slow and dull as a result. Bigelow would be gone soon and Henry would become a lovable country boy with Hillbilly Jim as his manager, which was the best thing that ever happened to him.

Former WWF Champion Bob Backlund looks for registered voters as he campaigns for President of the United States. Just go with it.

Shawn Michaels is talking a mile a minute and says he's giving himself a late birthday present by winning the Intercontinental Title.

Intercontinental Title: Shawn Michaels vs. Jeff Jarrett

Jarrett is defending and Roadie gives him a VERY long intro before we get to the match. The place goes nuts for Shawn, who is at his peak here as his path to the WWF Title is about to begin. Jeff poses on the ropes before the match but bails when Shawn grabs the belt to check out his looks. Back in and we have the first lockup after a minute, only to see Shawn punch Jeff into the corner for more stalling. Michaels lays on the top rope for a breather to tick the champion off even more.

Jarrett armdrags Shawn down and struts a bit before they run the ropes to speed things up, only for a right hand to drop Shawn to the floor. Jeff lays on the top as well in a nice mind game. Back in and they fight over a hiptoss before speeding things up again with Shawn hitting the hiptoss and clotheslining Jeff to the floor, only to skin the cat back inside. Jarrett teases walking out but slides back in at 9, only to head right back to the floor. Jeff counts along with the referee but breaks the count at nine again.

Shawn finally gets tired of waiting and heads out to the floor to bring Jarrett back in, only to dive into another right hand. Shawn holds the ropes to avoid a dropkick but has to knock Roadie to the floor. A charging Jarrett is thrown over the top onto Roadie, followed by a BIG dive off the top to take out both guys.

Back in and Shawn goes to the middle rope but Jeff dives to the mat to avoid a crossbody. Shawn held on though and catches Jeff with a sunset flip for two, only to be backdropped over the top and out to the floor. This has been great stuff so far. Back in again and a gordbuster (front suplex with Shawn landing on his head) gets two for the champ, followed by the abdominal stretch. Roadie helps Jeff but finally gets caught, allowing Shawn to hiptoss his way to freedom.

Jarrett takes Shawn's head off with a dropkick for two as Vince's mic goes out, leaving Lawler alone on commentary. Roadie gets caught cheating again as Vince's mic comes back on. Shawn is sent to the floor again but the referee won't let Jeff dive on him, allowing Roadie to get in a clothesline off the apron. Michaels makes it back in at nine and immediately rolls through a high crossbody for two. A Jarrett sunset flip is blocked for two but the counter is countered into the sunset flip for two more as this continues to be fast paced.

We hit a sleeper from the champion but Shawn fights up and suplexes his way out of it. Both guys are down but Shawn rolls over at nine and gets his arm on Jeff for two. Shawn is getting fired up and snaps off some right hands to take over. A backdrop puts Jeff down and a spinning ax handle off the top gets the same. The elbow drop gets the same for Shawn but he can't put Jarrett away.

Shawn slips under a boot in the corner and crotches the champion against the post. Jeff grabs the referee, allowing Roadie to crotch Shawn o the top rope. There's a superplex to Shawn but the Figure Four is countered into a small package for two. Now it's time to go after Shawn's leg but another Figure Four attempt is blocked, this one taking out the referee in the process. Shawn loads up Sweet Chin Music but Roadie takes out his knee. Jarrett gets two off another high crossbody but Roadie trips the wrong guy, allowing Shawn to superkick Jeff's head off for the pin and the title at 20:01.

Rating: A. This is an excellent match with both guys knowing exactly how to build a match into a frenzy at the end. The chess match here was excellent as they were constantly upping the other one until one of Jarrett's moves backfired and Shawn took the opening to get the superkick. Jarrett really doesn't get the credit he deserves for his in ring work, as he wrestles a very basic style but completely mastered it.

Doc Hendrix (better known as Michael Hayes) gives an INSANE report about how Roadie and Jeff Jarrett yelled at each other and got in a fight after getting back to the dressing room.

Tag Team Titles: Yokozuna/Owen Hart vs. Allied Powers

The Powers are Lex Luger and British Bulldog (Davey Boy Smith) and are challenging. Luger and his old WWF Title rival Yokozuna get us going as the fans chant USA. So do they hate Bulldog as well? Yokozuna shoves the very strong Luger into the corner but Lex comes back with right hands. A clothesline puts Luger down but he avoids a big elbow drop and tries to pound on Yokozuna a bit.

The big man's head is rammed into the top turnbuckle ten straight times and Yokozuna finally falls into the corner for the tag off to Owen. Yokozuna didn't want to tag though and shoves Owen down as a result. Hart hides from Luger in the corner before being armdragged down into an armbar. It's to Owen's real life brother in law Smith so they can fight over a wristlock. Bulldog tries a backdrop but Owen doesn't flip over, landing on his face instead.

It's off to a chinlock on Hart before he fights up and goes after the leg. Yokozuna comes in again and walks around a lot before putting on a nerve hold. Bulldog fights up but gets caught by an elbow to the jaw. Back to Owen who gets two off a clothesline before taking Davey's head off with an enziguri. Davey comes back with a clothesline as the fans chant USA.

The hot tag brings in Luger to punch Yokozuna some more, as well as taking Owen down off the top rope. He throws Owen at the big man to put both guys down. Everything breaks down but Owen breaks up a Luger cover. Yokozuna misses a charge into the corner and a double belly to back suplex puts the big man down again, only to have Owen come off the top to break it up. Luger is stunned from Owen's shot, allowing Yokozuna to drop the big leg to retain the titles at 10:54.

Rating: D+. This was a better choice than the Smoking Gunns but even power guys like Smith and Luger can only do so much when Yokozuna is that big. The double suplex was an impressive spot but it wasn't enough to save the match. The entire tag division was basically Owen/Yokozuna, the Smoking Gunns and a bunch of jobbing tag teams that would never make it onto a PPV. Nothing special here at all.

We recap Sid vs. Diesel which hasn't changed much since the first show.

Diesel says he's keeping the title and finishing Sid tonight.

WWF Title: Diesel vs. Sycho Sid

Diesel is defending in a lumberjack match with the Million Dollar Team and Diesel's friends on the floor to make sure no one tries to leave. Why this was a problem isn't clear but I don't think there was much thought put into this feud. Shawn escorts Diesel to the ring to try to get the fans to care about the match. Sid is quickly thrown to the floor twice before Diesel slams him down with ease. Back to the floor again though this time Sid winds up with his friends.

Diesel follows him out but gets jumped by the evil lumberjacks, triggering a brawl with the rest of the lumberjacks. Back in and Sid kicks Diesel down and starts going after the champion's ribs. A bad looking clothesline drops Diesel and Sid walks around a lot. The bad guys cheat again by choking Diesel, triggering another skirmish. Another kick to the head drops Diesel again but he comes back with right hands and a clothesline which clearly didn't make contact. The champion drops some elbows despite apparently having an elbow injury.

Diesel calls for the Jackknife but dives onto the lumberjacks instead of going after Sid. Back in and Diesel hits Snake Eyes in the corner, only to have Mabel pull him out to the floor and crush him against the post. A slam puts Diesel down and Mabel drops a big leg before throwing his body back in to Sid. He won't cover though and opts to choke Diesel even more to keep this match going.

We hit the chinlock on the champion before Sid hits his powerbomb and goes over to high five his friends. Diesel kicks out at two and backdrops out of another powerbomb attempt. Sid goes after Diesel's lumberjacks to mimic Diesel I guess, only to have Shawn dive off the top to take Sid out. Back in and Diesel has to knock down some lumberjacks before kicking Sid in the face to retain the title at 10:06.

Rating: D-. It's somehow even less interesting than last time if that's possible. The lumberjacks helped a bit but adding a gimmick for the sake of continuing a feud isn't something that works most of the time. These two just didn't work well together though this was probably a better idea than letting them have another regular match.

Diesel and pals celebrate to end the show.

Overall Rating: D+. This is another of those shows where there's only one good match, but in this case it's a VERY good match. The WWF was in desperate need of a shot of something to shake things up very soon because these shows are dreadful and were doing some horrible business. Shawn vs. Jeff was a bright spot but Jeff was literally gone the next day. Thankfully this show, as well as the rest of the two hour shows, was up to about an hour and forty five minutes of action instead of just 95 minutes the first time out.

After this mess, we headed into Summerslam which made the first two In Your Houses look like a day at the beach. Summerslam 1995 was one of the worst wrestling shows of all time featuring arguably the worst main event in the history of wrestling as Diesel defended the WWF Title against Mabel. Whoever saw this as a good idea should be drawn and quartered but thankfully it was just a one time thing.

Other than that the main story has been the rise of Shawn Michaels, who was still Intercontinental Champion but has been in the main event picture for a few months now. Thankfully the matches and feuds have changed up a bit since last time so it's not just part three of the same story this time around.

In Your House #3: Triple Header
Date: September 24, 1995
Location: Saginaw Civic Center, Saginaw, Michigan
Attendance: 5,146
Commentators: Vince McMahon, Jerry Lawler, Jim Ross

The title of this show refers to the main event, which is only one match. It's Michaels/Diesel vs. Yokozuna/Owen Hart will all titles on the line. In other words if Diesel and Shawn win then they're the Tag Team Champions but if Owen or Yokozuna beat Shawn or Diesel, the person with the pin gets the respective singles title. In other words, practically everything is on the line in one match so it better deliver. Let's get to it.

The opening video talks about the Triple Header match and refers to Owen and Yokozuna as perhaps the greatest tag team in company history. Uh, calm down a bit there guys. Also keep in mind that Shawn and Diesel are former Tag Team Champions.

The theme song talks about going home and being In Your House. Well you can't say they're being subtle at least.

Jim Ross' prediction for the main event is Yokozuna winning the Intercontinental Title.

Savio Vega vs. Waylon Mercy

Waylon Mercy is......interesting. He's based on Max Cady from the movie Cape Fear, but if you've never seen that, basically he's a 6'7 man (probably more famous as Dan Spivey) who dresses like a very laid back southern gentleman but turns into a psycho

20

when the bell rings. After the match is over, he's right back to being the kindest man you'll ever meet. The character had some staying power to him but a bunch of injuries forced him to retire just a few months after debuting the character. In more modern terms, Bray Wyatt without a cult.

Mercy offers a handshake to start so Savio dances a bit. Vega avoids a charge in the corner and cranks on the arm to start. He takes Waylon to the mat by the arm but comes back with a clothesline. We head to the floor with Mercy firing off chops and slamming Savio down before choking away back inside. A hot shot gets two for Mercy and he sends Savio into the corner but we cut over to Doc Hendrix in the back, saying that Owen Hart hasn't arrived yet. You can hear the "oh dear" from here.

Savio comes back with a hiptoss and some forearms but gets caught in Waylon's sleeper. Vega is in big trouble but manages to send Waylon face first into the buckle to escape. A belly to back suplex puts Mercy down before Vega takes over with some right hands. Vega kicks Mercy in the face and bulldogs him down for two. A side roll gets another near fall but Mercy comes back with a brainbuster for two of his own. Savio gets a quick German suplex for two before hitting a spinwheel kick for the upset pin at 7:06.

Rating: D+. The match wasn't too horrible but what in the world was the point of having Mercy lose here? Mercy was about to start feuding with the WWF Champion but you have him lose to Savio Vega in the opener of a pay per view here? My guess is that Mercy was about to leave due to the injuries so get the value you can out of him beforehand.

Cornette, Fuji, Yokozuna and British Bulldog are panicking in the back because WWF President Gorilla Monsoon is saying the Tag Team Titles might have to be forfeited. Gorilla says the title match is happening tonight.

Sycho Sid vs. Henry Godwinn

Henry turned down an official spot on the Million Dollar Team and got beaten down, turning him face as a result. Godwinn even slopped DiBiase for good measure, but got powerbombed on the floor by Sid. Henry pounds away to start and slams Sid face first into the mat as JR drops the term slobberknocker, blowing

Vince's mind. Sid gets suplexed back in from the apron but Henry hurts his back in the process. He can't pick Sid up for a slam and the Sycho takes over.

They head to the floor with Sid jumping off the apron with an ax handle to Henry's bad back. Back in and some kicks in the corner have Henry in even more trouble and we hit the camel clutch. Sid jumps down onto the back to slow Henry down again before ripping at his face. There's another camel clutch but Sid isn't even pulling back, making this look ridiculous. Back up and Sid misses a charge into the corner and Henry starts pounding away. A boot to the chest sets up the Slop Drop (reverse DDT) for two but DiBiase makes the save. DiBiase trips Henry again and Sid powerbombs him for the pin at 7:23.

Rating: D. Nothing to see here again but the fans were at least getting behind Henry a bit here. Sid was just worthless in the ring as he couldn't even perform a rest hold properly. Then again when you're that size you can do almost anything you want and the fans are going to buy it. Still though, not a good match here as the bad start to the show continues.

Post match Kama Mustafa comes out to help Sid and DiBiase try to slop Henry but Bam Bam Bigelow makes the save and pours the slop on DiBiase again.

Monsoon says that Cornette can find a substitute for Owen Hart and he'll have a chance at the Intercontinental or WWF Title in the main event just like Owen would have. The Tag Team Titles would still be on the line.

British Bulldog vs. Bam Bam Bigelow

Bulldog has a match on Raw tomorrow night against Undertaker so the announcers spend most of the match ignoring Bigelow to talk about that instead. Bigelow runs over Bulldog to start and then does it again for good measure. Bulldog bails to the floor and we go to a split screen to see Cornette recruiting Sid for the main event. Back in and Bigelow misses an elbow drop before being put in a quick chinlock.

Bigelow fights up but misses a headbutt, allowing Bulldog to hit a nice suplex. Bam Bam comes back with some clotheslines, only to miss a charge and fall out to the floor. Davey can't suplex

Bigelow back inside so Bigelow lifts him up for a crotching on the top rope. Smith goes after the knee and Bigelow is down again, giving Davey a nice target. Bulldog kicks away at the knee as the announcers speculate over who could be Yokozuna's replacement partner.

We get a leglock on the mat as the fans try to get Bigelow back in this. Back up and Bigelow is sent into the buckle but comes back with an enziguri. He can't follow up though due to the knee and Smith goes right back to the leg. We hit the half crab for a bit before a knee to the ribs gives Bulldog two. It's back to the chinlock for a bit before Smith fails at a slam attempt, giving Bigelow a two count. Bigelow sits down to block a sunset flip attempt but the moonsault misses. A missed charge in the corner lets Bulldog hit a quick powerslam (standing instead of running) for the pin at 12:00.

Rating: D+. Still nothing good here but it was WAY better than the previous match. Bulldog wasn't much by this point but he was fine for beating up guys on a lower level than he was. Bigelow was pretty worthless here and would be gone in just a few months, which is probably the best result for everyone.

Here's Bob Backlund who is thinking about running for President of the United States. He insults the fans for having a poor lexicon before talking about little victories in life, such as learning to read and write. Backlund introduces Dean Douglas (Shane Douglas as an evil teacher) for his match while praising him using words most fans don't understand.

Dean Douglas vs. Razor Ramon

This is a result of Dean insulting Razor for losing the Intercontinental Title match at Summerslam and Ramon has bad ribs coming in. Razor goes right for him to start and clotheslines Douglas out to the floor. Back in and they take each other to the mat a few times with no one being able to get an advantage. Dean fires off some right hands but gets hiptossed over the top and out to the floor. We cut to the split screen again with Mabel looking at Yokozuna and Cornette looking thrilled. Nothing is official though.

Back in again and Douglas cranks on the arm, only to have Razor counter into a top wristlock. Dean flips out of a hammerlock but gets caught in the fall away slam for two. Razor snaps Dean's arm over the top rope before putting on an armbar. Back up and Dean's sunset flip out of the corner gets two before Ramon clotheslines him down for the same. It's a back and forth match so far and we hit the armbar again. Dean gets back up and avoids a charge to send Razor out to the floor.

Razor gets slammed on the floor and they barely break the ten count. A knee to the back sends Razor into the steps before Dean rams him back first into the post. Back in again and a top rope ax handle gets two for Douglas. Dean's major flaw is really showing here: he's a pretty generic in ring worker and doesn't do anything particularly better than anyone else. He's much better on the mic but it doesn't help him in the ring.

Dean stays on Razor's back before cranking on the arms for a bit. Some right hands to Razor's bad ribs keep him in trouble and a gutbuster gets two. It's off to a reverse chinlock but Razor eventually gets to his feet with Dean on his shoulders for an electric chair drop. Ramon pounds away and rolls through Dean's middle rope crossbody for two. Dean sends Razor into the referee to knock both guys down but Ramon comes back with a quick Razor's Edge. There's no referee though and here's the 1-2-3 Kid to count the pin behind Razor's back. Ramon thinks he's won and Dean rolls him up for a quick pin at 14:53.

Rating: C-. The ending was more clever than a lot of others I've seen but it still wasn't anything special. As I said, Douglas was a much better character than wrestler which makes these fifteen minute matches fairly dull to sit through. Razor continues to be at about the same level he's been at for years while never really moving further up the card at all. He's still very popular though so it's not the worst thing in the world.

Shawn Michaels and Diesel talk about what it's like with being in love with a girl when you're younger but having it pulled away from you. That's how they feel with Owen backing out tonight.

Jean Pierre LaFitte vs. Bret Hart

LaFitte (later known as PCO) is a 275lb pirate, more famous as one half of the Quebecers tag team, who has been stealing the sunglasses that Bret gives to fans and then stole Bret's trademark leather jacket. Seriously that's the whole story. Bret dives through the ropes to take out LaFitte to start and the brawl is on in a hurry. Jean comes back with right hands and takes it into the ring, sending Bret into the corner over and over. Hart avoids a charge and takes him down by the arm.

Bret hooks the armbar but gets clotheslined down, sending Lawler into fits of glee. LaFitte stomps away as this is still in first or second gear. Bret gets pounded down in the corner before missing a charge into the post to damage his own shoulder. We get the required Bret chest first into the buckle bump as things speed up a little bit. Bret manages to backdrop Jean over the top to the floor but gets sent into the steps for his troubles.

Back in and Bret's comeback is stopped via a spinebuster for two and we hit the chinlock. Bret fights up for about the fifth time and gets two off a sunset flip, only to be caught in a side slam. Jean gets two off a guillotine legdrop before loading up his Cannonball (Swanton) finisher. Hart rolls away at the last second and both guys are down as the fans are getting into this. The Sharpshooter is countered with Bret being kicked through the ropes, only to avoid a dive over the top from LaFitte.

Bret sends Jean into the steps before whipping him chest first into the buckle in a nice callback from earlier. A Russian legsweep gets two on Jean but he gets the boot up to block Bret's middle rope elbow. Bret's crucifix is countered into a rolling fireman's carry senton but Hart gets a quick two off a rollup.

A bulldog is countered with Bret being sent chest first into the buckle again as Lawler is losing his mind on these kickouts. Jean's top rope splash misses and a double clothesline puts both guys down. With both guys on the mat we get one of Bret's favorites as he puts on the Sharpshooter from his back and turns it over for the submission at 16:37.

Rating: B. This started slow but got much better by the middle. Bret continues to be able to have good matches with anyone he's put in there with, which explains why he had such odd choices of opponents around this time. LaFitte was pretty much done after this match but it was a dead end character anyway.

Post match, Bret retrieves the jacket to end things with LaFitte.

British Bulldog will be Owen Hart's partner. Gorilla approves this move, saying that Bulldog can win or lose the Tag Team Titles as well as win either singles title.

Tag Team Titles/WWF Title/Intercontinental Title:
Yokozuna/British Bulldog vs. Shawn Michaels/Diesel

All titles are on the line here with the person getting the fall winning the belt of whomever they pin/make submit. Smith and Shawn get things going by trading some weak hammerlocks. A backdrop puts Smith down and a clothesline sends him to the floor with Shawn skinning the cat to get back in. Yokozuna comes in sans tag but Diesel punches him out to the floor, leaving the good guys to rule the ring.

Yokozuna comes in legally now and Shawn gets down in a sumo stance in a funny bit. Shawn of course moves from a charging Yokozuna but runs into a back elbow to put him down. A big elbow misses and there's the tag off to the WWF Champion Diesel. Yokozuna gets dropped by a running clothesline but Bulldog gets in a cheap shot to slow Diesel down. Smith actually gets Diesel up for his trademark delayed vertical suplex for a two count but Diesel is right back up.

Bulldog can't hit the powerslam and Diesel comes back with a corner clothesline to drop Smith. Back to Shawn who climbs onto Diesel's shoulders for a huge splash, getting two. Smith pops back up and gorilla presses Shawn before crotching him on the top rope to send him to the floor. They head inside again for a BIG backdrop for two on Shawn and we hit the chinlock, as required in tag matches.

Shawn scores with a crossbody but gets slammed down again, drawing in Diesel and allowing Yokozuna to come in for a nerve hold. Jim Ross (JR) asks a good question: why would Bulldog tag out? If Yokozuna gets the fall then Bulldog comes out with nothing. Shawn avoids the Banzai Drop and there's the hot tag to Diesel.

The big man runs over the Bulldog and puts him down with the side slam. Everything breaks down with Smith being sent into Yokozuna with the big man falling down onto him. Yokozuna breaks up a Jackknife attempt but Shawn superkicks him to the floor. Shawn breaks up a pin attempt by Davey but here's Owen

Hart who is immediately Jackknifed by Diesel for the pin and the titles at 15:42. You read that right and it's as confusing as it sounds.

Rating: C+. This was a decent match until the stupid ending. Naturally this didn't last and was overturned the next night, as it should have been. The fans popped for the finish but it was clear this wasn't going to last at all. At least Diesel had someone he could work with here as both Tag Team Champions could hang in a power match with him. Shawn was his usual good self.

Jim Ross points out how ridiculous this is to end the show.

Overall Rating: D. This makes three straight bad shows to start this series. I promise things will get better but it's going to take a little while to get there. This wasn't anything special and only a few decent matches aren't enough to make it worthwhile. Diesel just wasn't working as champion as he didn't have enough to carry the entire company. Shawn was popular but he was still several months away from a WWF Title push. Things will get better though, I assure you.

Not a lot would change between In Your House #3 and In Your House #4 as there wasn't another pay per view in between the two shows. Diesel and Shawn are still the singles champions, but the night after Triple Header saw new Tag Team Champions with the Smoking Gunns beating Owen and Yokozuna for the titles. The same cast is still around for the most part, though there will be some new arrivals for this show.

In Your House #4: Great White North
Date: October 22, 1995
Location: Winnipeg Arena, Winnipeg, Manitoba, Canada
Attendance: 10,339
Commentators: Jim Ross, Jerry Lawler, Vince McMahon

The main event tonight is Diesel defending the WWF Title against British Bulldog in a match that very few people cared to see. So few in fact that this show set a record for the lowest pay per view buyrate in company history which lasted for over ten years. Other than that we have Shawn defending his Intercontinental Title against Dean Douglas, allegedly. Let's get to it.

We open with a decision made by WWF President Gorilla Monsoon: Shawn Michaels has been stripped of the Intercontinental Title due to a real life attack by anywhere between 2-19 United States Marines (depending on how many Shawn feels like saying there were at the time). Therefore, he has to forfeit the title to Dean Douglas, his challenger for the night, though there will be a title match tonight.

Hunter Hearst Helmsley vs. Fatu

The undefeated Helmsley would eventually go just by his initials while Fatu would become Rikishi. At the moment though Fatu is trying to Make A Difference with wayward kids, which didn't work to put it mildly. Helmsley has a bottle of perfume to spray on Fatu but gets punched in the face for his efforts. Fatu takes him into the corner and pounds away, sending Helmsley to the floor before he can get his shirt off.

Back in and Fatu is sent face first into the turnbuckle to no effect whatsoever, so HHH throws him into the ropes with Fatu's neck getting tied up in the cables. Helmsley pounds away at the tied up Fatu before dropping him with a piledriver. The shirt is finally off about three minutes into the match and Helmsley walks

28

around for awhile. A neckbreaker puts Fatu down for two and a knee drop gets the same.

We hit the chinlock on Fatu, who looks to be nearly dead as a result. Back up and a clothesline turns Fatu inside out for another two count. A Pedigree is countered with a backdrop and Fatu scores with a superkick. Fatu hits a backbreaker to set up a middle rope headbutt for another two count. Lawler is losing his mind watching Helmsley get beaten up like this. A running Diamond Cutter puts Helmsley down again but Fatu misses the top rope splash, allowing Helmsley to hit the Pedigree for the pin at 8:06.

Rating: C-. This actually wasn't that bad despite Helmsley still being a glorified rookie. Fatu wasn't completely huge yet so he could move around the ring far better than he would be able to later in his career. This wasn't the best choice to open a show with but Fatu was popular enough to keep it from killing the crowd.

Post match Lawler talks to Helmsley when Henry Godwinn comes up with the slop bucket, sending Helmsley running away.

We look at British Bulldog pinning Diesel in a tag match from a recent episode of Raw. The Bulldog says he's ready to take the title tonight.

Tag Team Titles: Smoking Gunns vs. 1-2-3 Kid/Razor Ramon

The Gunns are defending while the challengers aren't getting along all that well, though they swear they're fine. The challengers both slick back their hair instead of shaking hands with the Gunns. It's the Kid starting things off with Billy and is easily shoved down. Since power doesn't work, the Kid opts for speed with a leap frog and an arm drag but Billy comes back with an armdrag of his own, giving us a stalemate.

Razor comes in again to crank on Bart's shoulder, only to be taken down by a fireman's carry. Now it's Bart working on a wristlock but Razor comes back with a big right hand, sending him to the ropes. With the referee and Razor's backs turned, the Kid pulls the ropes down, sending Bart out to the floor. Back in and it's off to the Kid legally with a dropkick to take Bart down again. Some running legdrops keep Bart down and it's back to

Razor for some power. There's the fall away slam and it's already back to the Kid for some kicks.

Razor comes in again but Bart scores with a clothesline as Dean Douglas is watching in the back. Apparently Razor will be the one getting an Intercontinental Title shot against the new champion Douglas later tonight. A double tag brings in Billy and the Kid with Billy cleaning house and getting two off an elbow drop. Back to Bart for some backbreakers but Razor comes in to break up the pin.

The Gunns hit a nice dropkick/suplex combo for two but the Kid avoids a Stinger Splash in the corner. The referee goes over to check on Razor so Bart pulls Billy on top of the Kid for two. He gets caught, so Razor comes in and puts Kid on top of Billy for two. Now it's a hot tag off to Ramon who cleans house with right hands and the Razor's Edge to Billy, but the Kid asks for the tag. The Kid takes forever to cover and gets cradled for the pin out of nowhere to retain the titles at 12:46.

Rating: C. This wasn't bad but the match was mainly about the angle at the end. Kid just wasn't working as a good guy for the most part so the turn and feud with Razor was the logical ending. The Gunns weren't great champions but they were the best that the company had at this point. Not a bad match here though.

Post match the Kid snaps and kicks the Gunns down, only to be calmed by Razor.

Marty Jannetty vs. Goldust

Goldust is a rather interesting character who was obsessed with movies and was pushed as being gay at first until the character got a bit too risque for 1995 and that aspect was toned WAY down. This is his debut as well as Jannetty's return to the company after a lengthy run in the indys. Golden glitter falls from the ceiling as Goldust gets in the ring for a cool visual. Marty jumps him in the corner and clotheslines Goldust out to the floor where another clothesline puts him down again.

Back in and Goldust stares at Marty for about 45 seconds before getting two off an O'Connor Roll. An uppercut staggers Jannetty and a second one puts him right back down again. Jannetty comes back with a hurricanrana and it's time to shove each other a bit more. Goldust takes his head off with a clothesline and drops an elbow for two. We hit the chinlock as the match stops almost dead. Goldust backdrops him down and pounds away before sending Marty into the steps on the outside.

Marty comes back by flipping Goldust back to the floor and sending him into the steps for some nice retaliation. Goldust will have none of this being in trouble though and sends Marty into the post to put him right back down. A suplex brings Jannetty back in and we hit another chinlock. Marty fights up but misses a crossbody in the corner, allowing Goldust to DDT him down for two. Jannetty scores with the Rocker Dropper (modified Fameasser) but his top rope fist hits a top rope boot. A gordbuster is enough to pin Jannetty at 11:15.

Rating: D. This went on WAY too long, running over eleven minutes instead of the five or so that it needed. The interesting thing though is how dull the match was. This is interesting because in just a few months, Goldust would be years better and challenging for the WWF Title. The lesson: you can't judge a wrestler by his debut match. You have to recognize the talent and work around them instead of bending them to your system.

We recap Yokozuna and King Mabel crushing Undertaker's face on Raw recently. As a result, Mabel and Yokozuna have a match tonight as punishment. I'm not sure I get that logic.

King Mabel vs. Yokozuna

They stare each other down to start before Yokozuna wins an early slugout, knocking Mabel out to the floor. Back in and they very slowly look at each other before Mabel slowly pounds him down and out to the floor. Back in again as JR uses his special code to apologize for how boring this match is. Yokozuna slugs Mabel down again but misses a legdrop. Mabel misses an elbow before trying a bulldog. I say trying because he grabbed Yokozuna's head and runs, but Yokozuna doesn't go down.....for a few seconds until he falls out of the ring. Mr. Fuji shoves down Cornette and Yokozuna splashes him, resulting in a double countout at 5:12.

Rating: F. I think this is one of those matches that doesn't need a lengthy explanation. Huge guys wrestling in short matches is a staple of wrestling, especially in the WWF so it's not like this is unheard of. The match of course was junk with about a minute and a half of "action" spread across five minutes of ring time.

Post match the guys get in the ring and stare each other down before raising each others' hands.

Here's Dean Douglas to be awarded the Intercontinental Title from the concussed Shawn. Shawn is very depressed of course so Douglas snatches the title away from him and puts it on. There's no announcement made here or anything so I guess the live fans are left figuring this out on their own. Shawn walks away and does the long look back before leaving. There is a title match tonight though.

<u>Intercontinental Title: Dean Douglas vs. Razor Ramon</u>

Razor, challenging of course charges to the ring and pounds away before being dropped by a right hand to the jaw. The champion bails to the floor before coming back in for some shoulders from Ramon. Razor cranks on the arm even more and we hit the armbar. Dean is sent to the mat by the arm and Razor slaps him in the back of the head to rub it in a bit. Back up and Razor stays on that arm and hangs on even through an armdrag.

Dean FINALLY sends him into the corner to escape and pounds away, only to be caught in the fall away slam. A clothesline puts Dean on the floor as this is one sided so far. Razor snaps the champion's throat across the ropes but Dean pokes him in the eye to get a breather. That's all it's good for though as Ramon punches him off the apron and out to the floor. Razor suplexes him back inside before whipping him right back to the floor. Ramon pours water over Dean's head and we head back inside for more work on the arm.

The Razor's Edge is countered with a backdrop over the top rope to give Douglas his first bit of control. Again it doesn't last long whatsoever though as Dean goes up, only to jump into a chokeslam. Douglas breaks up a belly to back superplex but his crossbody is rolled through into a near fall for Ramon. Back up and Razor grabs a quick belly to back suplex and awkwardly covers Dean for the pin and the title at 11:01, despite Dean putting his leg under the ropes.

Rating: D. This was a squash that happened to last eleven minutes. Dean got in almost no offense with his one big move being a counter to Razor's finishing move. This was the last you would see of Dean as anything of note in the WWF and he would be back to much friendlier pastures in ECW by the beginning of the year. Douglas' title reign lasted no more than fifteen minutes at most, easily the shortest reign on record. This was also Razor's fourth Intercontinental Title, a record that would stand for nearly four years.

Bret Hart comes out for commentary on the main event since he gets the winner for the title at Survivor Series. Lawler runs away in fear.

WWF Title: Diesel vs. British Bulldog

Diesel is defending and has no comment on the way to the ring. They shove each other around to start before Diesel puts him down with a forearm to the head. A crossbody is easily caught in a slam from Diesel, sending Bulldog out to the floor. Back in and the Bulldog goes after the leg, only to be sent into the corner for a clothesline. More elbows in the corner have Smith in trouble but he comes back with right hands of his own.

A dropkick puts the champion on the floor but he lands on his feet. Diesel gets in a shouting match with Bret, allowing Bulldog to take out Diesel's legs to take over. Back in and Smith works over the leg as the match slows down a lot. Bulldog can't hook something like a Texas Cloverleaf but he sends Diesel out to the floor anyway, allowing Cornette to get in a cheap shot to the leg.

Bulldog sends Diesel into the steps and gets admonished, allowing Cornette to get in some tennis racket shots to Diesel's bad leg. Bulldog puts on a half crab and then a full Boston crab to stay on the leg. Diesel powers out but gets caught in a second half crab. A legdrop gets two for the challenger and it's back to another leglock. Diesel finally fights up and scores with some more forearms, only to have Bulldog go right back to the knee. Bulldog loads up a cannonball down onto the knee, only to have Diesel kick him out to the floor.

Back in and Smith goes right back to the leglock to make sure nothing gets interesting in this match at all. Diesel scores with a quick suplex and its belly to back cousin gets him a breather.

Smith is up first and, after a point to Bret, puts on a sloppy looking Sharpshooter. Davey can't slam him though (after being able to slam the much larger Bam Bam Bigelow last month), allowing Diesel to hit a big boot to the face. Cornette is dragged into the ring and thrown at the Bulldog, sending Davey out to the floor. Diesel is sent face first into the post but Bulldog shoves Bret, drawing him in for a very lame disqualification at 18:14.

Rating: D-. This was terribly boring with the leg work going nowhere at all. The ending didn't do the match any favors either with the match taking forever to be set up and then having nothing for a finish. No one was interested in this match beforehand and it was clearly just a setup for Bret vs. Diesel next month.

Post match Diesel gets in Bret's face and they slug it out to end the show.

Overall Rating: F. This is one of the worst shows I've ever seen. The best matches are the first two and neither of those are anything past watchable at best. As mentioned earlier, no one seemed interested in seeing this show and it drew the lowest number of PPV buys for well over ten years. Just a horrible show and proof that a change was needed. Vince McMahon knew it too and ripped Diesel apart for the main event after the show, more or less guaranteeing that the title was changing hands very soon.

Bret Can Save Us

Thankfully that change would come the next month at Survivor Series with Bret Hart FINALLY taking the title from Diesel in one of Diesel's best matches ever. Other than that Shawn Michaels' injuries apparently weren't all that bad as he was back in action at Survivor Series as well, which I'm sure had nothing to do with him not wanting to be pinned for his title. The main event for In Your House #5 is Bret Hart vs. Davey Boy Smith, who has a legitimate claim to a title shot after the way his match with Diesel ended.

In Your House #5: Seasons Beatings
Date: December 17, 1995
Location: Hersheypark Arena, Hershey, Pennsylvania
Attendance: 7,289
Commentators: Vince McMahon, Jerry Lawler

In addition to the main event, this is the first In Your House to feature the Undertaker on the pay per view (he had wrestled in several post PPV dark matches already). It's rather interesting that one of the biggest and certainly most unique stars in the company hadn't appeared in the first four editions of a PPV series and I'm not sure why he hadn't. Anyway tonight he faces King Mabel in his signature match: the casket match. Let's get to it.

The opening video starts with various symbols of Christmas before transitioning to shots of the Hart Family splitting apart as well as the Bulldog pinning Bret Hart at Summerslam 1992 in a masterpiece.

Santa Claus is here handing out presents.

Jerry Lawler promises us a big surprise.

Razor Ramon/Marty Jannetty vs. Sycho Sid/1-2-3 Kid

The Kid is full heel now and a part of the Million Dollar Team. Goldust, in the crowd, rubs his chest while watching Razor come to the ring. Marty and the Kid start things off with Jannetty scoring with an enziguri for two. Some shoulder blocks and a clothesline get the same on the Kid and Marty goes over for the tag, freaking the Kid out. An atomic drop has Kid in trouble and now it's off to Razor for the showdown. The Kid bails to the floor for a second but gets a toothpick in his face back inside.

Razor is having a good time but a blind tag brings in Sid to take over for the Million Dollar Team. Back to the Kid for a kick to the face but Razor glares at him after some chops. Sid comes back in to pound Ramon down and get cheered by the crowd in a surprising reaction. Razor comes back with some right hands and a double clothesline puts both guys down. A double tag brings in Marty to run over the Kid again and a powerslam is good for two.

A front flip facebuster out of the corner gets two on the Kid and it's off to a camel clutch of all things. We go to Todd Pettengill in the crowd with Goldust, who quotes movie lines and expresses his lust for Ramon. This goes on for several minutes but at least we're on split screen. Goldust asks Todd to give Razor a letter. Back to the match and Marty punches his way out of the corner but his crossbody is caught in a powerslam for two.

Back to the Kid for a bad looking slam and a better looking guillotine legdrop for two before Sid comes in again. Ramon gets suckered into the ring but gets in a right hand to the Kid. Marty is turned inside out by a clothesline and it's off to a chinlock. Kid comes back in to drop a leg and then bring Sid back inside for some shots to the back.

It's the Kid in again but he misses a charge in the corner, allowing for the tag off to Razor as things speed up. The fall away slam puts Kid on the floor but Sid breaks up the Razor's Edge. Not that it matters as Razor hits a quick middle rope bulldog (his finisher before he was in the WWF) for the pin at 12:22.

Rating: D+. Not a terrible match but it went on too long for what they were going for. Jannetty was an odd choice as Razor's partner against DiBiase's boys as he was basically fighting everyone himself, but it was all about the him vs. the Kid anyway. Nothing much to see here and not the best choice for an opening match.

Here's Jerry Lawler in the ring with a present for the returning Jeff Jarrett. After sucking up to Jeff for awhile, the present is revealed to be a gold record of Ain't I Great, Jeff's single from six months earlier. Jarrett brags about how great he is and it doesn't make anything more interesting. The only thing of note is he enters himself in the Royal Rumble.

Dean Douglas vs. Ahmed Johnson

Douglas says he has a back injury and can't wrestle, so here's his prized student Buddy Landell.

Buddy Landell vs. Ahmed Johnson

This is actually a joke, as Buddy Landell is a Ric Flair ripoff and comes to the ring to Flair's WWF music in a Flair style robe. Douglas hates Flair in real life (never mentioned here of course), so it's supposed to be funny that Douglas is Flair's teacher or something like that. Not that it matters as Ahmed, a muscular monster with one of the most intimidating looks ever, destroys Landell and beats him with a Pearl River Plunge (double underhook powerbomb) in 32 seconds.

Post match Johnson paddles Douglas with the Board of Education, marking Douglas' last appearance with the company. Lawler interviews Johnson and calls him stupid, allowing Jarrett to break the gold record over Johnson's head. Jeff also gets in a few chair shots and rams Ahmed into the steps a couple of times, but Ahmed no sells them and chases Jarrett off.

Todd gives Razor the letter from Goldust and Ramon is disgusted, because it's 1995 and anyone gay has to be a heel right?

Hunter Hearst Helmsley vs. Henry Godwinn

This is a Hog Pen match, meaning there's an actual hog pen with pigs and mud near the entrance and the winner is the first man to send his opponent into said pin. Why is this match happening you ask? Simply put it's because Godwinn is a hog farmer so he associates with hogs. One note characters like him had a lot to do with the downfall of the WWF at this point, as there's no interest to such characters, meaning there's no reason to stick around and watch them. The guest referee is 1980s crowd favorite Hillbilly Jim.

Godwinn slops the ring announcer before the match starts for no apparent reason. Helmsley jumps Godwinn but is quickly sent to the floor for his efforts. Back in and Henry ties him in the ropes so he can rub more slop in Helmsley's face. After nearly retching, Helmsley takes it back to the floor, only to be bulldogged face first into the steps.

They head up the pen with Henry being whipped into the gate but still managing to block a Pedigree attempt with a backdrop. Helmsley lands on the edge of the pen and kicks Henry down before dropping an elbow to the chest. Lawler makes Jeff Foxworthy style redneck jokes about being from Arkansas as they head back inside where Godwinn hits a big wheelbarrow slam. Helmsley is whipped to two corners and out to the floor for another handful of slop. Henry hits the Slop Drop up by the pen but can't follow up. Instead he charges at Helmsley and gets backdropped into the slop to end things at 8:58.

Rating: C-. This actually wasn't that bad as it was a regular match until the ending. Again though, why am I supposed to care? It's the lowest level of comedy and storytelling possible, which doesn't mean it's necessarily bad, but we have no reason to care about either of these guys so why should I be interested in the match?

Post match Henry slams Helmsley into the pen for fun. That's a nice idea as at least the fans get the (limited) payoff.

We recap Diesel's change of attitude since he lost the WWF Title at Survivor Series, which has seen him act much more aggressive. This was what he should have been doing as champion.

Diesel vs. Owen Hart

This is a revenge match for Diesel as Owen kicked Shawn Michaels in the head and put him on the shelf as a result. Diesel launches Owen into the corner to start and hits a big side slam for no cover. The arena is full of smoke from Diesel's entrance. Owen comes back with some right hands but Diesel easily throws him to the outside for a meeting with Cornette.

Back in and Owen scores with a missile dropkick before going after Diesel's knee to take him down. A spinwheel kick gets two on Diesel but he easily kicks Hart away to break up a spinning toehold. Diesel comes back with a big boot and the Jackknife ("This is for you Shawn!") but he takes his foot off Owen's chest at two. The referee begs him to let it end so Diesel shoves him down for the DQ at 4:34.

Rating: D+. The match was going along pretty well until the stupid ending. I understand that they're trying to push Diesel as being more aggressive, but having him lose isn't the way to go about doing that. This is Diesel's third straight PPV loss which doesn't make me think he's a monster but rather a guy who can't finish his opponents.

Here are Savio Vega and Santa Claus to hand out presents to the fans, but Ted DiBiase interrupts them. He says everyone has a price and calls them both into the ring. DiBiase doesn't believe Santa can make it around the world in one night but he knows someone who can. Savio says he doesn't have a price and says he believes in Santa.

However, this isn't the real Santa. It's really.....XANTA CLAUS, Santa's evil brother from the south pole who steals presents from children. And yes, it is as awesome as it sounds. Xanta lays out Savio and leaves with DiBiase but Savio chases after them, only to get beaten up again. Vince: "SAY IT'S NOT SO!!!" Xanta is played by future ECW mainstay Balls Mahoney.

Mabel says he isn't scared of the Undertaker, who has returned after having his face crushed by Mabel and Yokozuna. Tonight it's a casket match, meaning you have to put your opponent in a casket and close the lid to win.

King Mabel vs. Undertaker

Mable now has a very questionable looking Mohawk to go with his ridiculous looking gold and purple pajamas. He jumps Undertaker to start but Undertaker comes back with rights and lefts in the corner. Mabel takes him down with a Boss Man Slam but Undertaker pops right back up. A clothesline gets the same result but a slam keeps Undertaker down for a bit. Mabel goes up for a middle rope splash but Taker moves to avoid probably death. Instead a belly to belly and legdrop keep Undertaker down and there's a splash for good measure.

Mabel and Sir Mo roll Taker into the casket but don't shut the lid because they're not that bright. Undertaker blocks the eventual lid closing as Mabel is dancing in the ring with his crown. Back in and Taker pounds away before kicking Mabel into the casket. Mo's save is easily thwarted with a chokeslam and he gets thrown in as well. Undertaker takes back the necklace made from the Urn (don't ask) and slams the lid shut for the win at 6:11.

Rating: D+. This was about as perfect as you could get to end the Undertaker vs. Mabel feud but it doesn't help that we had to sit through it for so many months. Thankfully Mabel was gone soon after this with his last notable appearance coming in January. Undertaker is a good force to have back in the company as he was probably the third most popular member of the roster at this point, if not a bit higher.

Post match Undertaker motions that he wants the WWF Title.

Jim Cornette walks us through Bret's history with the Bulldog, who is married to Bret's sister. Unlike in 1992 where the sister Diana was split on who to cheer for, she's firmly in her husband's corner tonight.

Bret says he's making up for 1992 tonight.

WWF Title: Bret Hart vs. British Bulldog

Bret is defending and Bulldog has Cornette with him. The much stronger Bulldog shoves the champion into the corner to start but Bret grabs an armbar to take over. Davey flips around a lot but ultimately takes Bret down by the hair like a true villain should. Back to the armbar by Bret as we take a look at Cornette's tennis racket cover which looks like Santa Claus' face. Bret gets two off a crossbody and goes right back to the arm. Smith comes back with another hair pull before tying Bret up in the Tree of Woe (hanging him upside down in the corner) to stomp away.

Off to the chinlock as the fans are solidly behind Bret. They soon get bored of cheering for him though and start chanting for the then upstart promotion ECW. With nothing going on, Vince informs us that the Undertaker has challenged the winner of this match for the Royal Rumble. After a Cornette tennis racket shot we're in the third chinlock less than ten minutes into the match. The required chest first bump into the buckle gets two on Hart.

A backdrop puts Bret down for two more and we hit the chinlock again. At least this time he makes it a headlock as the fans chant USA, in theory for the Canadian champion. Bret comes back with a monkey flip and a bulldog to the Bulldog for two. A piledriver lays Smith out for two more but Bulldog crotches Bret on the ropes to break up a superplex. Bret falls to the floor and the fans want a table. Instead they get the champion being sent into the steps as Bulldog is in control.

Smith sends him hard into the barricade and Bret is busted wide open. Back in and Bulldog piledrives Bret down for a near fall before pounding at the cut on the forehead. The delayed vertical suplex gets the same and there's a gorilla press slam for good measure. Bulldog channels his former partner the Dynamite Kid with a headbutt to the back for two. Smith seems to have hurt his knee though so Bret tries a quick Sharpshooter, only to have Smith break it up just as easily.

A hard shoulder puts Bret onto the floor so Smith can try to get some feeling back into his knee. Bret counters a suplex back inside into a rollup for yet another near fall before a double clothesline puts both guys down. They're quickly back up and a backdrop puts Smith on the floor. Bret is ticked off now and dives over the top to pound away on Smith even more. Davey will have none of that though and powerslams Bret down on the floor to suck the life out of the crowd.

The protective mats are peeled back but Bret blocks a suplex by crotching Davey on the barricade in a nice callback to earlier in the match. Bret clotheslines him off the barricade and heads back inside where a backbreaker gets two. Now the superplex connects for two and an O'Connor Roll gets the same. Back up and Bulldog charges into a boot in the corner so Bret can cradle him for the pin at 21:09 in a very quick ending. The look on Diana's face makes the ending even better as it almost says "HOW DARE YOU KEEP THE TITLE!"

Rating: B-. This got WAY better in the end but the first ten minutes or so of this were pretty dreadful. Also the ending didn't do it any favors as I was expecting a callback to the Summerslam 1992 match but we didn't get anything close to it. Still though, good match and by far the best thing we've had on one of these shows in the last two shows.

Paul Bearer (Undertaker's odd manager) and Undertaker are pleased that they get a title shot at the Royal Rumble. Diesel comes in and says it's his shot. The giants stare each other down to end the show.

Overall Rating: D+. While this isn't a good show, it's WAY better than the previous two entries in the series. Bret is just better as champion as he can work with almost any style and get a better match out of most people. The rest of the card was pretty horrible, but things would be changing quickly around here which is the best thing that could have happened for the WWF.

A lot has changed since last month for the first time in awhile. January's Royal Rumble saw Bret Hart keep the WWF Title by retaining over Undertaker due to Diesel interfering, continuing their three way feud over the title. Other than that Shawn Michaels made his grand return and won his second straight Royal Rumble, earning himself the WWF Title shot at Wrestlemania XII. The main event of In Your House VI saw Bret Hart defending the title against Diesel inside a steel cage to prevent any outside interference.

In Your House #6: Rage in the Cage
Date: February 18, 1996
Location: Louisville Gardens, Louisville, Kentucky
Attendance: 5,500
Commentators: Jerry Lawler, Vince McMahon

This is the final show before Wrestlemania XII, meaning almost everything has been set up for the show already. There main question is who will be facing whom for the WWF Title. Other than Diesel vs. Bret tonight, there's also the case of who gets to face the winner for the title. As mentioned Shawn has won the right to fight for the title, but he also wants revenge against Owen Hart for putting him out, so tonight Shawn is putting his Wrestlemania title shot on the line for a shot at Owen. Let's get to it.

The opening video talks about the mindsets of Diesel and Bret and what role the Undertaker might play in the whole thing.

Vince and Jerry preview the show for us.

Razor Ramon vs. 1-2-3 Kid

This is a Crybaby Match, meaning the loser is put in a diaper. It's also the final encounter in a story that has run over two years and seen both guys turn at one point. The Kid also cost Razor the Intercontinental Title at the Rumble. He throws a diaper in Razor's face and gets punched in the jaw for his efforts before a big clothesline sends Kid over the top

The Kid snaps Razor's throat over the top rope and comes back in with a springboard clothesline before kicking away in the corner to take over. A big spin kick takes Razor's head off and he fires off chops in the corner, only to be reversed into a big hiptoss to give Ramon control again. There's the fall away slam but the Kid bails to the floor to escape the Razor's Edge. To play up the gimmick of the match, DiBiase slips the Kid some baby powder to throw in Razor's eyes (not a DQ for no apparent reason) to give the Kid two.

A pair of legdrops and a top rope splash gets another two count on Ramon and Kid hooks a sleeper. The hold stays on for almost three minutes but Razor finally fights up and crotches the Kid on the top rope for the break. Back up and Ramon scores with some right hands before rolling through a high crossbody for two. Kid comes back with a big spin wheel kick for two but gets caught in a middle rope fall away slam to knock him silly. DiBiase gives the Kid more powder but Razor kicks it into Kid's face before planting him with the Razor's Edge. He pulls Kid up at two though before hitting a second Edge for the pin at 12:01.

Rating: C+. Not a bad match here and a good choice for an opener but the sleeper went on too long. This is one of those stories that went on so long that it was hard to care about either guy at the end of it, but it got the Kid to a higher level than he would have been at otherwise which is a good sign. This was probably their best match in the entire story too.

Post match the Kid has a baby bottle poured down his throat, gets put in a diaper and covered in baby powder.

Hunter Hearst Helmsley vs. Duke Droese

Helmsley is accompanied by Elizabeth Hilden, a Penthouse Pet of the Year (not mentioned here of course). Droese is another of those one note characters, this time a wrestling garbage man. Helmsley cut Duke's hair recently so this is about revenge. Droese charges the ring and pounds away on Helmsley in the corner before slamming him down hard. Duke takes off his vest to whip Helmsley before booting him in the jaw.

A backdrop puts Helmsley down as Lawler hits on the Penthouse chick. Helmsley's Pedigree attempt is countered with an atomic drop and a clothesline puts him down again. Droese misses a charge and gets backdropped out to the floor, possibly injuring his shoulder. Helmsley whips him into the post for two and pounds away but Duke comes back for a slug out. A jumping knee to the face gets two on Droese and a snap suplex gets the same. Helmsley charges into a boot in the corner and a double clothesline puts both guys down.

Hilden is at least watching and seems to be interested in what's going on. That's all you can ask for with "celebrities" like her so I'll take what I can get. A spinebuster puts Helmsley down and a big backdrop does the same. There's a powerslam for no cover but Duke says it's time to take out the trash. He hits his tilt-a-whirl powerslam (the Trash Compactor) but goes to get his garbage can instead of covering. The referee throws it out but the distraction allows Helmsley to blast Duke with the can lid for the pin at 9:40.

Rating: C-. Not terrible here with Droese having some nice power stuff. The story doesn't really work because it's such a low level idea but the hair cutting stuff from a few weeks ago gave it a personal touch. Not a great match or anything but it did its job well enough. Helmsley is getting some character development over the months too which is what he needs more than anything.

We recap the collapse of Camp Cornette, which culminated in the British Bulldog accidentally hitting Yokozuna and costing them a tag match. Cornette berated Yokozuna after the match and the big man erupted, turning face in the process ala Andre the Giant at Wrestlemania VI.

Yokozuna cuts his first promo ever, saying it's his time to take the spotlight from Cornette.

Yokozuna vs. British Bulldog

Bulldog gets slugged down within seconds and there's a slam for good measure. Yokozuna misses an elbow drop though and Bulldog starts the very slow choking. It only lasts a few seconds though as Yokozuna crushes him in the corner but Cornette breaks up the Banzai Drop attempt. We get a VERY slow fight on the floor until Bulldog avoids a charge into the post and they head back inside. A top rope ax handle gets two for Smith but Yokozuna hits a quick (by comparison) Samoan drop, drawing in Cornette with a tennis racket shot for the DQ at 5:05.

Rating: D. This didn't have time to go anywhere but what we got was as bad as it sounded. There's just nothing you can do with a guy Yokozuna's size unless you're a monster yourself. Smith is a powerful guy but he's hardly a giant. Nothing much to see here though but at least it was short.

Post match Yokozuna goes after Cornette until Vader, the new monster of Camp Cornette, comes out to slug Yokozuna down into the corner and handcuff him to the ropes. The beating ensues and goes on longer than it should have.

Goldust is on AOL for an interview and flirts with the guy typing.

We recap Shawn vs. Owen which we've covered for the most part. Owen is bragging about injuring Shawn's head but tonight Michaels is back and putting up his Wrestlemania title shot for a chance at revenge.

Shawn says this is the biggest match of his career because if he doesn't win, he can't achieve his destiny at Wrestlemania.

Owen Hart vs. Shawn Michaels

The Wrestlemania title shot is on the line. Shawn comes in from the roof of the house set, dancing atop the garage. Feeling out process to start with Shawn sliding through Owen's legs and all the way out to the floor to show Owen up a bit. Michaels kisses a woman in the front row on the cheek, sending her nearly into delirium. Back in and Owen slides through the legs just like Shawn did, only Michaels goes up top and dives to the floor to take Owen out. Back in and a top rope ax handle to the head gets two for Michaels.

Owen gets taken down with ease and Shawn walks up his back to show off even more. We hit a headlock for a bit with Shawn messing up Owen's hair. Owen gets a quick takedown but Shawn kicks him away, allowing both guys to nip up at the same time. A hurricanrana takes Owen down and Shawn pounds away, only to walk into a belly to belly suplex to give Owen his first advantage.

A neckbreaker gets two for Owen as he starts going after Shawn's head. Scratch that actually as Shawn has to kick out of a Sharpshooter attempt but gets caught in an armbar. The hold is shifted into a camel clutch before Owen gets two off a rollup. Off to a chinlock as the rest holds continue to abound. Back up and the spinwheel kick sends Shawn out to the floor, possibly injuring Shawn's head again.

Back in again and Shawn throws Hart to the floor and dives off the apron, only to get caught in a powerslam down to the floor. A missile dropkick gets two for Owen and Shawn is in big trouble. The hard whip into the corner turns Shawn upside down in the corner and he gets his head taken off with a hard clothesline for no cover. There's the Sharpshooter as Owen completely changes his offensive strategy for the sake of using a signature move.

Michaels is dragged back to the middle of the ring but finally grabs the bottom rope. Back up and Owen hits his enziguri, sending Shawn out to the floor and seemingly out on consciousness. Back in and Owen only gets a two count but Shawn comes back with a flying forearm to the head. He nips up and the energy is rolling. The top rope elbow connects, followed by a right hand to Cornette, setting up Sweet Chin Music to send Shawn to Wrestlemania at 15:57.

Rating: B. This was good but it didn't hit the level they were going for. That being said, this was exactly what they were supposed to be doing with Shawn coming back from his injury and winning the match completely clean in the middle of the ring. Shawn was on a roll at this point and the fans were WAY into him.

Post match Shawn dances with an 8 year old girl in the ring for a nice moment.

Here's acting president Roddy Piper with something to say. He thinks Michael Jackson is guilty (topical at the time) before officially announcing Shawn as #1 contender to the WWF Title. Second he doesn't feel sorry for Yokozuna because he let himself get cuffed to the ropes. Piper thinks Vader is inbred and that his mask looks like a jockstrap. Vader vs. Yokozuna is officially made for Wrestlemania.

This brings out Cornette but Piper immediately cuts him off and demands respect. Cornette talks about how the old Piper was afraid of nothing but now he's afraid of Vader. Piper cuts him off again and says that if Vader loses at Wrestlemania, Cornette has to face Yokozuna one on one. This was a way to give the ring crew time to set up the cage.

WWF Title: Diesel vs. Bret Hart

Bret is defending in a cage of course and you can win by escape only. Diesel pounds him into the corner to start but Bret comes back with right hands of his own, only to be shoved down with ease. The big man fires off more right hands in the corner before talking some trash. A HARD whip across the ring shakes the cage and Bret is in big trouble early. The champion slips away from Diesel, sending his head into the cage. Bret rams it in again and drops some elbows on Diesel's head as this is very physical so far.

Bret goes up but Diesel makes the stop and rams Bret back first into the cage wall. He tries to get out but Bret crotches him with the ropes and fires off even more right hands to the head. Neither guy can escape so Bret goes after the knee to slow Diesel down. Bret fights back up and clotheslines Hart down as Lawler wonders why they're not running to escape as soon as the other guy is down. A sidewalk slam puts Hart down again but he takes out the knee again to regain control.

Hart goes for the escape but only gets one leg out when Diesel makes another stop and launches him off the top rope in a slam. Diesel charges into a knee in the corner and gets bulldogged down but Bret can't follow up. We get another escape attempt by Bret but this time Diesel suplexes him down for the stop. They're getting a little repetitive here.

Diesel misses a charge in the corner and hurts his knee again, giving Bret an opening. The champion goes after the bad wheel and drops a middle rope elbow on it for good measure. Diesel counters a whip to give us the chest first buckle bump, which sounds AWESOME because of the cage shaking. The challenger pounds away with elbows in the corner but Bret kicks him in the knee for a breather.

Hart goes up again and gets all the way out of the cage but Diesel pulls him up by the hair in a painful looking sequence. Diesel stays on Bret's back by cannonballing down onto the spine, only to be rammed face first into the cage for his efforts. The big man pokes Hart in the eye and the fans are entirely in his corner at the moment.

Bret fights up and slugs away before taking Diesel down with the Russian legsweep. There's the middle rope elbow but Diesel pulls Bret down again to put both guys on the mat. Diesel goes for the door but the Undertaker pops up through the mat and pulls Diesel down under the ring. Smoke pours out of the hole as Bret climbs out to retain the title at 19:13.

Rating: D+. This was a pretty boring match for the most part with a very repetitive sequence going on throughout the twenty minutes. Diesel needed to be more physical out there and this is one of the few instances where pinfalls could have helped a cage match. Diesel wasn't going to escape, but the threat of a Jackknife could have helped things out a lot.

Diesel and Undertaker crawl out of the hole with Diesel escaping from further torment to end the show.

Overall Rating: C-. It's a better show overall due to the really good Shawn match and some other nice stuff in between but it's still no classic. They're definitely getting the formula down though and things will be changing even more with the events of Wrestlemania. Better show here and thankfully these are getting much easier to sit through. That's a sign of the times in the WWF, which would actually lead to much darker days, which we'll get to soon enough.

The show following Rage in the Cage was of course Wrestlemania XII where a lot of things changed. First and foremost, Shawn Michaels beat Bret Hart for the WWF Title in a one hour Iron Man match, sending Bret away in a huff for the next seven and a half months. Shawn Michaels is now the man that will lead the WWF in the coming war with WCW. However, Shawn needs a win to cement himself as the new top guy.

The other major match at Wrestlemania saw Diesel face the Undertaker in a battle of the monsters. If you know your WWF history, you'll know there's no way Undertaker loses at Wrestlemania, meaning Diesel was planted with the Tombstone. Since Diesel needs to get a win under his belt (after losing every PPV match he's had since November), he's the #1 contender against his old friend Shawn Michaels in a no holds barred match.

In Your House #7: Good Friends, Better Enemies
Date: April 26, 1997
Location: Omaha Civic Auditorium, Omaha, Nebraska
Attendance: 9,563
Commentators: Vince McMahon, Jerry Lawler

Other than the WWF Title match, there really isn't much to talk about on this show. There are some Wrestlemania rematches and a few thrown together matches, with the biggest being the Intercontinental Title match. Champion Goldust will be defending against the returning Ultimate Warrior, a former star of the 1980s who hasn't been a regular competitor since 1992. He returned at Wrestlemania and beat Hunter Hearst Helmsley in a squash, earning a title shot. Let's get to it.

The opening video sums up the main event and highlights Diesel running over everyone in sight on the path back to the title.

Owen Hart/British Bulldog vs. Jake Roberts/Ahmed Johnson

This is a rematch from Wrestlemania minus Vader and Yokozuna on the respective teams. Apparently Davey Boy Smith has a horrible fear of snakes as learned on a recent tour of Germany. Naturally Jake the Snake Roberts has a snake with him, but Camp Cornette's attorney Clarence Mason has an injunction to prevent him from bringing it out. Jake responds by pulling the snake out and throwing it on Cornette, who faints as a result. The snake has to be taken to the back but the damage has been done.

Jake pounds away on Owen as Ahmed, a VERY muscular and intimidating looking strongman, is still making his entrance. Owen bails to the corner and brings in Smith to face Johnson. The Bulldog sees him come in and immediately tags back out to Hart in a funny bit. Ahmed easily launches Owen into the corner because he wants the Bulldog one on one. He still doesn't get his wish though as Hart grabs a headlock and is against tossed across the ring.

Here's Roberts again but Owen is quickly out the back door to avoid a DDT. Owen bails to the corner to avoid another attempt and now it's off to Bulldog to slam Roberts down. Smith runs from Johnson again with Hart getting annoyed at having to fight the monster over and over again. A test of strength goes badly for Owen and Johnson clotheslines him down with ease. Owen gets in a shot to the ribs to take Johnson down and it's finally off to Smith for some cheap shots.

Ahmed shrugs off all of the offense and scares Bulldog into the corner for yet another tag off to Owen. Johnson easily slams the Canadian down and it's off to Jake who gets dropkicked in the face to give the villains control again. Smith comes back in to stomp Jake down, allowing Owen to get in some extra choking on the side. Jake avoids a charge in the corner to send Owen chest first into the buckle ala his big brother. Roberts gets poked in the eyes to stop his hot tag bid and it's back to Owen with a top rope elbow to the face for two.

We hit the chinlock as the match slows down a bit with Owen still in full control. A jumping back elbow to the face looks to set up the Sharpshooter but Jake kicks him away. Bulldog cheats from the apron and comes back in for another chinlock. The fans are staying into the match with their cheering for Jake but this time Owen cheats from the apron to keep him in the ring.

Jake gets caught in a sleeper but he suplexes Hart down to escape. Now we get the hot tag off to Ahmed who cleans house before everything breaks down. Owen and Bulldog are sent to the floor but Smith gets in a tennis racket shot to Jake's knee. A simple leglock is enough to make Roberts submit at 13:47.

Rating: D+. WAY too long here and it dragged the match down a lot. The match wasn't going to be much to see in the first place but this should have been about five minutes shorter. Bulldog and Owen are becoming one of the longest running tag teams in the 90s and they're reaching a fairly high level in a hurry. Match was still too long though.

Intercontinental Title: Goldust vs. Ultimate Warrior

Goldust is accompanied by both Marlena (his regular valet) and an unnamed bodyguard here and is defending. This match basically becomes a game to see how many movie references Jerry Lawler can make in under ten minutes. He makes so many that I can't even keep track of them but I'd say it's at least twenty of them.

Now here's the problem with the match: Goldust has a legitimate knee injury and can't have a match, but we're going to have a "match" anyway. Warrior's entrance is enough to fire up the crowd (Lawler: "He's like a raging bull." Just picture about 25 of those kind of lines and you'll get the idea.) but that's about all of the good.

Goldust ("He's got such a brave heart.") limps into the ring but hides back on the floor before trying to leave with his lady Marlena. Warrior takes Goldust's cigar and puffs away like a real hero does. He brings Goldust's director's chair into the ring while wearing the champion's blonde wig and robe because a replacement wrestler was too complicated I suppose. Goldust is walking up and down the aisle while this is going on and I'm not even sure the match has started yet.

After walking around for about five minutes Goldust grabs a mic and threatens to come into the crowd and kiss everyone in the audience if they don't shut up. Warrior holds up the rope like a bullfighter's cape as Marlena gets in the ring for some reason. There has been no contact at all so far.

Goldust gets in the ring behind Marlena and Warrior holds up the robe so the champion can put it on. This has been going on for nearly eight minutes now. Now he's sitting in the chair with his legs crossed as Warrior puffs on the cigar. Goldust holds out his hand and gets burned, earning himself a clothesline. That's enough to send him to the floor and there's a countout to FINALLY end this at 7:38

Rating: N/A. I can't rate this because it wasn't a match. This was some bizarre performance piece and I have no idea who thought this was the best idea. There was nothing here for the fans to watch and it was basically a way to rip them off while knowing that there was nothing to offer them at all. This is one of the most insane things I've ever seen in wrestling which covers a lot of ground.

Post match Warrior beats up the bodyguard which would have made for a much better match.

British Bulldog is ranting and raving about something while trying to get into Shawn Michaels' dressing room. We'll come back to that later.

Razor Ramon vs. Vader

Vader recently broke Yokozuna's leg so Ramon is here as his next target. Cornette also manages Vader so Razor has someone else to worry about. Razor is easily launched over the top and out to the floor before being shoved down in the ring. Vader is tired of throwing him around now though so here are some hard punches to the ribs. A hard shot puts Razor down onto his knees and there are some heavy punches to the head as well.

Razor comes back with some rights of his own but gets easily clotheslined down by the monster. Ramon hits a running right hand but a Razor's Edge attempt is easily blocked with a backdrop out to the floor. Back in and Razor pounds Vader down in the corner for his first real advantage and a discus punch drops Vader. A clothesline does it again and a second clothesline puts Vader to the floor. Razor is WAY over with the crowd here.

Vader slides in to break a few near countouts as the match slows way down. A Cornette distraction lets Vader come back in but Razor catches him with another right hand to the jaw. Vader is tired of this being on defense stuff though and takes Razor down with another stiff clothesline. Razor ducks another clothesline and hits a nice belly to back suplex for two but can't follow up.

Vader drags him over to the corner and hits his Vader Bomb but Ramon somehow kicks out at two. That's a very rare sight to see. A belly to back puts Razor down this time but Vader just takes him into the corner and pounds away to bust up Razor's insides even more. Razor actually comes back with a vertical suplex for two but Vader snapmares him back down. A middle rope clothesline is caught in a powerslam for two by Razor but he still can't follow up because of the punishment.

Razor gets two off a middle rope bulldog but a shoulder block puts him right back down. Another Vader Bomb is countered into a Razor's Edge attempt but the bad ribs give out to stop Razor in his tracks. Vader loads up the moonsault but Razor pulls him down in a nice looking electric chair drop. Razor tries the Edge again but Vader backdrops him down and drops down onto the bad ribs for the pin at 14:49.

Rating: B-. This was a fun match as Razor was the perfect choice to put Vader over. He's very popular but at the same time he's big and strong enough to be able to throw Vader around and make it look good. Vader was definitely a monster though and was on for bigger and better things in the near future.

The match however is more important for being Razor's last significant match in the WWF until 2002, as he was wooed away by millions of dollars to WCW. This would be a huge blow to the company and we'll get into how big of a deal it was in a little while. Razor wouldn't be the only one to take off after this show.

Doc Hendrix tells Vader and Cornette that Vader will face Yokozuna at the next In Your House. Cornette freaks out, as only he can.

Tag Team Titles: Godwinns vs. Bodydonnas

The Bodydonnas, the champions, are fitness enthusiasts Skip and Zip and managed by the gorgeous Sunny. The Godwinns are Henry and his cousin Phineas (Middle initials O and I respectively, meaning their full initials are H.O.G. And P.I.G.) with the latter having a big crush on Phineas. The Bodydonnas won the titles in a tournament final at Wrestlemania so this is a rematch.

Henry throws Zip around to start but has to double clothesline both Donnas down. Off to Phineas who bites Zip's arm and cranks on it a bit before tagging Henry back in. Skip, the more talented of the champions, comes in and jumps into something vaguely resembling John Cena's Attitude Adjustment. A nice wheelbarrow suplex sends Skip out to the floor as this is one sided so far. Zip tries to sneak in but the referee catches them since the Bodydonnas aren't exactly twins.

Back in and it's Phineas vs. Zip with Phineas getting some kicks to the head and grabbing a headlock. Skip low bridges the hog farmer to the floor and the champions take over for the first time. The Donnas get two off a slingshot suplex as the camera keeps looking at Sunny but I can't say I blame them much this time around. Off to a chinlock from Skip followed by a standing hurricanrana for two.

Phineas gets all riled up (Vince's words) and cleans house as everything breaks down. Sunny runs to the back and comes back with a framed photo of herself to give to Phineas. Why he's fascinated by the photo when the real thing is right in front of him isn't explained but Phineas wasn't all that bright. Henry hits the Slop Drop on Zip but the distraction at ringside allows Skip to sneak in and small package Henry to retain the titles at 7:17.

Rating: D. Much like most of the Bodydonnas' matches, Sunny was the best thing going on. She was just so good at being evil and the looks didn't hurt anything at all. The tag division was just such a mess at this point though and this didn't do it a lot of favors. That would be the case for years to come.

Marc Mero (former WCW star Johnny B. Badd) wants a piece of Hunter Hearst Helmsley over Helmsley mistreating one of his valets named Sable. Helmsley interfered in Mero's match on the preshow and laid Mero out with a Pedigree. Mero says Helmsley unleashed the wild man.

We recap Shawn vs. Diesel. The idea is simple: they used to be friends but now Diesel wants the title and will do whatever it takes to get it back. Shawn is in WAY over his head in a no holds barred match because it's not his forte, but he's got a big heart and won't back down no matter what.

Shawn guaranteed a win earlier tonight.

Legendary wrestler Mad Dog Vachon (from Omaha) is at here.

WWF Title: Shawn Michaels vs. Diesel

Shawn is defending and remember this is no holds barred so

anything goes. No flashy entrance from Shawn as he just power walks to the ring and takes the belt off on the way. He pounds away on the much bigger Diesel but a knee to the ribs puts the champion down. A big dropkick sends Diesel to the floor and a moonsault press takes him down onto the concrete.

Shawn steals a boot from the Spanish's announcer and lays out Diesel back inside for two. Back up and Diesel whips Shawn up and over the corner before hammering him off the apron and face first into the barricade with a nasty bump. Back in and Diesel runs Shawn over again before walking around very slowly. Snake Eyes (a face first drop onto the buckle) drops Michaels again and Diesel yells at Shawn's trainer Jose Lothario that this is how we do it in the 90s.

A big side slam drops Shawn again and Diesel chokes the referee with his wrist tape for no apparent reason other than evil. Diesel steals the referee's belt to whip Shawn even more before wrapping it around Shawn's neck and hanging him over the top rope. He even ties the belt around the middle rope so he can grab a chair to blast Shawn in the back. They get back in the ring and another chair shot to the back puts Shawn down yet again. A third shot hits the top rope, sending the chair bouncing back into Diesel's head.

Now Shawn grabs the chair but Diesel hits him low before Shawn can swing it. A BIG backdrop keeps the pressure on Shawn's back and gets a two count. Diesel cranks on Shawn's neck but Michaels fights up, only to be dropped with a series of forearms, knocking him out to the floor. In the big spot of the match, Diesel Jackknifes Shawn through the announcers' table (big deal back then), further destroying his back. That looked AWESOME and Vince begging Shawn to "just let it be over" makes it even better.

Diesel tries to pull Shawn back in but Michaels finds a fire extinguisher under the ring and blinds the big man so he can pound away. The fans are going NUTS over this comeback. Shawn pulls in a chair and goes to town on Diesel but lets Diesel get back up for a clothesline and a big boot to the jaw. Diesel loads up another Jackknife but Shawn punches his way out of it and drops a top rope elbow to the big man's chest. Shawn tunes up the band for the superkick but Diesel blocks the boot and clotheslines Shawn down again.

A third clothesline puts Shawn on the floor as Vince gets in the very almost famous line of "We said it would be no holds barred but we didn't expect this." Diesel drops Shawn throat first on the barricade before going over to Mad Dog Vachon. He chokes Vachon down and RIPS OFF HIS PROSTHETIC LEG. Back in and Shawn hits Diesel low, blasts him in the face with the leg and hits Sweet Chin Music to retain the title at 17:53 to blow the roof off the place.

Rating: A+. This was a WAR and one of the best brawls you'll ever see. They were beating the tar out of each other out there with Shawn bumping around like a maniac and making Diesel's offense look great. This gave Shawn the credibility that he needed as champion to show he could fight as well as wrestle and it was a great performance to boot. It's one of my all time personal favorite matches and still more than holds up over seventeen years later. Probably the best In Your House match to this point.

Unfortunately for the WWF, this was also Nash's swan song as he and Razor were the two that left for WCW less than a month later. We'll be talking about that in much greater detail soon.

Shawn poses with an awesome look on his face that says he can take on the world to end the show.

Overall Rating: C+. The rest of the show isn't great but the main event more than makes up for it. That's a major perk of having shows under two hours: a match that runs about fifteen to twenty minutes like Shawn vs. Diesel can save a bad card and this one saves it in a big way. The only other good match on here is Vader vs. Ramon and even that's just ok. Shawn vs. Diesel however is a classic and bordering on a masterpiece, making it well worth seeing if you haven't before.

It's only a month later but a lot has changed in the WWF. We no longer have Razor Ramon or Diesel, leaving Shawn with a lot more of the pressure to carry the company on his shoulders. The main event for the next show is Shawn defending against the British Bulldog who you might remember freaking out about something Shawn did at the last show. The story went that Shawn made a pass at Smith's wife, setting the Bulldog off. There isn't much else of note on the show, but this is one of the most interesting shows in WWF history.

There are actually two versions of this show but only one ever saw the light of day. The original show was scheduled for Sunday, May 26 in Florence, South Carolina. The first match went by perfectly well but after that, a bad thunderstorm rolled into the area and knocked out the power to the arena. The PPV feed cut out and the fans at home missed about an hour of the show. The feed did come back on in time for the main event, but no one saw the middle four matches. Those matches actually took place in the dark but to the best of my knowledge they have never been released.

Obviously this wasn't fair to the people who paid for the show, so the company held a second PPV in North Charleston, South Carolina on Tuesday, May 28th. The show featured the two matches from the original show and three new matches that aired live. The airing of the matches was a little odd as the WWF Title match was aired second on the second PPV while the rest of the matches were aired after, meaning the last thing on the PPV is an Intercontinental Title match instead of the WWF Title match.

In Your House #8: Beware of Dog
Date: May 26/28, 1998
Location: Florence Civic Center, Florence, South Carolina/North Charleston Coliseum, North Charleston, South Carolina
Attendance: 6,000/4,500
Commentators: Vince McMahon, Jerry Lawler/Jim Ross, Mr. Perfect

Other than the Shawn vs. Bulldog match, the biggest match here is probably a Caribbean strap match between Savio Vega and newcomer Steve Austin. Austin isn't a big star yet but it's clear that the potential is there and that he could become something very big if he's given the right amount of time. Vega was his first major feud and tonight is the blowoff between the two of them. Let's get to it.

58

The opening video talks about Shawn while also focusing on the allegations of him breaking up Bulldog's marriage.

Vince thanks the people that keep us free to be here tonight, which I'd assume is a shout out to the military.

Hunter Hearst Helmsley vs. Marc Mero

These two have been feuding since Wrestlemania. It's a brawl to start before Mero's theme music is even off. Mero takes him into the corner and pounds away before punching Helmsley out to the floor. A big plancha over the top takes Helmsley down again and we head back inside for a two count.

Helmsley pokes him in the eye to get a breather but gets flipped upside down in the corner for another near fall. Mero misses a charge and goes shoulder first into the post followed by Helmsley throwing him shoulder first into another post to really take over. A DDT on the arm stays on the bad shoulder as Vince warns of potential technical difficulties due to the storm but promising that they won't last long. Mero gets pounded down and Vince isn't pleased with the officiating so far.

A jumping knee to the face gets two on Mero and it's off to another armbar. Mero tries to come back with a backslide but the arm gives out, allowing Helmsley to wrap it around the post again. The arm goes around the post a fourth time and Mero is in big trouble. Helmsley wraps the arm around the ropes and rams it into the buckle before putting on a cross armbreaker of all things.

After nearly a minute in the hold Mero is able to get to a rope, drawing almost no reaction from the crowd. They don't seem all that interested in what's going on, even though this is good stuff so far. Helmsley drops a knee onto the arm and puts on an armbar for a few moments. The shoulder is sent into the buckle again but Mero grabs a quick rollup with his feet under Helmsley's arms for two. Helmsley wraps the arm around the ropes again and drops a top rope ax handle into the shoulder. That arm is being destroyed so far.

A hammerlock slam puts Mero down again but he gets up fast enough to crotch Helmsley on the top rope. Mero is able to snap off a top rope hurricanrana to put both guys down as the arm is too banged up. Helmsley gets taken down with a headscissors and a running knee lift before a top rope sunset flip (one of Mero's finishers) is good for two.

Mero sends him to the floor and tries a flip dive over the ropes, only for Helmsley to move, injuring Mero's knee in the process. Back inside and Helmsley loads up the Pedigree but Sable covers her eyes, making Helmsley drop the move. He demands that she watch but the delay lets Mero counter the second attempt into a catapult into the post for the pin out of nowhere at 16:23.

Rating: B. This was a really nice surprise with both guys looking great out there. I loved seeing Mero wrestle with one arm as so often you'll see someone have a limb injured and then just hold it while wrestling as usual. Very good showing here and a good example of letting the young guys set up the rest of the show in style.

Camp Cornette has a big surprise for Shawn but for now he'll just get a smaller one: Owen Hart has a one night only manager's license so he'll be at ringside with the Bulldog.

Remember that the following match happened about an hour after the previous match.

Shawn says that he's ready for the match but as he's walking to the ring, Mr. Perfect smirks at him for some reason. They have a history together but haven't had any issues for years.

WWF Title: British Bulldog vs. Shawn Michaels

Shawn is defending. Before the match, attorney Clarence Mason says that Shawn has tried to break up the Smith family so he'll be filing a lawsuit against Shawn for "attempted alienation of affection." Shawn is given the subpoena, rips it up, and gets jumped from behind to get things going. That's about the extent of this story and no one remembered it after the show. Shawn slides between the Bulldog's legs and pounds away, sending Smith to the floor to run away from the kick.

Michaels dives over the top to take Bulldog out and we head back inside so they can circle each other. Shawn grabs a headlock to take him down to the mat with the hold lasting for a good while.

Back up and Bulldog grabs a quickly broken bearhug, only to drop down to avoid a charging Shawn and getting caught in a rollup for two. Shawn goes to a short arm scissors but Smith rolls over and lifts Shawn into the air in the same counter he made famous against Shawn back in 1992.

Bulldog stomps Shawn down a bit more and poses for good measure. We hit the chinlock before the Bulldog puts on an over the shoulder backbreaker to stay on the back. The Bulldog slams him down and hits a Samoan drop to keep Shawn in trouble. Off to another chinlock as Owen goes around ringside talking trash about Shawn.

While in the hold, something clearly goes wrong with Shawn. The referee then gets up and goes over to the timekeeper, completely ignoring the hold. Allegedly this was saying that the match's time had been cut due to the technical issues and Shawn was throwing a fit. Great way to react by the champion there. Anyway Shawn fights up and escapes the hold but misses a charge and falls out to the floor in a heap. Bulldog rams him into the announcers' table as well as the apron before heading back inside for a breather.

Shawn fights back and scores with a slingshot clothesline from the apron to put both guys down again. Back up and they hit heads to knock both guys down for the third time. Shawn is up first and scores with the flying forearm before nipping up. A top rope ax handle gets two but the Bulldog accidentally runs over the referee, knocking him out to the floor.

Shawn hits the top rope elbow but has to take out Owen instead of superkicking Smith. Another referee comes out as Smith loads up the powerslam but Shawn escapes. The champion hits a belly to back suplex and all four shoulders are down. The second referee gets back in and we have a double pin at 17:21.

Rating: B-. This was a solid match and set up the rematch well enough. That being said, this would have felt better if it came at the end of the show rather than in the middle, but you can't blame the company for a bad storm. Good stuff here though with Shawn looking good and Bulldog being a good opponent for him. It also reinforces the idea that Diesel just wasn't all that good in the ring as Smith has had his second solid title match in a few months.

Post match both guys are announced as winners by different referees. President Gorilla Monsoon comes to the ring and we get a lot of replays which show the same double pin over and over again. Since it's a tie, Shawn retains the title, all but guaranteeing a rematch.

Everything from this point on is from Tuesday's show and is airing live on PPV instead of being taped.

Savio Vega vs. Steve Austin

This is a Caribbean strap match, meaning they're tied at the wrist and the first person to touch all four corners without interruption is the winner. Austin debuted a few months prior and is just the Ringmaster at this point, meaning he's as generic of a heel as you could ask for. There's potential there, but the gimmick is crippling him. The idea here is that it's Savio's signature match and if he wins, Austin's manager Ted DiBiase leaves the company forever. DiBiase has a chauffeur's hat which goes on Savio if he loses.

Austin immediately bails to the floor to start before coming back in to pound away on Vega. Savio comes back with a backdrop and Austin bails to the floor, only to have Savio pull the strap to send him ribs first into the apron. Back in and Vega whips Austin's back with the strap and Steve just tries to get out of the ring to safety. Savio suplexes Austin back inside and the strap goes across the chest even more. Vega gets two corners but Austin trips him up to stop the streak, thereby erasing the two corners Savio touched.

Now it's Austin's turn to whip Vega but Savio pulls him to the mat and they go outside again. Austin gets in a HARD whip to the back before sending him back first into the barricade. Steve pulls him back up onto the apron to try and hang Savio but opts to just whip his chest instead. The strap is wrapped around Savio's ankle so Austin can drag him around the ring but Vega breaks it up just before the third corner.

Savio starts whipping Austin again but gets backdropped out to the floor before he can get too far. The strap comes back to haunt Austin again though as Vega pulls him to the floor instead of giving Austin a breather. Vega suplexes Austin on the floor and takes him back inside where he ties Austin's arm and leg together. Austin makes a stop and just goes nuts with the whip to take Savio's breath away. Vega somehow gets up and crotches Austin down on the top, setting up a great looking superplex.

Savio slaps three corners but Austin makes a last second save with a spinebuster. Both guys are down again and Austin's back is red from those strap shots. Austin chokes Savio across the ropes and with the strap before blasting him in the back for good measure. Austin gets two corners but Vega pokes him in the eyes before the third. They trade Tombstone piledriver attempts but Savio falls over the top and out to the floor before either guy can hit one.

Austin hangs Savio over the ropes yet again before going up top, only to be pulled down onto the barricade. Savio pulls him into the post before taking Austin back inside for a fireman's carry. Austin puts up a fight after two buckles but it isn't counted as breaking the momentum so Steve pulls him down after the third. A piledriver lays out Vega again but DiBiase wants another one. Savio counters into a backdrop but Austin comes back with his Million Dollar Dream sleeper.

Vega manages to stay on his feet so Austin jumps on his back. Savio walks around and gets two corners, only to climb up the ropes and drive Austin back first onto the mat for the break. Austin comes right back with more choking, wrapping the strap around Savio's throat and pulling him across. Steve gets two but Savio slaps both of them as he passes by. Both guys get number three so it's next buckle wins. In a very interesting ending, they get in a tug of war over the last corner but Austin looks down at DiBiase and catapults Savio into the buckle to lose the match at 21:27, but also intentionally get rid of DiBiase.

Rating: A-. This is by far the best four corners strap match I've ever seen. They beat the tar out of each other and the story made it even better. Steve intentionally losing makes him look very smart and all the more evil because he's willing to throw DiBiase out the door to make himself a bigger star in the future. Really good stuff here.

Savio has the fans sing the Goodbye song to DiBiase.

Vader vs. Yokozuna

Vader broke Yokozuna's leg a few months ago so tonight is about revenge. They slug it out to start with Vader getting the best of it to start, only to have Yokozuna punch him to the floor. Cornette nearly has a fit as Yokozuna is asking for a sumo challenge. Vader gets down in a three point football stance but steps to the side instead of charging ahead. They set up again and Vader does the exact same thing. The third attempt actually happens and Vader goes down like he's barely even there before Yokozuna clotheslines him out to the floor.

Back in and Vader pounds away at the side of the head, only to have Yokozuna sweep the leg out and fall down on Vader's leg. Vader rolls to the floor again, making sure we don't have more than a few consecutive seconds of action in this match. He gets back inside and just pops Yokozuna in the face with right hands. Yokozuna sweeps the leg again and drops another elbow to complete the same sequence we just saw.

This time Vader doesn't go to the floor but rather get up and pound away on Yokozuna's back. He can't slam him though, allowing Yokozuna to come back with a Rock Bottom for no cover. A Samoan drop puts Vader down again but Yokozuna goes after Cornette instead of hitting the Banzai Drop. Vader saves Cornette and hits two Vader Bombs for the pin at 8:53.

Rating: D-. This was nine minutes of the same sequences going over and over until we got to the ending. These battles of huge men rarely go anywhere because there's only so much they can do. Yokozuna would fade away pretty quickly after this due to his immense weight. He would try for years to get back into the company but he just couldn't get his weight under control.

Intercontinental Title: Goldust vs. Undertaker

This is a casket match. The video before the match show us the setup of Goldust vs. Ahmed Johnson from last night instead of telling us about Goldust vs. Undertaker. Goldust had given an unconscious Ahmed mouth to mouth, thereby infuriating Johnson. The lights go out (JR: "On purpose this time.") and Undertaker appears behind Goldust in the ring. Undertaker throws the champion around on the floor before taking him inside for more of the same.

They head back outside again with Goldust being sent into steps. Back inside again as the destruction continues. A legdrop keeps Goldust in trouble and Undertaker hits what would become known as Old School. Goldust comes back with a quick slam and a Tombstone of his own but Undertaker sits up almost immediately. The champion puts him in the casket but can't get the lid shut as Undertaker comes back with right hands. Instead Goldust sends him out to the floor and into the steps before choking with an electrical cord.

Back in and Undertaker gets caught in a bad looking sleeper hold to drag the match down even more. Goldust still can't get him in the closed casket though as Undertaker blocks two attempts. They head back inside with Undertaker clotheslining both guys out to the floor, only to head back inside where the champion powerslams him down. A middle rope clothesline puts Undertaker down and Goldust goes for a cover out of instinct.

Goldust tries Old School of his own, only to be slammed down with ease. There's the real Tombstone but Undertaker opens the casket and finds the recently debuted monster Mankind waiting on him. Mankind puts Undertaker in his Mandible Claw submission hold before putting Undertaker inside the casket and closing the lid for the win at 12:36.

Rating: D. This feud was just a holding pattern for Undertaker until the real feud Mankind could get going. No one bought Undertaker as a guy who would be in the Intercontinental Title picture for more than a few weeks and that's exactly what happened. Nothing to see here and not a good way to end the show.

Post match Mankind locks Undertaker inside the casket but as Mankind leaves, smoke starts coming out of the casket. Paul Bearer opens the casket and there's no one inside. The lights go out again to end the show.

Overall Rating: B. This is a really solid show with three awesome matches to open things up followed by two that weren't so good. If you stop the show after the strap match though, you have an awesome PPV with storyline development and awesome action. Really good stuff here....for the first hour or so.

Maybe It's Time To Change

Wrestling really started to change around this time and it was the WWF that was being left behind. On the Monday between the two In Your House #8 shows, something happened on the WCW TV show called Monday Nitro. In the middle of a worthless match, an unnamed man jumped the guardrail and said everyone knew who he was but no one knew why he was there. Wrestling fans knew him as Razor Ramon but everyone thought he still worked for the WWF.

This began a multi-year long storyline with the group that Ramon (later named Scott Hall) would help form, eventually named the New World Order (NWO), would attempt to take over WCW. The story was incredibly popular and destroyed the WWF and Monday Night Raw in particular for the better part of two years. The old style of production that Raw was presenting wasn't cutting it anymore and something new was needed.

At the pay per view in between In Your House 8 and 9, Steve Austin won the King of the Ring tournament. This didn't mean much at the time but it was certainly his biggest accomplishment to date. The more important thing though was the speech that Austin gave after his win. While on the stage, Austin first uttered the phrase Austin 3:16, which launched a marketing campaign and a slew of t-shirts over the years and ultimately launched Austin to the stars. We'll cover that in more detail later though.

The next show we'll be covering is In Your House #9, which served as a bridge between Beware of Dog and the feud that would headline Summerslam 1996. The main event is a six man tag with Camp Cornette teaming up against the People's Posse, comprised of Shawn Michaels, Ahmed Johnson and the returning Sycho Sid. However, the result has been telegraphed though as Cornette has guaranteed the fans their money back if his men lose the match. I think you know where this is going.

In Your House #9: International Incident
Date: July 21, 1996
Location: General Motors Place, Vancouver, British Columbia, Canada
Attendance: 14,804
Commentators: Vince McMahon, Jerry Lawler, Jim Ross

The People's Posse originally had the Ultimate Warrior teaming up with Johnson and Michaels, but Warrior bailed on the company again for asking for too much time off. Warrior claimed he was leaving due to not getting money he was owed and Vince McMahon claiming that he didn't buy Warrior's excuse of grieving over his father's death. Either way, we get Sid tonight which might actually be the better option. Let's get to it.

Earlier tonight on the Free For All, Cornette swung the tennis racket at Jose Lothario but got punched in the face for his efforts. Vader and Shawn came in to prevent any further violence.

Smoking Gunns vs. Bodydonnas

The Gunns' Tag Team Titles aren't on the line, though they do now have Sunny with them (she goes with the titles you see). The Bodydonnas have turned face with a new manager named Cloudy (a man in woman's clothing), but no one cares about them at all either way. Sunny won't let Vince hold the Tag Team Titles so she'll just do it herself. The Gunns are sent to the floor to start before we get down to Bart vs. Zip. They trade chops with neither guy seeming all that interested in selling for the other. Zip takes him down with an armdrag into an armbar before bringing in Skip to crank on it as well.

Bart gets tired of having his arm pulled apart so he throws Skip down and brings in Billy to fire off some right hands. A nice headscissors puts Billy down and Skip spins out of a few hiptosses, only to be punched down for his efforts. Skip grabs another armbar as the match slows down all over again. Out of nowhere Sunny collapses but as Skip goes to check on her she slaps him in the face, allowing the Gunns to clothesline him down.

Back in and the Gunns take over with Bart whipping Skip HARD into the corner to take him down. Skip comes back with a quick clothesline and goes up top, only to dive into a sweet powerslam for two. With Skip draped throat first over the top and Bart holding his legs up, Billy tries to jump over his partner's back to land on Skip's back but can't get up and over Bart. If you can't do the spot, don't try it.

Skip and Bart mistime something out of the corner and awkwardly stop in the middle of the ring. Bart goes up top but jumps into an atomic drop, allowing for the hot tag off to Zip.

Billy trips Zip down but can't get in place for the Sidewinder (side slam/guillotine legdrop combo), allowing Skip to hit a missile dropkick on Bart to give Zip the pin at 13:05.

Rating: D. This was a horrible choice for an opening match with WAY too much time and the botches dragging things down. On top of that, why in the world would you make this a non-title match? To set up a future rematch? Why in the world wouldn't you do this on Raw and then have the title match here? It wasn't even good in any way.

Camp Cornette rants about the fight with Cornette and Lothario while guaranteeing a win later.

Mankind vs. Henry Godwinn

Mankind is one of the most bizarre characters in wrestling history. He debuted the night after Wrestlemania and immediately targeted the Undertaker, easily beating him down like no one else ever had before. Mankind lives in a boiler room, often sits on the mat and rocks back and forth and is known to pull out his hair. He also wears a leather mask that covers half of his face and is missing part of an ear. Henry is substituting for Jake Roberts who didn't show up for the show.

Mankind jumps Godwinn from behind to start but Henry is more than comfortable in a slugout. He punches Mankind in the face a few times and powerslams him down for two. Mankind pounds him down with shots to the back as Lawler makes jokes about Roberts' substance abuse issues. Henry sweeps Mankind's legs out and hits some HARD shots to the face, only to have Mankind choke him for a breather.

A running knee to Henry's face has him in even more trouble so Mankind goes to the floor and pulls back the mats. Henry gets taken down by a swinging neckbreaker onto the concrete. Back in and Mankind misses a charge into the corner but he easily sends Henry out to the floor. Godwinn comes right back by slamming Mankind to the concrete but the Slop Drop is countered with into the Mandible Claw for the win at 6:54.

Rating: D+. Nothing great here but it was a nice brawl while it lasted. Henry was stuck in a stupid gimmick but he could throw some great right hands and brawl with the best of them. There's nothing wrong with having a guy like that around as you're going to get an entertaining match more often than not. Still though, nothing great here.

Post match, Mankind sprints up the aisle but stops at the entrance because he's a bit strange.

Marc Mero vs. Steve Austin

This is a rematch from the King of the Ring tournament. Austin jumps him right after the bell but Mero comes back with a quick armbar. That gets him nowhere so Steve grabs a headlock and takes him down to the mat. Back up and they slug it out with Mero, a former New York Golden Gloves Champion, easily taking control. Austin is knocked to the floor and goes after Sable, only to be jumped from behind.

Back inside and Steve gets rolled up for two but manages to send Mero out to the floor to take over. A catapult sends Mero face first into the post and another shot knocks him off the apron and into the barricade. Back in and a middle rope elbow gets two for Austin and we hit a reverse chinlock. Austin slaps Mero in the back of the head but misses a charge and lands on the middle rope to give Marc a breather.

Steve goes up but gets crotched down, allowing Mero to pull him down and hook a hurricanrana to send both guys to the floor. A moonsault press off the apron takes Austin down again and a slingshot moonsault gets two back inside. Mero pounds away with right hands in the corner but Austin shoves him to the side, crotching Mero on the top rope. Marc blocks Austin's Stunner finisher and gets two off a slingshot legdrop. For some reason Marlena comes out to watch the ending. Not that it matters though Austin comes back with a quick chop block and the Stunner connects for the pin at 10:48.

Rating: C. Good stuff here for the most part but the match felt off for some reason. It's very interesting to see Austin evolve the Stunner over the years as there's no kick to the ribs yet and he just snaps it off. Mero wasn't bad in the ring at all but he never quite fit in the WWF.

Former WWF Champion Bob Backlund is running for President of the United States and looks for registered voters in the crowd.

Highlight video on the Undertaker's feuds with Mankind and Goldust, which is set up like a music video for some reason.

Goldust vs. Undertaker

Goldust, who has since lost the Intercontinental Title to Ahmed Johnson, bails to the floor to start and does so again after Undertaker moves towards him. He gets in again and hides behind the referee for a few moments before doing his trademark deep breath. It only earns him an uppercut to the jaw, sending Goldust right back to the floor for more stalling. Lawler makes movie references as Goldust teases walking out and VERY slowly gets back in the ring.

Undertaker finally goes out after him and chokeslams Goldust down onto the steps in an awkward looking sequence. Undertaker picks up the steps but won't crush Marlena along with Goldust. Apparently he's a zombie with a heart. Back in and Goldust gets clotheslined down before a legdrop gets two for Undertaker. This has been one sided so far. Goldust finally comes back with some knees in the corner to take over but Undertaker grabs him by the throat and throws him into the corner to hand out a beating.

The fans chant Rest in Peace (Undertaker catchphrase) as he connects with Old School and some uppercuts. Goldust clotheslines Undertaker over the top rope but Undertaker lands on his feet and keeps firing off uppercuts. Something resembling a Stunner across the top rope snaps Goldust's neck back but he uses the distraction to pull the turnbuckle pad away. Undertaker is sent back first into the exposed steel to finally give Goldust control.

They head outside again so Goldust can drop the steps on Undertaker's back to further his advantage. Back in and Goldust puts on a reverse chinlock to keep the match at a very slow pace. The fans chant for Undertaker so Goldust breaks the hold like any idiot heel would do. Undertaker comes back with a big boot to the face and a small package of all things for two. The flying clothesline takes Goldust down and there's the Tombstone, drawing Mankind up through a hole in the ring for the DQ at 12:07.

70

Rating: D-. Way too long here and horribly boring due to all of the stalling. Goldust and Undertaker had some of the least interesting matches I can ever remember for two guys with as much talent as they have. It was clearly just a backdrop for Undertaker vs. Mankind, which isn't something you spend three months on.

Post match Mankind pulls Undertaker through the hole with the Mandible Claw before crawling back out on his own. The lights flicker and Undertaker's music plays but he comes out of another hole to sneak up on Mankind. They brawl to the back to one of the only good reactions of the night.

The announcers talk about the main event while the ring is repaired.

We go to the back to see the brawl between Undertaker and Mankind continue.

Goldust and Marlena are in the boiler room where Mankind and Undertaker were fighting earlier. Goldust quotes Kramer vs. Kramer when Mankind pops up and calls Goldust mommy. Mankind rams his head into a cabinet while screaming about what mommy wants, mommy gets.

The announcers ignore what we just saw and talk about the main event a bit more.

We recap the main event six man tag which started at King of the Ring. Shawn pinned British Bulldog in the rematch but Vader and Owen Hart came in for a post match attack. Ultimate Warrior and Ahmed Johnson came in for the save, setting up the six man. Ultimate Warrior was suspended a few weeks after, so Shawn and Ahmed brought in Sid to take his place. It's not clear if Sid can be trusted though.

The People's Posse says they can trust Sid and they'll win tonight.

People's Posse vs. Camp Cornette

If Camp Cornette loses, Cornette has to pay back all of the fans, which would cost him millions. Also Owen has a broken arm coming in. Vader and Ahmed start things off but Vader wants the WWF Champion instead. Shawn is happy to oblige and is easily shoved away by the monster. Vader lifts Shawn into the air in a choke but Shawn punches his way to freedom. Shawn speeds things up and actually hits a running hurricanrana to take Vader down. A crossbody sends Vader to the floor and Michaels follows with a nice plancha to take the monster down.

Shawn tries another hurricanrana but gets hit a bit low to give Vader control. Vader pounds away in the corner and Shawn is in quick trouble. Michaels manages to escapes a belly to back suplex and makes the hot tag off to Sid for a battle of the giants. Sid cleans house and sends all of Camp Cornette out to the floor, drawing a HUGE reaction from the crowd. Owen tries to sneak in from behind but is easily taken down by another clothesline. It's off to Johnson who actually rolls German suplexes on Owen.

Johnson misses an elbow drop and it's off to the Bulldog to pound away for a bit until he gets caught in a spinebuster. Ahmed hits his Pearl River Plunge tiger bomb but it's Owen making the save. Off to Vader for some power but Ahmed pounds him down in the corner to keep the fans into things the entire way through. Vader easily reverses a whip into the corner and hits a hard splash followed by even more fists to the head and body. Another splash attempt is caught in a slam which Ahmed made look far easier than should be possible.

Owen comes in and takes Johnson down with a spinwheel kick but Johnson pops up at two. Johnson keeps coming back with a gorilla press slam and it's back to Sid for a big boot to the face before firing off some very fast right hands in the corner. Sid whips Owen into the Cornette corner and it's time for the Bulldog vs. Sid power match. Smith actually lifts him up in the delayed vertical suplex and a Vader elbow is good for two. Vader runs Sid over again and brings Smith back in for some headbutts.

Sid is able to get in a shot to the face and makes the tag off to Shawn, but Bulldog quickly avoids a charge to send Shawn shoulder first into the post. Shawn sends Bulldog into Vader to knock the big man off the apron and get a pair of two counts on Smith. Back to Owen to trade some VERY fast rollups with Shawn for two each before Shawn gets two more off a crossbody. A victory roll gets the same for Michaels and they head to the mat before bridging into Ric Flair's trademark pinfall reversal sequence. That was outstanding.

Back to Bulldog for a legdrop but Michaels avoids an elbow drop to get a breather. Owen finally uses the cast on the bad arm to put Shawn down and it's back to Vader to pound away on the WWF Champion. Shawn is whipped across the ring and goes over the corner and out to the floor in a big crash. After Owen and Bulldog get in some cheap shots on the floor it's back in for a half standing chinlock/half bearhug on Shawn with Vader's arms wrapped around his neck and under his arms. Not a bad looking hold actually.

The hold stays on for awhile as a fan tries to interfere and is easily run off by Bulldog and the referee. After several minutes of the hold, Vader throws Shawn down and splashes him but Ahmed comes in to break up a cover. Bulldog comes in and puts on an over the shoulder backbreaker followed by a fall away slam for two. Smith misses a charge into the corner but it's Hart breaking up the hot tag attempt yet again.

Shawn punches Owen down but can't follow up, allowing for another tag back to Davey, whose cover is quickly broken up by a Sid legdrop. Vader gets the tag and Shawn crawls over to make one as well, but the referee doesn't see Ahmed get the tag. Johnson protests but Shawn gets triple teamed, giving Bulldog another two count. Owen tries a missile dropkick but hits Bulldog by mistake, allowing Shawn to FINALLY make the tag off to Sid.

The big man cleans house and chokeslams every member of Camp Cornette before launching Shawn off the top onto Vader for two. Everything breaks down and Cornette throws in the tennis racket but Shawn intercepts it to clock Vader in the head. Somehow that's only good for two so Shawn tunes up the band, only to have Cornette trip him up. Vader runs Michaels over and hits the Vader Bomb for the pin at 24:38 to suck the life out of the crowd.

Rating: A-. REALLY good match here with everyone working hard and having a match that had the fans going nuts. Sid's popularity is nearly astounding as the guy was just crazy over on about three moves. The ending was obvious, but on rare occasions that's not a bad thing with this being a good example of that.

Post match Sid and Ahmed clean house with powerbombs to

Owen and Bulldog but Vader is pulled to safety. Shawn dives over the top and takes out Vader, sending Camp Cornette running off. A lot of posing ends the show.

Overall Rating: D. The only thing that is holding up this show is the main event. Let's look at this entire card: what in the world would you want to pay for on this show? There are five matches, zero titles on the line, and the one match that might draw some interest had a telegraphed ending. This was a terribly uninteresting show which set a record for the lowest buyrate in company history as not many people cared about seeing this show. It also doesn't help that two weeks prior to this, Hulk Hogan turned heel in WCW, lighting the fire that would burn the WWF as close to a crisp as you can be for the next year and a half.

Following this mess, it should be pretty clear where things were heading at Summerslam. One main event was Undertaker vs. Mankind in a boiler room brawl with Mankind winning after Paul Bearer shocked the world by turning on the Undertaker and siding with Mankind. The win was enough to get Mankind a WWF Title shot at the next In Your House.

The real main event of Summerslam though was Shawn defending the title vs. Vader in the final blowoff of the summer long Shawn vs. Camp Cornette feud which while decent, didn't do the best business in the world. Shawn successfully defended the title after Cornette kept asking for the match to be restarted, ultimately costing his man the title match. That brings us to Shawn defending the title vs. Mankind at In Your House #10.

In Your House #10: Mind Games
Date: September 22, 1996
Location: CoreStates Center, Philadelphia, Pennsylvania
Attendance: 15,000
Commentators: Vince McMahon, Jim Ross, Mr. Perfect

Much like the rest of the series so far, there isn't much to this show aside from the main event. The company is really starting to feel the heat from WCW's NWO angle but it really doesn't seem like the WWF is trying anything to fight back. Shawn is doing what he can, but when he has nothing backing him up, what is he supposed to do? Let's get to it.

The opening video focuses on how evil Mankind can be and how only Shawn can stop him. We also get something about Goldust vs. Undertaker despite almost no one being interested in the feud. Tonight is their final match, thank goodness.

Justin Hawk Bradshaw vs. Savio Vega

This is fallout from about five minutes ago on the pre-show. Bradshaw is a big Texan and a newcomer who hasn't lost a match yet but is mad that he can't get a spot on the pay per view. He attacked Savio after his Free For All match so a Caribbean strap match was quickly made. It's the touch all four corners variety again and remember if your momentum is stopped, you lose any corners you've touched. Savio charges in but gets taken down with clubbing forearms and some shots to the back with the strap.

Vega is knocked to the floor and choked up against the post but he manages to pull Bradshaw shoulder first into the steel. Now it's time for the most interesting part of the match, as a local independent wrestler throws beer on Savio and slams the can into his own head. This would be the Sandman, an ECW mainstay with his cohort Tommy Dreamer next to him. Philadelphia was ECW's home base and this was near the peak of ECW's popularity. The theory was this being a shoot but it turned out to be the two companies working together. Paul Heyman, ECW owner, can be seen holding them back as security takes them out.

Back in and Bradshaw hooks a headlock on Savio and gets three buckles before Savio makes the save before the fourth. Some HARD strap shots to the back have Bradshaw down and Savio gets three buckles as a result before Bradshaw pulls him down to reset the score. A spinwheel kick puts Bradshaw down again but he makes the save after two corners this time.

Bradshaw takes him down with a big boot and a HARD clothesline to get three corners but just like in the first strap match with Austin, Vega follows along and gets them as well. Bradshaw makes the mistake of pulling on the strap though, sending Savio into his fourth buckle for the win at 7:09.

Rating: D. So remember the Austin vs. Vega match where there was a ton of drama and hard hitting shots which got people into the match? None of that applies here. This was paint by numbers stuff which wasn't anything interesting at all and was only interesting because of the ECW involvement.

We recap Jose Lothario vs. Jim Cornette. This is really just an extension of Shawn vs. Camp Cornette as Jose trained Shawn to wrestle but Cornette swears he can beat up the old man. Jose was 61 years old at this point.

Before the match we cut to the back to see "Diesel and Razor Ramon" attacking Savio Vega. We'll get to this idea later on but I'm putting it off as long as I can. In short it's part of Jim Ross turning heel which has never worked and will never work.

Jose Lothario vs. Jim Cornette

Jose drops Cornette with a single punch and does it a few more times for good measure. Two more punches end Cornette at 56 seconds. If there was a point to this being an actual match, it eludes me.

Savio isn't sure what happened to him but doesn't think it was the original Razor and Diesel. If it was the real Razor though, Savio has something for him.

Here's Brian Pillman, who had guaranteed that Bret Hart would be here tonight. However, we get a clip from Bret saying that both Pillman and Owen (who said Bret would be here too) are liars. Brian talks about how this is a nice facility they're in here, but this is just a small percentage of the cesspool that Philadelphia has become. Pillman rips on the fans and brings out Owen to class up the place a bit.

Brian sucks up to Owen, praising him for being so much better at everything than Bret is. Owen says that Bret is getting older and slower and had finally admitted that Owen was the best Hart ever. Then Bret lied about being here in Philadelphia where he had promised to praise his brother and family friend Pillman in front of the world. The only thing that could keep him away is a fear of Steve Austin.

This brings out Austin, who said everyone, including Austin himself, knew Bret wasn't going to be here tonight because he's such a coward. Austin's opinion of Bret Hart is you need to add an S to his nickname (Hitman). Austin threatens to beat Bret from one side of the ring to the other if he ever comes back. This would be the start of the angle that kept the WWF afloat for the majority of 1997 and made Steve Austin the biggest star in the wrestling world.

We see newcomer Mark Henry walking around some of the tourists attractions of Philadelphia.

Tag Team Titles: Owen Hart/British Bulldog vs. Smoking Gunns

The Gunns are defending and the challengers have no Cornette with them due to the beating he received earlier. We see Cornette in the back with attorney Clarence Mason having him sign something. Also I have no idea why Owen left ringside after the previous segment when his match was next. Billy walks behind Bart with his arm around Sunny which probably isn't a good sign. Before we gets started, Sunny tries to unveil a giant poster of herself by having it drop from the rafters but now it has a big beard painted on it for a nice touch. Clarence Mason comes to ringside, apparently replacing Cornette for tonight.

Owen hits a few crossbodies for two each on Billy before it's off to a headlock. A small package gets two more for Owen as JR is still playing the heel on commentary, ensuring Vince that the REAL Diesel and Razor are back. Remember that line because it becomes important in a few months.

It's off to Bart vs. Davey with the Bulldog hitting a few dropkicks to take over before cranking his arm for a bit. Owen comes back in for a chop block as the target shifts to Bart's knee. Owen and Bulldog take turns working on the leg with Owen putting on a modified Indian deathlock. A Boston crab doesn't last long as Bart quickly makes the rope but Bulldog comes in for a vertical suplex to put him down again. Bulldog even throws in a front flip to show off his athleticism a bit.

Back to Owen for more leg work but his spinning toehold is countered into a small package for two. Owen comes right back with an enziguri for two of his own but Billy finally interferes, pulling Bulldog out to the floor and sending him into the steps. Back in and Bart is able to make the tag off to Billy. The champions take over but Billy almost immediately tags back to Bart.

The Sidewinder connects but Mason distract the referee, allowing Owen to come in off the top with a shot to the back of Bart's head. Bulldog can only get two though and it's back to Billy who again only hits a few stomps before tagging out to the weakened Bart. Bart loads up a powerslam on the Bulldog but gets rammed into Billy who wasn't paying attention. Davey hits the real powerslam for the pin and the titles at 10:59.

Rating: D+. The title change was the right idea but this was one of the longest eleven minute matches I've ever seen. Both teams were heels here so the fans didn't have anyone to cheer for and the Gunns were boring in the first place. It wasn't terrible but the match didn't do anything for me at all.

Post match Sunny yells at the Gunns and calls them no good cowboy wannabes. She's had enough and fires both of them.

Paul Bearer guarantees that Mankind will win the title tonight and blames Undertaker's fans for him turning his back on Undertaker. Mankind promises to make Shawn miserable tonight.

Mark Henry vs. Jerry Lawler

Henry is a newcomer to the WWF at this point and was on commentary during Jake Roberts vs. Jerry Lawler last month. Lawler had tried to pour whiskey down recovering alcoholic Roberts' throat, drawing Henry off commentary for the save. This is Henry's in ring debut and his chance to prove that he's the World's Strongest Man. Lawler spends his entire walk to the ring badmouthing the Olympics (Henry was an Olympic weightlifter) and Henry in general, riling up a crowd as only he can. Lawler may not be the most skilled grappler he is one of the greatest of all time and making a crowd want to chase him down with pitchforks.

Lawler offers to start with a very basic headlock to let Henry get his feet wet. Mark easily counters into a hammerlock and shoves Lawler down, sending pure fear into Lawler. Henry puts on a headlock of his own and Jerry counters the same way Mark did earlier, but Henry counters the counter into another hammerlock. A gorilla press slam sends Lawler down again and his own shoulder block has about the same result.

Henry sidesteps Lawler and sends him flying to the floor in a big crash. Since plans A-C haven't worked, Lawler pulls out a foreign object and socks Henry in the jaw a few times to take over for the first time. Mark will have none of that though and fires off knees into Jerry's ribs before finishing him with an over the shoulder backbreaker at 5:03.

Rating: D. This was what it was. The match was designed to make Henry look like a monster and that's exactly what it did as Lawler could do this match in his sleep. That being said, it wasn't exactly interesting as you can tell Henry is a big strong guy just by looking at him. At least it wasn't long or anything though and it didn't get too repetitive.

Post match the New Rockers and Hunter Hearst Helmsley come out to try to make a name for themselves against Henry and are easily dispatched.

Owen and Bulldog are in the back with Clarence Mason. The paper that he had Cornette sign was turning over the contract of the new champions to Mason, making him their new manager.

We recap Undertaker vs. Goldust which has been going on for about five months now. There really isn't even much of a story to it. Basically Goldust is weird and likes that Undertaker is weird too so they had a series of boring matches. Mankind is in there too as an ally for Goldust and is the real adversary for Undertaker.

Goldust vs. Undertaker

This is called a Final Curtain match, meaning there must be a pinfall winner so there are no disqualifications. Goldust doesn't even get a full entrance. Undertaker jumps him to start and whips Goldust from corner to corner before lifting him up in a big choke. A legdrop gets two on Goldust and an uppercut easily stops his big deep breath. Taker suplexes him down before hiptossing Goldust across the ring. Old School connects and Undertaker throws him to the floor, only to have Goldust take something from Marlena's purse.

With Marlena distracting the referee, Goldust throws powder into Undertaker's eyes and gets his first advantage. Goldust takes it to the floor and shoves Taker's head into the steps to keep him in trouble. They head back inside with Undertaker avoiding an uppercut but walking into a clothesline for two. Undertaker finally comes back with a belly to back suplex but is still blinded by the dust.

Goldust comes back with a hiptoss of his own for two before trying to smother Undertaker. That goes nowhere so Undertaker grabs him by the throat and launches Goldust into the corner to pound away. A double clothesline puts both guys down but Goldust goes up top, only to be chokeslammed back down. The Tombstone finally ends both Goldust and the feud at 10:23.

Rating: D. NOW NEVER WRESTLE AGAIN. This was one of the least interesting feuds I've ever seen and it just kept going. Undertaker never lost a match clean to Goldust and there was never any reason to think he would. Undertaker was just a bigger deal and there was nothing Goldust could throw at him as a real challenge. Thankfully this was the last match they would have and it's not a minute too late.

Shawn Michaels says he can't wrestle a maniac like Mankind, but thankfully Shawn is a bit cuckoo himself, so he's walking out with the title.

WWF Title: Shawn Michaels vs. Mankind

Shawn is defending. Druids wheel out a casket during Mankind's entrance and he pops out for a disturbing visual. A quick elbow to the jaw puts Shawn down and there's a shot to the throat for good measure. Mankind's signature clothesline (Cactus Clothesline) puts both guys out onto the floor where Mankind peels back the floor mats. Shawn dropkicks them into Mankind's face and jumps up and down on Mankind before hitting a crossbody off the top and out to the floor.

A flying shove sends the back of Mankind's head into the concrete again but he doesn't seem all that bothered. Back in and a top rope ax handle drops the challenger again and Shawn peppers him with left hands. Michaels drops the top rope elbow for no cover before tuning up the band, only to have Mankind bail to the floor where he holds the urn and rocks back and forth. Back in and Shawn slugs away even more so Mankind slaps him in the face, sending it down to the mat in a brawl.

Mankind trips Shawn down in a nice amateur style move where he tries the Mandible Claw but Shawn blocks the hand. He elbows Mankind in the jaw to escape and pounds away as they're in what would be called full mount/guard positions respectively in MMA terms. Mankind throws him out to the floor and sets up the announcers' table next to the ring, only to have Shawn dive over to pummel Mankind even more. A suplex slams Mankind's legs into the steps and he's in big trouble.

Back in and Shawn stomps at the leg but stops to yell at the referee. Mankind gets in a few kicks with the good leg but Michaels catches him in a dragon screw leg whip. There's a figure four but Mankind gets in a shot to the face to break it up. Michaels goes right back to the knee with a dropkick and an old Mr. Perfect move called the Robinsdale Crunch (Perfect: "That's one of my moves!"). Shawn goes to a half crab but Mankind is quickly in the ropes for the break.

They get back up and Shawn tries a running hurricanrana, only to have Mankind catch him in the air and fall back to drop Shawn throat first across the top rope. Mankind grabs a pen to stab into his own leg to wake it up a bit in a bizarre yet smart move. Shawn gets rammed face first into the casket and a running knee to the face keeps him in trouble. Mankind's knee going into Shawn's head slows the challenger down a bit so he rams Shawn face first into the mat to get a breather.

Michaels comes back with a quick belly to back suplex but can't get any momentum going with Mankind right back on him. It turns back into a slugfest until Mankind whips him into the corner and gets Shawn tied up in the Tree of Woe. An ax handle to the face knocks Michaels free and a boot to the face puts him out onto the floor. Mankind follows him out but gets whipped knees first into the steps, followed by a drop toehold into the steps for good measure.

They fight for a suplex on the apron but Shawn winds up landing on the apron where he kicks Mankind's leg out again to take over. Back inside and Shawn gets two off a powerslam before whipping Mankind in the ropes where he flips over, getting his neck tied up in the ropes. Shawn goes over but gets caught in a quick Mandible Claw to stop Shawn cold. The Claw goes on again on the floor but Shawn launches him face first into the barricade for the break.

Back up again and Shawn grabs a chair to block a right hand, hurting the Mandible Claw hand in a brilliant move. More chair shots to the hand have the challenger in trouble so Shawn bites away at the fingers. Back inside and Michaels stomps at the hand before going to the other hand to make sure it doesn't feel unloved. Mankind manages to backdrop Shawn back to the floor and drops an elbow off the apron in another signature move. A swinging neckbreaker puts Shawn down on the floor as these guys are getting tired.

Back in again and Mankind gets two each off a double arm DDT and a piledriver. The fans sound ready to explode on Shawn's comeback. Mankind is so frustrated that he pulls his own hair out. As most psychos do you see. We get a couple of chairs thrown in but instead of using them, Mankind opens up the casket.

Shawn fights his way out of it and hits the forearm into the nipup that he's famous for. Michaels stomps away in the corner and gets two off a high crossbody. Mankind crotches Shawn on the top to slow down the comeback before loading up a belly to back suplex to the floor. Since that would kill Shawn though, he counters in midair into a crossbody to drive Mankind through the table, sending both guys down in a heap.

Mankind sets up a chair in the ring and brings in a second one, only to have Shawn use the chair as a springboard to superkick the second chair into Mankind's face in a cool looking spot. That would look to be the finish but Shawn has to pull off and go after the interfering Vader, drawing the DQ at 26:25 for the only negative part of the match.

Rating: A+. This isn't just the match of the night or the match of the year or the match of In Your House so far. This match is in the running for the greatest match of all time. It tells an amazing story with Shawn having to completely change his style and get crazy to hang with Mankind. On top of that you have the brutal physical aspect with both guys just beating the tar out of each other for nearly twenty seven minutes. Absolutely amazing stuff and well worth seeing if you never have before or if you haven't seen it in a while.

Post match Shawn knocks Vader to the floor but gets blasted in the back of the head by the urn. Sid shows up to fight Vader to the back but it's Mankind up first. He puts the Mandible Claw on Shawn and goes to put him in the casket, but somehow the Undertaker is inside this time. Paul Bearer freaks out and the crowd comes unglued as Undertaker shoves Mankind to the floor and stalks the villains up the aisle.

Shawn poses a lot to end the show.

Overall Rating: C-. The main event is the only thing worth seeing on here, but you have to remember this is a show lasting less than two hours and the main event is about 35 minutes of that counting introductions and post match shenanigans. It's a very good thing to have over a fourth of your show be outstanding, but it doesn't say much for the rest of it. The dark days are continuing for the company business wise, but the on screen stuff is coming in just a few months.

In Your House #10 and #11 are in back to back months again so there isn't much new stuff going on. The next one is actually a B-level show even by In Your House standards with the main event being a special Buried Alive match (exactly what it sounds like) between Mankind and Undertaker. Shawn isn't in action on the show but we'll find out who faces him at Survivor Series in a #1 contender's match.

In Your House #11: Buried Alive
Date: October 20, 1996
Location: Market Square Arena, Indianapolis, Indiana
Attendance: 9,649
Commentators: Vince McMahon, Jerry Lawler, Jim Ross

This is another of those shows where there just isn't much to say. There are only five matches on the card and only two of them are worth much of anything. It's always interesting to see a main event with the focus being something other than the WWF Title feud and Undertaker vs. Foley would be going on for a lot longer after this. Let's get to it.

The opening video talks about Undertaker spending his life at war with Mankind and warns Mankind to enjoy his last breaths before he's buried alive.

There's a big mound of dirt with a Tombstone next to an open grave.

<u>Hunter Hearst Helmsley vs. Steve Austin</u>

The first of many, many times and it's heel vs. heel here. Before the match Austin says that he's fine with fighting Helmsley since Savio Vega is injured tonight. Apparently Bret Hart is coming back to Raw and Austin hopes it's to announce his retirement. Before we get to the match though, I should note JR is in full heel mode here, constantly ranting about how he won't be silenced and how he's the real voice of the WWF. The fact that the mics aren't all working ticks him off even more.

Feeling out process to start with Helmsley armdragging Austin down. JR has his microphone changed as Austin goes to the floor to jaw with a fan. Back in and Austin armdrags Helmsley down and flips him off. The feeling out process continues as JR takes credit for Bret coming back while his mic cuts in and out. Austin gets tired of this slow paced stuff and slaps Helmsley in the face to speed things up a bit. Helmsley bails to the apron as we're nearly five minutes into this match and we've had two armdrags and a slap to the face.

Back in and an elbow to the head puts Helmsley down and we hit an armbar from Austin. Helmsley fights up and pokes Austin in the eye as we've got a split screen of the match and the commentators for no apparent reason. It's back to the armbar for a bit before Helmsley fights up and buries a knee into Austin's ribs. A backdrop puts Austin down as Hunter has his first advantage. There's a knee drop to the head for two and Helmsley is getting frustrated. The mics still aren't working with JR cutting in and out on almost every other word.

We hit the chinlock on Austin and it's back to the split screen for a few moments. Austin fights up and they trade sleeper holds until a jawbreaker puts Helmsley down for two. A Stun Gun (hot shot) gets two more for Austin but Helmsley hits a jumping knee to the face and a middle rope right hand for two. They clothesline each other down and here's Mr. Perfect who will be facing Helmsley tomorrow night. Perfect comes to the ring to put his arm around Helmsley's valet, allowing Austin to get in some cheap shots.

That's not cool with Perfect either so Austin throws a soda at him, only to have Helmsley jump him from behind. Perfect leaves with the valet, which causes Helmsley to drop the Pedigree attempt. Austin goes after him but gets suplexed in the aisle to put both guys down. Helmsley is catapulted into the post and they head inside where the Stunner ends this in a hurry at 15:30.

Rating: C+. This was more an historical note than anything else as Helmsley was still slowly coming up the card and Austin was ready to move up the ladder. Still though, these two fighting each other is always worth a look. The JR stuff got old fast though as the constant breaks in commentary were distracting.

We recap the Smoking Gunns vs. Owen Hart/British Bulldog. There isn't much to this one as the Gunns lost the titles last month and are having problems due to Sunny. She fired both of them after losing though so she won't be a factor tonight.

Billy Gunn says they'll get the titles back and Sunny will be back at their side. He doesn't seem interested at sharing the glory with Bart though.

Tag Team Titles: Smoking Gunns vs. Owen Hart/British Bulldog

Owen and Bulldog are defending. Billy takes Owen down with a headlock to start as the microphones continue to mess up, annoying JR even more. Eventually he does manage to say Owen got a haircut. Lawler: "How analytical." Billy goes up top but jumps into a punch to the ribs, giving the champions their first advantage. Bulldog comes in to crank on the arm as the announcers debate cowboys. Bart gets in a cheap shot to put Bulldog down as Sunny can be seen watching in the back.

Bart comes in legally but misses a high crossbody, giving Bulldog two. Back to Owen for a missile dropkick and some headbutts in the corner for good measure. The champions put Bart down again with a double clothesline as JR rips into Vince for his obvious points on commentary. Owen drops a leg and puts on a chinlock and JR is now claiming a conspiracy by Vince. Bulldog distracts Billy by posing and Bart is whipped into the ropes, knocking his partner down to the floor.

Billy trips Owen down and accepts the tag from his brother like nothing happened. A double Russian legsweep gets two on Owen, followed by an elbow from Billy. There's a neckbreaker dedicated to Sunny but she doesn't seem all that interested. It's back to Bart who breaks up a tag attempt as the Gunns continue to double team Owen. Bulldog is knocked off the apron but he sneaks back in to pull Bart down, breaking up the Sidewinder. Owen pops back up and hits a spinwheel kick to take out Billy for the pin to retain at 9:17.

Rating: D+. This was again more storytelling than a match but no one thought the Gunns were going to get the belts back, nor did most people want them to. Owen and Bulldog were a much better team and the Gunns' time was over. Not a terrible match or anything, but it was all about the story instead of the match, which is fine in this case.

Bart leaves on his own.

Vince talks about Faarooq, a newcomer feuding with Ahmed

Johnson, being attacked earlier but JR gets in the ring. Before he gets to the point, he says he won't talk about Vince firing him and trying to ruin his life. Bret Hart will be in Fort Wayne, Indiana tomorrow night and it's not because of Vince. It's because JR went to South Africa to talk to him because JR loves the fans more than Vince. JR rants about Vince destroying the microphones (which the fans in the arena wouldn't know about) and throws his mic to Vince before storming off.

Back to Faarooq, he says he's ready for Ahmed no matter what. Johnson lost the Intercontinental Title because of Faarooq so Ahmed jumped him on the Free For All, injuring him.

Here's Mr. Perfect to replace JR on commentary.

Intercontinental Title: Goldust vs. Marc Mero

Mero is defending after winning a tournament due to Ahmed being injured and stripped of the title. Mero defeated Faarooq in the finals and this was supposed to be a rematch but Johnson prevented that from happening. Another feeling out process to start, complete with Goldust doing his big deep breath. Some armdrags and a hiptoss put Goldust down and we hit the armbar. Goldust fights up and pounds away in the corner before doing the same in the opposite corner.

Mero is tired of the beating and takes Goldust down to fire off right hands of his own. A backdrop sets up a clothesline and Goldust bails to the floor. The champion hits a BIG flip dive over the top to take Goldust out again and a slingshot legdrop gets two back inside. Mero goes up again but gets powerbombed down and sent to the floor. Back in and we hit the chinlock on the champion before a knee to the ribs puts Mero down again.

We hit another chinlock as Mero is in some trouble. The champion fights up again but gets clotheslined down. Goldust asks for a microphone, threatening to come into the crowd and stick his tongue down everyone's throat if they keep booing him. Mero uses the distraction to take Goldust down and gets two off a spinning moonsault press. Goldust's Curtain Call (reverse suplex) is countered into a rollup for two and we head to the floor again.

Mero is sent into the barricade and Perfect is tired of the referee doing nothing. He gets up and helps Marc back inside, drawing Helmsley back out for a showdown. Perfect drops Goldust with a right hand, allowing Mero to bring it back inside for a Samoan drop and the Wild Thing (Shooting Star Press) to retain at 11:38.

Rating: C+. Mero was pretty awesome in the ring at this point and could fly with the best of them. He could also talk and had a good look, but somehow this was pretty much the peak of his career in the WWF. This was a fun match but cutting out a minute or two in the middle would have helped a lot. Still though, not bad and it even advanced Perfect vs. Helmsley for tomorrow.

We recap Sid vs. Vader, which is set up as a fight over who is the master of the powerbomb. This was supposed to be the main event of WCW's Starrcade 1993 with the same story but a lot of problems prevented it from happening. Tonight it's a result of Shawn vs. Camp Cornette as seen at the end of Mind Games when Sid saved Shawn from Vader.

Sycho Sid vs. Vader

The winner gets a WWF Title shot at Survivor Series so Shawn comes out to do commentary. They slug it out to start with Sid knocking Vader down and dropping a leg for two. Sid pounds away in the corner but Vader blocks a slam with a right hand to the face. Now it's Vader pounding Sid down in the corner before hitting a running splash. Sid falls to the floor and lays there for a very long time without getting counted out.

Back up and Sid pounds away from the apron before actually trying a sunset flip, only to have Vader sit down on his chest. Sid gets up again and a double clothesline puts both guys down one more time. Vader slugs him into the corner but a splash is broken up by a boot to the face. Sid goes up top but a high crossbody is caught in midair with a SCARY display of strength.

A slam and a splash get two for Vader and there's a middle rope splash for the same, but this time Vader pulls Sid up before three. Instead he loads up the Vader Bomb but it lands on knees, allowing Sid to slam Vader down. He sets up the powerbomb but has to take care of Cornette. Another powerbomb attempt is countered by a Vader low blow. Now it's Vader loading up the powerbomb, but he pulls out and punches

Sid in the head, allowing Sid to grab a quick chokeslam for the pin and the title shot at 8:04.

Rating: D. They kept this short which is the right idea, but the match was nothing all that great. There's only so much you can do in a match like this and they pretty much firmly hit that ceiling. Also, shouldn't there have been at least one powerbomb in a match built around who is the master of the powerbomb?

Post match Shawn congratulates Sid on his win.

After a Survivor Series ad, JR horns in on a Sid interview and pesters Sid into saying he'll do anything to beat Shawn.

We recap Mankind vs. Undertaker. Mankind jumped Undertaker on April 1 and laid him out like no one had in years if ever, triggering a months long feud. Eventually Paul Bearer turned on Undertaker to join Mankind, ending a six year partnership. Tonight Undertaker has vowed to bury Mankind alive.

Mankind vs. Undertaker

As mentioned there's a big mound of dirt with an open grave in the middle. You win by dragging your opponent to the grave and covering them with said dirt. The brawl is on to start as the arena is still full of smoke from Undertaker's entrance. Mankind comes back with right hands in the corner, only to be grabbed by the throat and tossed in himself. Undertaker kicks him to the floor and into the barricade, setting up a HUGE dive off the top to send Mankind onto the concrete.

They brawl up the aisle (by brawl I mean Undertaker punches and Mankind stumbles) towards the grave site where Undertaker grabs a shovel. It takes too long though so Mankind tries a suplex, only to be caught in a small package of all things, sending them tumbling down the dirt. They fight back to ringside with Undertaker still firmly in control. Undertaker chokes Mankind with a microphone cord and they head into the crowd. More right hands have Mankind in trouble, including Undertaker diving over the barricade with a clothesline.

They head back inside where Old School is countered to give Mankind his first advantage. He chokes Undertaker down in the corner and blasts Taker with some kind of jagged object handed to him by Bearer. Undertaker comes back with a shot to the throat and takes away the object for a few shots of his own. A jumping clothesline puts Mankind down and Undertaker goes after Bearer. Mankind tries a chair shot but gets kicked in the ribs, only to have Paul blast Undertaker with the urn, allowing Mankind to hit Undertaker with the chair.

A running knee drives Undertaker's head into the steps and it's back up to the grave site again. Undertaker gets knocked into the grave but Mankind can only get in a few shovels full of dirt before getting pulled in as well. They fight out of the hole with Undertaker throwing Mankind off the dirt and down to the floor again. Back inside again with Mankind hitting a pulling piledriver and covering which means nothing here.

A double arm DDT onto the chair knocks Undertaker out but Mankind grabs the urn to rock back and forth. Undertaker sits up and CRACKS Mankind in the back with the chair before legdropping it down onto his face. Mankind comes back with a Stunner onto the top rope and peels back the mats on the floor. His piledriver is countered into a kind of backdrop onto the steps to put further destroy Mankind's body.

The steps are brought inside and dropped onto Mankind's back, setting up the Tombstone to knock him out cold. Undertaker carries what used to be Mankind to the grave site but on the way he wakes up and grabs the Mandible Claw to take over. It doesn't last long though as Undertaker gets a quick chokeslam to send Mankind into the grave. The burial is quick and Undertaker wins at 18:25.

Rating: B-. Good match here between two guys who could bring the brutality when they had the chance. Mankind was one of the only guys that could give Undertaker a run for his money and there were moments where he looked like he had a chance. It's the best match of the show and that's what a main event should be most of the time.

Undertaker keeps burying him and shoves the referees away when they try to stop him. Out of nowhere here's a man in an executioner hood to blast Undertaker in the back of the head with a shovel. He gets Mankind out of the grave and throws Undertaker in instead. Thunder starts rumbling and the lights flicker as Mankind and the hooded man bury Undertaker.

90

The lights straighten out as the grave fills up with dirt and here are Goldust and some other villains to help. This goes on for a good while until thunder rumbles some more and the shovel is stuck down in the dirt. Mankind and Bearer leave before a bolt of lightning hits the grave and Undertaker's hand sticks out of the dirt to end the show.

Overall Rating: C. It's not a great show but this is a really easy sit through with nothing being all that bad. The worst match is pretty easily Sid vs. Vader and that only runs about eight minutes. It's interesting that the best show in awhile didn't have Shawn in action which might have been a sign. There's nothing great to see here but it's definitely not a bad show, making it one of the better entries in the series so far.

After Buried Alive the company headed back home to New York City and Madison Square Garden for Survivor Series. A lot of things changed at that show with the most important being Steve Austin facing Bret Hart in an all time classic with Bret escaping with a win. Austin had arrived though and there was no doubt that he was the next big thing in wrestling. No one knew how big he would be however.

The other major change was the crowning of a new WWF Champion as Sid turned heel by hitting Shawn with a camera to win the title. As hard as Shawn worked over the summer, it just wasn't working well enough at the box office and something had to be done. Sid wasn't a long term solution but he was definitely a change of pace. By beating Austin, Bret earned the first title shot at In Your House #12.

The third note which didn't mean anything yet was the debut of the a third generation athlete named Rocky Maivia who beat Goldust to be the last man standing in an elimination tag. Again everyone knew there was potential there but no one knew how much potential he had. We won't be seeing Rocky for awhile but once he becomes a big deal, he isn't going away for a good while.

In Your House #12: It's Time
Date: December 15, 1996
Location: West Palm Beach Auditorium, West Palm Beach, Florida
Attendance: 5,708
Commentators: Jim Ross, Jerry Lawler, Vince McMahon

The title of this show was odd and a good example of how fast things can change in wrestling. It's Time was Vader's catchphrase and tonight was supposed to be a showcase of him as the new WWF Champion, but obviously that didn't happen. Actually Vader isn't even on the card due to an injury, making the title all the more inappropriate.

The opening video shows quick clips of Bret and Sid with the words IT'S TIME in between.

Lawler promises to knock Shawn out if he comes out here.

Leif Cassidy vs. Flash Funk

Cassidy is more famous as Al Snow but is one half of the New Rockers here. Funk is more famous as 2 Cold Scorpio and is

92

basically a pimp without calling him as much. He has Funkettes (dancers) and funk music, basically making him the original Brodus Clay. Even Vince dances to the theme song a bit. After a long dance sequence by Funk and his girls we're ready to go. Funk shoves Cassidy into the ropes to start and dances a bit, only angering Leif as a result.

They trade wristlocks until Flash spins around and grabs an armbar on the mat. Cassidy spins up but a flying snap mare takes him right back down. Funk flips out of a Boston crab attempt and takes Leif down into a headlock. Back up and Flash tries to go up but slips off the ropes, only to pop back up and hit a crossbody to set up another armbar. A headscissors out of the corner is countered into a reverse powerbomb by Cassidy.

Cassidy blocks a right hand and traps Funk's arms for some headbutts, followed by a belly to belly over the top and out to the floor. Leif follows it up with a springboard moonsault to the floor in a great looking dive. Back in and we hit the chinlock but Flash fights up and dances a bit more. Another powerbomb attempt by Cassidy is countered and Flash lands on his feet, dancing again. Leif comes back with a sitout spinebuster for a very delayed two count. Off to a modified dragon sleeper but Leif lets him go very quickly for some reason.

Funk avoids a middle rope moonsault as you can see a lot of empty seats not that far from the ring. A cartwheel into a spinning kick to the head sends Leif outside in a heap. Another big dive takes Cassidy down before a gorgeous top rope moonsault gives Funk two. They trade some quick rollups for two each until Flash scores with an enziguri and the Funky Flash Splash (450 and yes that's the real name) gets the pin at 10:34. We even get an error from JR who calls it a Shooting Star Press.

Rating: B-. This took a while to get going but for its time, this was pretty awesome. Funk is a personal favorite of mine who could fly like few other mainstream guys at this time. Cassidy was no slouch either but it would take an absurd gimmick to get him noticed, which is a shame at the end of the day.

Tag Team Titles: Diesel/Razor Ramon vs. Owen Hart/British Bulldog

Diesel and Razor are challenging and this is the story that I didn't want to get to earlier on but I'm stuck with it now. No these aren't the real versions returning, but rather people that JR brought in and who are being used as something resembling a parody of the guys who were on top of the wrestling world at this point.

Originally JR talked about how the person didn't actually matter and the gimmicks were what got Hall and Nash over, which is actually a nice jab at them. That didn't last long though and eventually became a basic parody, though Rick Bogner (Fake Razor) looks like he's wearing a Razor Ramon costume.

On the other hand, Glenn Jacobs (Fake Diesel) actually looks like the real thing from behind and when he's wearing sunglasses, making him far more bearable in the costume. We'll be hearing from Jacobs again in a few months. As for the match, the idea is that the champions are having problems because Steve Austin has been messing with their heads.

Diesel starts with Owen as JR gets into full analytical mode now that some of his buddies are in there. Diesel drives Owen into the corner and fires off some elbows before shoving Owen off the ropes. Owen comes back with some right hands but gets slammed down with ease. Two guys from Mexican wrestling company AAA named Pierroth and Cibernetico are in the aisle to distract the Bulldog, which doesn't quite work.

Off to Bulldog vs. Razor with the latter doing a pretty decent imitation of the real Razor's mannerisms, but the whole thing falls apart as soon as you see his face. Bulldog fires off some forearms as the AAA guys leave, only to be replaced by Austin. Bulldog hits a quick crossbody but goes to the floor to get in a fight with Austin. Steve is taken to the back but the distraction allows Razor to hit a spinning right hand, sending Bulldog into the corner for a tag off to Owen.

Hart gets a quick two off a missile dropkick but Diesel pulls the top rope down to send him out to the floor. Diesel rams Owen back first into the post before sending him back in for an armbar from Razor. It's back to Diesel for a sidewalk slam but he stomps away instead of covering. Ramon comes back in and hits a pumphandle fall away slam for two, followed by a reverse chinlock. The fans are almost entirely behind the champions, despite them being huge heels at this point.

Diesel gets two off a big boot (which clearly missed by several inches) but the fans all think he sucks. Owen gets a boot of his own up in the corner and takes Diesel down with a nice enziguri. There's the hot tag off to Bulldog who cleans house with clotheslines and forearms all around. A quick vertical suplex gets two on Razor as everything breaks down. Owen is whipped into Diesel who catches him in midair but Bulldog dropkicks his partner in the back, sending them both to the floor. Owen slides back in to spinwheel kick Razor in the face to break up a Razor's Edge attempt and score a quick pin to retain at 10:45.

Rating: C-. As stupid as the gimmick was, the match wasn't too bad at all. Diesel was actually very solid in the ring and would be around for many more years under a different gimmick. Razor was just kind of there though and the match was definitely weaker when he was in there. Not bad stuff for the most part though.

Post match Austin immediately hits the ring for some cheap shots on the Bulldog, possibly injuring his knee.

Here's Ahmed Johnson for an interview. He's looking forward to the Royal Rumble for his shot at Faarooq because he's lost everything due to the injury Faarooq caused. Johnson has lost his car, his girlfriend and his house so now it's time for revenge. All he has left are the people, but before he can go into that here's the Nation of Domination, Faarooq's semi-militant black power group. Faarooq goes into a rant about how Johnson's people have no future but everyone is looking to Faarooq for their hope. Johnson wants to fight right now and starts his trademark YOU'RE GOING DOWN chant.

We recap Hunter Hearst Helmsley vs. Marc Mero for the Intercontinental title. Helmsley took the title from Mero the night after Buried Alive with Mero replacing Mr. Perfect. It turns out that Perfect had been grooming Helmsley to steal the title from Mero and their rift from a few months ago was all a ruse. Helmsley won the title and threw Perfect out of the WWF, leading to a rematch tonight.

Intercontinental Title: Hunter Hearst Helmsley vs. Marc Mero

Mero is challenging and thankfully Helmsley has officially been nicknamed HHH by this point, making my typing far easier. The champion grabs a hammerlock and takes Mero down to the mat, only to be countered into a hammerlock as well. Back up and they fight over a top wristlock before Mero scores with a hiptoss. A dropkick and clothesline put Helmsley on the floor and Mero hits a nice dive to take him out again.

Back in and Mero keeps the pressure on with a backdrop and some right hands in the corner, only to have HHH drop him face first on the buckle to take over. That doesn't last long either though as a Pedigree attempt is countered into a backdrop over the top rope, sending HHH back to the floor. Mero gives chase but HHH hides behind Sable like the coward that he is. It's Mero being sent into the steps now with HHH firmly in control.

Helmsley grabs a chair but the referee takes it away, only to allow Helmsley to send Mero into the steps again. Back in and a backbreaker puts Mero down again as Vince apologizes for satellite transmission problems. Another backbreaker gets two and we hit the abdominal stretch. It's nice to see a basic story here and it's working quite well. Things don't have to be complicated to work which is a lesson so many wrestling companies and wrestlers in general can't understand.

The referee catches HHH using the ropes for additional leverage and breaks up the hold, triggering a shoving match between referee Earl Hebner and the champion. This would actually become a recurring bit between the two of them over the years. Mero tries to speed things up but charges into a boot in the corner to put him down again. HHH goes up but dives into a boot to the face as well, giving Mero the breather he needed. A hard whip turns HHH upside down in the corner and a knee to the ribs puts him down again.

Mero gets two off a headscissors and a top rope hurricanrana looks to set up the Wild Thing. Helmsley is nothing if not resourceful though and sends Hebner into the ropes, crotching Mero down onto the buckle. The Pedigree is countered into a slingshot which sends Helmsley head first into the post but only gets a two count. A moonsault press (the Merosault) gets another two but Marc clotheslines the referee down.

Helmsley scores with a neckbreaker but there's no one to count. The title belt is brought in but Mero avoids a shot to the head and gets a rolling cradle but there's still no referee. Helmsley is whipped int the corner and goes flying to the outside where Mero scores with another dive. Cue Goldust for no adequately explained reason to swing another Intercontinental Title at HHH but hitting Mero by mistake. The referee is back up to count and only Mero gets back in to beat the count, earning a countout win at 14:03, meaning no title change.

Rating: C. Again not a bad match at all with Mero still being great in the air and Helmsley really starting to get into the heel mode that would make him a legend. The Goldust stuff didn't do much for me but he would be feuding with Helmsley more extensively soon enough. Good stuff here though.

Post match Mero hits the Wild Thing on HHH for fun. Goldust gets in some cheap shots in the aisle as his face push continues.

Sid is very happy to be here even though he and Shawn got in a brawl earlier this morning. Bret tried to intervene and took a beating from Sid as well. Sid whispers a lot, saying that he beat Shawn and Shawn beat Bret, ergo he can beat Bret.

We recap the Executioner vs. Undertaker, which should be obvious if you read the previous show. Undertaker was back at Survivor Series, basically looking like Batman and wearing a better looking outfit. The Executioner attacked him again at Survivor Series, setting things up here.

Executioner vs. Undertaker

This is an Armageddon match, meaning after a fall the person who was pinned or submitted has a ten count to get to his feet. Basically it's a last man standing match but the counts don't start until after a fall. Executioner is former Freebird (legendary 80s team) Terry Gordy who was about ten miles past his prime here. Undertaker runs him over to start and backdrops Executioner before booting him in the face. A whip into the corner gets Executioner tied up in the Tree of Woe so Undertaker can stomp away even more.

He takes too much time glaring at Paul Bearer though and misses a splash in the corner. It doesn't seem to affect Undertaker that much though as he's right back up, only to miss an elbow drop. A clothesline puts Undertaker over the top but he lands on his feet and pulls Executioner to the floor. Paul blasts him with the urn to little effect but being sent into the post works a bit better. A clothesline puts Executioner back down though and Undertaker peels the mats back, only to have Mankind roll out from under the announcers' table to double team Undertaker down.

They head inside but Undertaker clotheslines both of them out to the floor and fights them up the aisle. Undertaker throws Mankind through the In Your House set window, punches him around the back and knocks him through the door as well. Executioner gets back up and they head back to ringside with Undertaker being caught by the numbers game again. Security comes out and spray mace at Mankind to little effect as the other two head back to the set. They brawl backstage and outside as Mankind has been put in a straitjacket.

The camera only shows us the steps and never goes outside with Undertaker and Executioner, so we cut back to the arena to see Mankind in the jacket stumbling around ringside. We finally get a camera outside and see a wide shot of Undertaker knocking Executioner into the water. He heads back inside to get some more of Mankind who charges at him while still in the straitjacket. Eventually a dry Executioner comes back to the ring and gets Tombstoned for the easy pin and ten count at 11:31.

Rating: D-. To call this a mess is an insult to messes. The Armageddon stuff was worthless because there wasn't even a fall attempted until the very end. This was also the last major appearance for Executioner and I can't say I'm surprised. He was just a generic big guy that never did anything of note. Terrible match here that was trying WAY too hard.

Bret looks at the video from earlier today with the three way fight between himself, Shawn and Sid, saying he wouldn't put anything past Shawn. He gets cut off by Shawn's music and is even more ticked off.

WWF Title: Sycho Sid vs. Bret Hart

Sid is defending and Shawn is on commentary due to getting the winner at the Royal Rumble. He immediately jumps on Bret (verbally), blasting him for not putting people over and making it all about himself. Bret jumps Sid from behind and pounds away with Shawn still getting in jab after jab at him. A hard whip into the corner and a clothesline put Bret down though as the champion takes over. Sid hits a running kick to the side of the head before stomping away in the corner. Bret comes back with a shot to the ribs and drops some elbows as Shawn rips into Bret for his lack of emotion.

Sid punches him to the floor for nothing of note before going back inside where Bret gets backdropped right back to the floor. The mats are peeled back again but Bret pushes Sid into the post to break up an attempted powerbomb. Bret picks him up and rams him back first into the post before heading back inside for some kicks to the spine. It's off to a reverse chinlock, which is usually a heel move but Bret is a face, despite wrestling a heel style here (Got that?). Sid is allegedly a heel but the fans like him, though not as much as Bret. 1996 was weird.

Bret stomps away in the corner but uses the referee's break to untie a turnbuckle pad. Sid blocks a ram into the buckle but gets suplexed down for two. The Russian legsweep gets the same and Bret follows up with a snap suplex for no cover. A middle rope elbow to the back gets two more as Bret isn't hooking the leg for some reason as per his custom, but for once the announcers are calling him out on it.

Bret goes up but gets slammed off and punched HARD in the face. There's a big boot for two and Shawn makes sure to point out Sid hooking the leg. Sid misses an elbow drop but kicks Bret to the floor to break up the Sharpshooter. Cue Steve Austin out of nowhere with a chop block to take Bret's knee out. This brings out the Bulldog and Owen to take out Austin but the damage has been done. Bret gets back in with a bad limp but Sid is tentative to go after him, possibly due to Bret's history of goldbricking but I don't think Sid is that bright.

The champion finally pounds Bret down into the corner and stomps away with pure power. Bret escapes Snake Eyes onto the exposed buckle but gets sent chest first into it instead which suits him very well. A big chokeslam gets two for the champ but Sid misses a charge, allowing Bret to hit a Cactus Clothesline and send both guys to the floor. Bret grabs a chair (Shawn: "There's your role model!") but Sid takes it away with ease. Sid shoves Shawn down, bringing Michaels to the apron. Bret is sent into Shawn, allowing Sid to powerbomb him and retain at 17:03.

Rating: C+. Much like the rest of the show, this wasn't all that bad. The face/heel dynamic here was very strange to say the least but it actually worked in the end. Bret is the kind of guy that can work with any style and bouncing around for a monster is one of his specialties. Good main event here though not great. In an impressive note, Sid has now pinned Shawn and Bret at consecutive PPVs, which is quite the feat.

Post match Shawn is injured from being knocked off the apron and Bret pounds away on him. Bret leaves in a huff and Shawn promises to kick Bret's teeth down his throat to end the show.

Overall Rating: C+. For a two hour show at a cost of $20, this was actually pretty solid stuff. The Undertaker match was dreadful but other than that there isn't anything bad on the card. We're definitely past the worst point and things should start going up from here. The three way feud over the WWF Title is interesting stuff and the promos that built it up were even better. There's nothing groundbreaking or worth going out of your way to see here, but it was a pleasant surprise after so many awful shows so far.

Let The New Era Again

A lot would change as we head into 1997. Business was still bad, but it was clear that things were starting to swing up from a quality perspective. The next major show was the Royal Rumble in Shawn's hometown of San Antonio, where Shawn won the WWF Title back in front of over 60,000 fans. The incredible reaction Shawn received was enough to cancel a proposed heel turn for the time being and his title reign was back on.

However it didn't last long, as Shawn was scheduled to face Sid in a rubber match on a special episode of Raw. As was a tradition with Shawn, he developed a "career threatening" knee injury just before the match and had to vacate the title in the famous Lost Smile speech. The common theory states this was due to Shawn not wanting to lose the title at Wrestlemania but that's only speculation. Really strong speculation but speculation nonetheless. Over the years Shawn has hinted that the knee injury was faked but has never flat out admitted to making it up.

With Shawn vacating the title, a new champion had to be crowned. Instead of giving the title to the #1 contender, it was decided instead that Sid would get the first shot at the new champion. However, there was confusion as to who should hold the title in the first place. A good idea might have been to award it to the winner of the Royal Rumble, but that wasn't so simple either.

Steve Austin had won the thirty man Royal Rumble, but only after returning to the ring when the referees didn't see him being eliminated. The solution was to have a four way match between the final four competitors in the Rumble with the winner being named the new #1 contender. With the title vacated though, the match was made a title match with the winner defending against Sid the next night on Raw.

In Your House #13: Final Four
Date: February 16, 1997
Location: UTC Arena, Chattanooga, Tennessee
Attendance: 6,399
Commentators: Jerry Lawler, Jim Ross

The problem with having four top guys in a single match is that it takes away from the rest of the show. Luckily there was a title match on the special episode of Raw that saw newcomer Rocky Maivia upset HHH for the Intercontinental Title, meaning there's a rematch tonight. Other than that there isn't much here to say the least. Let's get to it.

The opening video talks about what it means to be WWF Champion and how the desire for the belt has changed people's lives, implying Bret turning to the dark side after being screwed out of the title at It's Time.

Marc Mero vs. Leif Cassidy

Cassidy doesn't even get an entrance. Instead he slaps Mero in the face and gets taken down by an armdrag for his efforts. We hit the armbar for a bit with Mero in control but Cassidy fights up and shoves the referee before bailing to the floor. Leif wraps Mero's leg around the rope but Sable goes after him, allowing Mero to come back with right hands. Back in and a slingshot legdrop keeps Cassidy in trouble with Mero shouting to stay away from Sable.

Cassidy comes back with a pair of dropkicks to the knee and Mero is in trouble. More kicks to the knee have Marc on the mat and Leif slaps on a leg lace. Mero's knee is slammed down into the mat as the fans are starting to wake up a bit here. Back to the leglock as Mero's offense is stopped cold again. Mero finally reaches over and grabs a rope so Leif keeps stomping away.

The leglocks continue until Mero fights up and scores with an enziguri, setting up a rollup for two. Cassidy will have none of this being on defense and puts on a lame figure four leglock until Sable helps Marc get to the ropes. Leif goes after Sable so Mero dives through the ropes to take him out. Back in and Marc rams him face first into the mat a few times, followed by a Samoan drop to set up the Wild Thing for the pin at 9:30.

Rating: D+. I didn't hate the match and the psychology was working, but the execution was rather boring for the most part. This was more about pushing Sable as having more backbone and Mero being more protective of her, but I see no reason for this to have been on PPV. This could have been accomplished in half the time on TV which brings this down. Not a horrible match though.

Former Intercontinental Champion the Honky Tonk Man comes out for commentary as he searches for a protege.

We go back to that special Raw where Shawn forfeited the title due to a knee injury. We see nearly the entire speech, which would be undone when his knee miraculously healed about a month after Wrestlemania. The announcement of the Final Four match becoming a title match is included as well.

Sid says he doesn't feel bad for Shawn because Sid never got his title shot due to Shawn's injury. He'll get his chance tomorrow night and will rule the world again.

Nation of Domination vs. Bart Gunn/Goldust/Flash Funk

The Nation is Faarooq, Savio Vega and Crush. It also includes two white rappers, Clarence Mason, and several unnamed actors who were there to make the Nation look bigger in a brilliant move. Bart had a match against Faarooq where the rest of the Nation interfered so he wants revenge. The same thing happened to Goldust in a match with Crush while Flash is just there to make it 3-3.

Faarooq has something to say before the match but Goldust jumps him, starting a six man brawl. The Nation is sent to the floor so Funk dives over the top to take all three of them out. We finally get going with Goldust vs. Faarooq and the golden one in control. It's quickly off to Funk who gets caught in a spinebuster to give the Nation control. Funk fights up and hits a quick springboard hurricanrana but Crush breaks it up.

Bart comes in to fight Crush and the Nation bails to the floor, only to have Gunn launch Funk over the top and onto all three of them. However it's a bad idea to have Funk dive on all three of them as the three on one beating begins. Crush gets two off a belly to belly suplex before it's off to Faarooq for some cannonballs down onto Funk's back. This works just fine until Funk turns over to crotch Faarooq on his knees.

Goldust tries to come in but the distraction allows Crush and Vega to spike piledrive Flash for two. Funk comes back with a quick double clothesline to Vega and Faarooq, allowing for the tag off to Gunn. A powerslam gets two on Faarooq as everything breaks down. Bart hits a top rope bulldog on Faarooq but Crush hits a guillotine legdrop to knock Bart out, giving Faarooq the pin at 6:43.

Rating: D. This match exists and that's about all there is to say about it. It was a glorified squash with the Nation never being in any real danger at all. Much like the opening match, this was something that could have been on any given television show and no one would have known the difference.

Doc Hendrix asks Austin if he's worried because he's never beaten any of the other people in the Final Four match. Austin says he won the Rumble and is tired of the BS and politics that have been holding him back because it ends tonight.

Intercontinental Title: Rocky Maivia vs. Hunter Hearst Helmsley

Maivia is defending, having won the title from Helmsley three days ago so this is the rematch. Helmsley grabs a headlock to start before taking over with an armbar and slapping Rocky in the head. Rocky trips him down and hooks a hiptoss followed by a dropkick. There's an armdrag and armbar from the champion who slaps Helmsley in the back of the head as payback. Helmsley fights up but gets taken down into another armbar seconds later.

Rocky gets up but hits the ropes once too often and gets sent out to the floor. A baseball slide sends Rocky into the barricade as things slow way down. There's a knee drop to Rocky's head for two and we hit the chinlock with Helmsley putting his feet on the ropes for extra leverage. Earl Hebner breaks up the hold so Helmsley has to put Maivia down with a running knee to the face. Rocky comes back with a quick small package for two but HHH stomps him right back down.

A backbreaker gets two on Rocky and it's right back to the chinlock. Rocky fights up again and scores with a crossbody but avoids a dropkick, sending Maivia back down to the mat. HHH clotheslines him down again but goes up top, only to jump into a shot to the ribs. Rocky speeds things up and hits a powerslam before hitting his high crossbody for two. Maivia charges into a boot in the corner but comes back with a spinning DDT to put both guys down. Rocky comes back with a facebuster and neckbreaker but here's Goldust to distract Helmsley. The distraction lets Maivia suplex him down to retain at 12:34.

Rating: C-. The match wasn't great but both guys would get so much better. These two would go on to have one of the best feuds of all time and carry the company in years to come. At this point though, Rocky was still very young and inexperienced, meaning the match wasn't all that great yet. Still though, worth a look for historical purposes if nothing else.

Post match Goldust gets on the apron when an overly muscular woman reaches over the barricade to choke Marlena. Security takes the woman away as Goldust demands she be put in jail. We'll get back to her soon enough.

Vader, now managed by Paul Bearer, promises to win the title and run through all three other men to do so.

Tag Team Titles: Doug Furnas/Phillip LaFon vs. British Bulldog/Owen Hart

Owen and Bulldog are defending and this could be interesting. Furnas and LaFon are a team of smaller but very strong guys who mostly wrestled in Japan but are here to try to breathe some life into the tag team division. During the entrance, Owen sneaks in front of Bulldog to make sure he gets the spotlight, which is partially what broke up Shawn and Diesel. Owen also eliminated Bulldog from the Rumble to further the potential split.

Furnas and Hart get things going with Doug grabbing an armbar. It's off to LaFon who counters a monkey flip into a sunset flip for two before rolling Hart into a leg bar. Bulldog comes in and forearms Phillip instead of accepting a handshake. A spinwheel kick gets two for LaFon but Owen gets in a cheap shot from behind, allowing for a double team by the champions. Owen comes in legally with a backbreaker for two before it's back to Bulldog. Smith stomps away as well but gets caught in a sunset flip, only to have Owen distract the referee to prevent a near fall.

Hart's Sharpshooter attempt is kicked away but he still blocks a tag attempt. Off to a leglock from the champion before Bulldog comes in and lifts up LaFon with Owen adding a crossbody for a nice combo move. The referee yells at Bulldog as Phillip rolls up Owen, but the Bulldog comes in to turn the small package over. While he's being put back into the corner, Furnas comes in and turns it over again to give LaFon two.

LaFon rams the champions' heads together and Owen

accidentally spinwheel kicks Bulldog in the face, furthering the tension even more. Bulldog powerslams Owen down and LaFon gets two off a top rope splash. The hot tag brings in Furnas for a dropkick and belly to belly suplex as everything breaks down. A DDT and a legdrop get two on Owen but he comes back with the enziguri to Furnas.

The double tag brings in LaFon vs. Bulldog with Davey throwing the smaller man around. LaFon gets a sunset flip for two as everything breaks down again with the champions being thrown together. Bulldog drops LaFon face first onto the buckle and loads up the powerslam, only to have Owen hit LaFon with his Slammy Award for the DQ at 10:31

Rating: B-. This was really good stuff but the ending went for the story development instead of the good match ending. LaFon and Furnas are guys who have grown on me over the years and this is one of their best matches in the WWF. Owen and Bulldog were guys that could work well with anyone and when you give them talented people to work with, the matches were always going to work well.

Post match the champions argue and Bulldog breaks the Slammy. They eventually make up, though the tension is still there.

Undertaker says he has his edge back and will take the title tonight.

We recap the main event. Again these are the final four in the Rumble but the ending was such a mess that the only way to settle it is this Final Four match which is now a title match due to Shawn forfeiting the title.

WWF Title: Bret Hart vs. Vader vs. Steve Austin vs. Undertaker

The title is vacant coming in. This has some unique rules in that it's elimination style with eliminations coming from pinfall, submissions or over the top rope with both feet hitting the floor. Other than that, anything goes. Undertaker and Vader go at it while Austin gets pounded into the corner. Undertaker goes after Bret before punching Austin as well before getting VERY risky with Old School. Vader comes back with a belly to belly suplex on Undertaker but that just means a sit up.

The two monsters fight through the ropes to the floor, meaning they're still in the match. Vader's chair shot hits the post instead of Undertaker before Undertaker kicks it back into Vader's face. Undertaker sends Vader into the steps, busting him open before pounding away on the cut. Both guys head inside where Bret has been working over Austin's back to join the fight. Now it's Vader pounding away on Undertaker's face as Austin breaks up a sleeper from Bret. Undertaker chokeslams Vader but Austin tries a Stunner, with Undertaker turning to the side to make it more of a neckbreaker.

Bret pounds on Vader but gets hit low and they head outside. Undertaker beats Austin down in the corner but gets caught with a neckbreaker (meant to be a neckbreaker this time). Vader hits Bret in the back with a chair a few times as his eye is just gushing blood. All four guys are on the floor with Undertaker backdropping Austin on the concrete. Undertaker goes after Bret while Vader stumbles out to the floor to beat on Austin. Steve sends Vader into the steps and drops them on Vader's back as Undertaker gets two on Bret via something we couldn't see.

Bret takes over and goes after the Undertaker's knee as Vader sends Austin into the barricade as this match is really hard to call with everything that's going on. Austin hits Vader with the belt a few times but Vader fights back and drags Bret to the floor for no apparent reason. Austin tries to come off the top on Undertaker but gets crotched as Vader and Bret fight up the aisle. Vader is sent into the crowd and Undertaker gets a two count on Austin. Undertaker tries to throw Austin out for the first time but Austin comes back with a clothesline for two.

Sid is watching in the back as Vader puts Bret in a Sharpshooter of all things on the floor. Austin breaks it up for no apparent reason so Bret goes after Steve in retaliation. Undertaker pounds on Austin but Bret wants some of Undertaker, allowing Austin to hit the Thesz press on Vader and fire off even more right hands. Undertaker goes after Austin but Bret drops Undertaker, leaving Hart as the only man on his feet. Vader hits a nice clothesline on Undertaker as Bret hits a good looking piledriver for two on Austin.

The 450lb Vader misses a moonsault onto Undertaker, firing the crowd up even more. The monsters head to the floor to brawl even more as Vader's eye is looking horrible. Austin tries to throw Bret over the top rope but Bret saves himself and slugs Steve down as Vader chokes away on Undertaker. Bret drives some elbows into Austin's face for two but Undertaker goes after Austin instead. Hart comes back with a low blow on Vader, sending the blood down onto his chest in a scary visual.

Austin stomps on Undertaker, earning himself a backdrop out to the floor. Vader tries an armbar of all things on Bret as Austin has Undertaker over the top rope and onto the apron, but it appears that Austin has hurt his knee in the process. Keep that in mind as it comes into play later. Bret goes after Austin as Steve can barely even stand up. Not that it matters as he's thrown out just a few seconds later for the first elimination.

Back in the ring and Undertaker splashes Vader in the corner so Bret goes after Undertaker and Vader helps him, sending Undertaker under the ropes and to the floor. Bearer gets in an urn shot to Undertaker as Vader goes up top, only to be superplexed down. Vader's face is COVERED in blood now.

There's a Sharpshooter to Vader but Undertaker breaks it up out of instinct. Cue Austin to go after Bret and send him into the post. Back inside and Vader loads up the Vader Bomb but Undertaker gets to his feet and low blows him out, leaving us with two men. Undertaker chokeslams Bret and loads up the Tombstone but Austin breaks it up. Undertaker goes after him, allowing Bret to get a rollup for two. Bret pounds away on Austin before clotheslining Undertaker out to the floor for the win and the title at 24:06.

Rating: A. This is such a unique match that I'm surprised they've never used the rules again. The key to the match was keeping the pairings moving, giving you a string of matches instead of the same guys fighting over and over again. Vader's eye looked HORRIBLE and made the match that much better. As for Austin's knee injury, a popular rumor says that he was going to win the title here and lose it the next night but everything went as planned.

Sid comes out to stare down Bret to close out the show.

Overall Rating: B-. Much like Mind Games, when you have one classic match take up thirty minutes of a 105 minute show, it's hard to call the show a failure at all. The Tag Team Title match helps a lot as well, giving you two very solid matches out of five and nothing was really bad, leaving this as probably the best overall show so far. Things would get WAY better soon though.

Sid did indeed get his WWF Title match the next night on Raw and, thanks to the interference of Steve Austin, Bret lost the title. This eventually set up Sid vs. Undertaker for the title at Wrestlemania while Austin and Hart would have the sequel to their classic at Survivor Series in an I Quit match. Vader would be shunted down the card into a tag team with Mankind and never approach the top of the card again.

This brings us to Wrestlemania XIII where Undertaker pinned Sid to win the title in one of the most forgettable Wrestlemania main events of all time. Part of the reason no one remembers this match is because Austin vs. Hart is probably one of the top ten matches of all time for a variety of reasons. Other than the incredible hatred between the two, the iconic image of blood running down Austin's face as he tries to escape the Sharpshooter, the key to the match was a double turn, making Austin into the anti-hero and Bret into the top villain.

The feud wasn't over though, as the next night on Raw Bret interrupted a match between Owen Hart and British Bulldog. He talked about how the American fans were ripping the family apart and that the Canadians and British Harts needed to stand together. This was the formation of the Hart Foundation, eventually joined by Bret's old tag partner Jim Neidhart (Anvil) and crazy man Brian Pillman.

The team praised Canada and ran down the United States at every chance they could, with Steve Austin as their top foe. The first battle would be at In Your House #14, which featured a double main event of Austin vs. Hart for the title shot at the next PPV and Mankind challenging Undertaker for the WWF Title.

In Your House #14: Revenge Of The Taker
Date: April 20, 1997
Location: War Memorial Auditorium, Rochester, New York
Attendance: 6,477
Commentators: Jim Ross, Vince McMahon, Jerry Lawler

While the main event picture has picked up a good bit, there's still a lot of trouble for the company as a whole. WCW is absolutely destroying them in business and the WWF is just trying to hang on at this point. Undertaker as champion is a new idea, but the real strength of the company will come through the Border War storyline of Canada vs. the USA. Let's get to it.

The opening video focuses on exactly what you would expect it to: the Undertaker coming for revenge on Mankind.

Tag Team Titles: Owen Hart/British Bulldog vs. Legion of Doom

Owen and Bulldog are defending. The Legion of Doom (LOD) were the most dominant tag team in wrestling in the 80s but have been in WCW for years. They're now back to try for one more run at glory. The champions come out to the Hart Foundation song which is Bret's old theme music. Also Bulldog is the first ever European Champion, having won the title in Germany by beating Owen in a tournament final. Animal (of Animal and Hawk Hawk) starts by pounding Owen into the corner and runs over him with a flying tackle. Owen tries to run Animal over but literally bounces off of him.

Instead it's off to the Bulldog but the LOD are even stronger than he is, with Hawk getting two off a clothesline. Bulldog gets pounded in the corner but comes back with a great looking delayed vertical suplex on the huge Hawk. It's off to Owen with a top rope forearm to Hawk's head but Hawk easily breaks up a Sharpshooter attempt and clotheslines Hart down. Back to Animal for a powerslam and we hit the chinlock. We go to a split screen to see Steve Austin arriving late.

Animal gorilla presses Owen down and it's back to Hawk for a mostly missed top rope splash which gets two. Owen whips Hawk chest first into the buckle and they ram heads to put both guys down. Hart scores with the enziguri and it's back to Bulldog for some stomping. Hawk fights out of a chinlock but gets taken down by a knee to the ribs.

Owen comes back in with a sleeper as JR and Lawler get into a big argument over whether Oklahoma (JR's home state) is part of the civilized world or not. Hawk rams the champions into each other and lifts Davey up to Animal for a second rope powerslam for the pin and the titles out of nowhere.

Rating: D+. Not much to see here but the fans popped big for their childhood heroes getting another run at glory. Bulldog and Owen were an awesome team and did a great job of holding the titles until another team could eventually take them away. I'm surprised it didn't end with the LOD's signature Doomsday Device though. Anyway, nice surprise finish.

Actually never mind as another referee comes out and says

Animal pinned the illegal man, so the fall doesn't count and the match continues. Owen and Bulldog try to walk out on the match but are told if they leave they also lose the titles. That's enough to get them back in and Owen takes Animal down with a quick spinwheel kick.

Owen gets two off a neckbreaker and legdrop before it's back to Bulldog for some stomping. That only lasts a few seconds as it's already back to Hart who misses a top rope splash. Hawk gets the tag and cleans house as everything breaks down. Animal puts Owen on his shoulders for Hawk's clothesline (the Doomsday Device) but Bret runs in for the quick DQ at 10:11.

Rating: D. That's for the whole thing. The second part didn't add anything to the match other than screwing the fans over yet again. You know, in case getting on their nerves wasn't enough the first time. The match was nothing special overall as we got the idea the first time around.

Owen and Bulldog say that was all skill with no luck. They're upset that Austin is here.

Intercontinental Title: Savio Vega vs. Rocky Maivia

Rocky is defending. Savio is now in all black instead of his old red attire and has almost the entire Nation with him here. Rocky successfully defended the title at Wrestlemania but lost to Savio via some cheating on Raw. Savio tries to jump the champion as he gets in the ring and the fight is on quickly. Maivia grabs an armbar as Faarooq comes out with his arm in a sling to do commentary. Vega fights out of the armbar and snaps Rocky's throat over the top rope to take over.

We hit a quick nerve hold as Faarooq issues a challenge for Ahmed Johnson to run the Nation gauntlet. If Johnson can beat all three of them, the Nation will be abolished. A small package gets Rocky nowhere so it's back to the nerve hold. We're almost five minutes into this match and almost nothing has happened. Rocky gets a quick fisherman's suplex but Crush distracts the referee to prevent a count. They finally get back up so Maivia can hit his floatover DDT for a delayed near fall.

A rollup out of the corner gets the same for Vega but the kickout sends him shoulder first into the post. Rocky gets two off a belly to back suplex and the move that would become known as the Rock Bottom gets the same. Vega sends Rocky through the ropes and out to the floor where Crush lays him out with a heart punch (exactly what it sounds like), drawing a countout at 8:33.

Rating: D. Other than seeing the beta version of the Rock Bottom there was nothing here. The main reason this match existed was to let Faarooq issue his challenge because the wrestlers clearly weren't putting in a ton of effort out there. The match wasn't even nine minutes long and about half of that was spent in rest holds.

Savio is mad at Crush for costing him a chance to win the title, but Faarooq tells them to beat up Rocky instead. Ahmed Johnson runs in with a 2x4 for the save and accepts Faarooq's challenge.

Sable is proud to have won Miss Slammy and Marc Mero says he'll be back from his knee injury soon. As they're talking, Austin is seen going into the men's room when a commotion is hurt. Bulldog and Owen leave the room with Davey holding a board as Hebner says Austin has been attacked.

Jesse James vs. Rockabilly

Oh let's get this over with. Jesse James is the returning Roadie, who was revealed as being the voice that Jeff Jarrett was lip syncing to. The debuting Rockabilly is Billy Gunn, but now as a dancer under Honky Tonk Man's tutelage, following months of Honky Tonk Man looking for his new protege. It's even more confusing since Billy punched Honky Tonk Man two weeks ago. Billy kicks away at Jesse's ribs and comes back with a dropkick, sending Billy to the floor. A clothesline off the apron takes Billy down and Jesse says he's coming for Honky Tonk Man next.

Back in and Billy scores with a dropkick of his own before posing a bit. The match slows down a lot as Billy is more interested in dancing than going for a win. Now it's off to a chinlock before Billy rakes the eyes to slow James down. A corner splash misses and Billy hits the post and eventually James gets up to pounds away in the corner. Billy sends him to the floor before bringing it back inside for more dancing. As usual this goes badly as his suplex is countered into a small package by Jesse for a fast pin at 6:46.

113

Rating: D. Egads this show has been horrible so far. This is another feud that went on for months with no one caring, though in this case there would be something good to come out of it. We'll get to that later, but for now there was nothing to see here and no one was interested in these two at this point.

Austin says he'll fight tonight. President Gorilla Monsoon puts Bret vs. Austin on last to give Austin time to recover.

The Hart Foundation (Just Bret, Owen and Bulldog at the moment) say Austin started it and they were just defending themselves.

We get a really creepy video for both main events rolled into one which is supposed to be like looking into the mind of a crazy person. To be fair I don't think it's that far off actually.

WWF Title: Mankind vs. Undertaker

Undertaker is defending and I think we've covered the backstory for this one enough already. For perhaps the only time in his career, Undertaker charges from the floor into the ring and the fight is on. Undertaker has a bandage on his head from where Mankind burned him recently. They slug it out to start and a running right hand to the head puts Undertaker down. The Cactus Clothesline puts both guys on the floor but Undertaker of course lands on his feet. A HARD whip sends Mankind into the barricade and a standing chokeslam does it again.

The third whip sends Mankind into the crowd and the Undertaker is in full control. Mankind is whipped into the barricade yet again as we head back to ringside. Back into the ring with Undertaker still pounding away and driving him down with shoulder blocks. Undertaker lets go of the hand on Old School so it's a diving clothesline instead of a forearm to the back. Paul Bearer gets on the apron to prevent the Tombstone and a quick shot with the urn gets two for Mankind.

The champion gets pounded down in the corner and a running knee to the head puts him down again. We hit the nerve hold on Undertaker before Mankind turns it into a reverse chinlock. The much stronger Undertaker is able to turn around though and fire off right hands to the ribs to escape. A very hard shot sends

114

Mankind out to the floor and Undertaker sends him face first into the steps. Mankind comes back with a pitcher of water and shatters it over the champion's face to put him back down. A chair to Undertaker's head still doesn't draw a DQ and JR demands to know why. Good question actually.

Mankind drops an elbow from the middle rope to the floor in one of his signature spots. The bandage is ripped off of Undertaker's head and the injury is just ugly looking. Undertaker finally gets back inside where a pulling piledriver gets two for the challenger. The same move gets no cover but Mankind does screech a lot. Undertaker staggers around for a bit before hitting a jumping clothesline out of nowhere. The referee is knocked down and Mankind gets the Mandible Claw to knock Undertaker out cold.

Another referee comes in and gets the Claw as well for reasons of Mankind is insane. Bearer throws in a chair but Mankind wants the steps. In perhaps the only time in his career, Undertaker dropkicks the steps into Mankind's face, and now it's time to fight. A BIG chair shot to the head knocks Mankind silly and Undertaker throws him into the ropes to tie Mankind up by the neck.

The champion rips Mankind's mask off and smashes the steps into Mankind, knocking him off the apron and head first through the table in a scary looking crash. Back inside and a chokeslam only gets two, shocking the crowd. Taker isn't playing anymore though and it's a Tombstone to retain the title at 17:26.

Rating: B. This got really good once they stopped the pretense of a wrestling match and started fighting. A ticked off Undertaker is just fun to watch and this was no exception, especially when you had a human pinball like Mankind to bounce all over the place like he did. The match wasn't particularly good, but it was fun which is what this has show desperately needed.

Post match Undertaker goes after Bearer but has to fight off Mankind. Undertaker kicks something out of Mankind's hands and kicks Mankind to the floor. Mankind dropped a lighter and flash paper, so Undertaker lights it up in Bearer's face to burn him like Mankind burned Undertaker.

Side note: on the home video version of this show, there's an ad here which shows the main event of next month's show, which is Undertaker defending against the winner of Bret vs. Austin. Nice job guys.

The Hart Foundation says they're in a war here and if Bret has to beat Austin a third time, so be it.

Steve Austin vs. Bret Hart

Winner gets Undertaker for the title next month. Hart tries to have Owen and Bulldog accompany him but they're stopped by referees because this is one on one. Naturally the fight is on as soon as the bell rings with Austin getting the better of it. They head to the outside with Bret being sent into the steps as it's all Austin so far. Another whip into the steps has Bret writhing in pain before they head into an empty space next to the crowd. Back in and Austin shoves him to the mat for two, sending Bret running to the floor.

Austin trips chasing after Hart, allowing Bret to slide a chair into the ring. Steve knocks it out of his hands though and picks it up himself, only to have Bret dropkick Austin in the back, knocking the referee down in the process. Bret goes after Austin's bad knee with the chair, despite the fact that Gorilla Monsoon is at ringside. Bret helps the referee up after the damage has been done before going after the leg even more.

Hart slams the leg into the apron but Austin kicks away from out of the corner, using the ropes to hold himself up. Bret lures him into the middle of the ring though and puts a Figure Four on around the post. Three straight chair shots to the knee have Austin in agony but he gets a rush of adrenaline to fire off elbows to Bret's back. A single kick to the knee puts Austin right back down though and it's off to a basic leglock. Bret takes Austin's knee brace off and cannonballs down onto the leg again.

Austin rolls out to the floor but Bret takes the opportunity to send the knee into the steps. Back in and Austin scores with a quick low blow before choking away on the mat. A middle rope elbow misses and Austin bangs the knee again to stop another comeback bid. Bret suplexes him down and puts on a Figure Four to keep the pressure on the leg. Austin eventually rolls over to break the hold but stops to yell at the referee for some reason, allowing Bret to kick the knee out again.

116

Bret tries the Figure Four around the post again but settles for just ramming Austin's ribs into the barricade. Austin backdrops a charging Canadian into the crowd and slugs away before dropping Bret chest first onto the steel. Back in and Bret is sent chest first into the buckle before Austin just rains down right hands. Austin tries a piledriver but the knee buckles, preventing any pain to Hart. A whip across the ring sends Austin down again as the knee gives out one more time.

They head to the corner and Austin is able to drop Bret face first onto the buckle for two. The Stunner is blocked so Austin just pounds away on Bret's back. Bret pays back Austin with a low blow of his own before sending both guys crashing down off a superplex. Hart loads up the Sharpshooter but Austin grabs his knee brace and blasts Bret in the head. Now it's Austin putting the Sharpshooter on Bret but here are Owen and Bulldog to interfere. They're ejected pretty quickly and Austin puts the Sharpshooter on again. Owen and Bulldog come in again and blast Austin with the brace, finally drawing a DQ at 21:09.

Rating: B. I liked the match but Austin's selling wasn't exactly great. He would just pop up after a long beating and be fine before a single shot took him down again. The ending didn't quite work either as we get a DQ after all the chair shots and knee brace shots. Austin winning via a rollup or something like that would have been fine here as he never actually pinned Bret.

Post match Bulldog and Owen are sent out again and Austin beats on Bret's knee with a chair. The Sharpshooter goes on for the third time but Bulldog and Owen are held back. Austin is finally pulled off and Bret is helped to the back to end the show.

Overall Rating: C+. As has been the case several times in this series, the majority of the matches were horrible, but when two great matches take up half the show, how can the show not be called good? You can see the seeds being planted of feuds that are going to help bring the company back to life, but they would take time to grow. Good show here but it's still not the great one the company needs.

If Austin vs. Hart at Revenge of the Taker is called a battle, their actions the next night on Raw would be considered a war. The night consisted of Austin practically hunting the Harts, eventually getting Bret alone in the ring and destroying his knee before attacking Hart again in the ambulance. The Border War was officially underway and it would dominate the company over the next several months.

In Your House #15 was the following month, but this time there was no Bret Hart due to the attack by Austin. The main event is Undertaker defending against Austin with the second biggest match arguably being the in ring pay per view debut of Ken Shamrock. Ken was a UFC fighter who had come to the WWF to referee Austin vs. Hart at Wrestlemania. His first major match is against Vader in what could be a war.

In Your House #15: A Cold Day In Hell
Date: May 11, 1997
Location: Richmond Coliseum, Richmond, Virginia
Attendance: 9,381
Commentators: Jerry Lawler, Jim Ross

Things are still bad for the WWF but there's a light at the end of the tunnel, assuming you have a telescope with you. At the moment nothing is working from a business standpoint due to WCW and the NWO angle destroying everything that dares cross their path. Things will eventually improve and a lot of it is because of what's going on right now. Let's get to it.

The opening video is nearly religious in nature with shots of a cross and narrated by Undertaker, talking about how Armageddon is near. Austin counters by saying there's nothing that can save Undertaker. Well done stuff here.

The announcers run down the card to start the show. Kind of an odd choice given that the people seeing it would have already paid for the show at this point.

There are five empty front row seats for the now complete Hart Foundation if they show up later.

Hunter Hearst Helmsley vs. Flash Funk

The Funkettes are now gone but the house set's window has been replaced by a standard small video screen. HHH now has

118

Chyna (you knew we'd get back to her) as his full time bodyguard. Flash pushes HHH into the corner before shaking his hips a bit. A hiptoss and a dropkick put Helmsley down and we hit the armbar. Back up and another dropkick puts HHH on the floor and a middle rope clothesline drops HHH again. The referee goes out to break things up but the distraction allows Chyna to blast Flash in the back of the head.

Back in and a facebuster puts Funk down again and a Chyna forearm gives HHH two. A knee drop gets the same and we hit the chinlock. That goes nowhere so it's a jumping knee to the face to put Funk on the apron again. HHH pounds away at the chest and another knee sends Funk to the floor, ramming him head first into the stage.

They head back inside with HHH going up but jumping into Flash's boot to put both guys down. A hard clothesline puts HHH down and a spinning legdrop is good for two. There's a high crossbody for the same but Flash pulls up at two for some reason. Flash goes up for the moonsault but gets crotched down. A release belly to back superplex from HHH sets up the Pedigree for the pin at 10:05.

Rating: C-. Not bad here and a decent little squash here for HHH. It also helped to establish Chyna as a bonus threat in HHH's corner which would become a much bigger deal for him in the future. Funk was going to change his gimmick soon and be just Scorpio, as he probably should have been the entire time.

Post match Chyna easily lifts Funk onto her shoulders, walks him across the ring and crotches him down on the top rope.

We get some UFC footage of Ken Shamrock before the letters UFC meant anything to most fans.

Ken Shamrock says he'll be in his zone for the match with Vader.

Rocky Maivia vs. Mankind

Maivia has lost the Intercontinental Title to Owen Hart so this is a non-title match. Before the match Rocky says he thinks success might have come to him too soon. Rocky scores with a few dropkicks to start and clotheslines Mankind out to the floor. Back in and a powerslam puts Mankind down again and it's off to a hammerlock. Mankind finally ducks a shot from Rocky to send him to the floor. A cannonball attack off the apron puts Maivia down again and Mankind is in control.

Back in again and Mankind pounds Rocky down into the corner before driving a running knee into his head. Rocky fights back but a double clothesline puts both guys down. Something resembling a snapmare over the top puts Mankind on the floor again as the match turns into a brawl.

The move that would become known as the Rock Bottom slams Mankind into the steel ramp and back inside they go. Rocky gets two off his floatover DDT but Mankind comes right back with a discus lariat. A dropkick stuns Mankind so Rocky can go up top for his crossbody, but Mankind rolls through and puts on the Mandible Claw for the win at 8:46.

Rating: C. I liked this better than the opener with Rocky continuing to lose after having such a hot streak to open his career. The counter to end the match worked quite well and that's what you need for a match like this. We'll definitely be coming back to this pairing near the end of the series.

Ad for the Austin 3:16 shirt. I'd think that did pretty well.

We recap Crush trying to beat three guys in a row on Raw to show up Ahmed Johnson. In true wrestling fashion, Ahmed was the third man and destroyed Crush.

Nation of Domination vs. Ahmed Johnson

This is a gauntlet match and if Ahmed can win, the Nation has to disband. Gorilla Monsoon ejects all the other members so that it's one on one the entire time. It'll be Crush starting for the Nation but Ahmed pounds away on him to start. An ax kick to the back of Crush's head puts him down but Ahmed misses an elbow drop. Crush kicks Johnson in the chest and gets two off a middle rope clothesline. A suplex gets the same but Johnson comes back with an ugly looking sitout gordbuster for two of his own.

We hit the sleeper from Crush and Ahmed is in trouble for a few moments. Crush waves the Nation down to ringside but they all stand pat. A piledriver puts Johnson down again but Crush looks at the Nation again instead of covering. Crush's heart punch is countered into a spinning heel kick to the face for a fast pin.

A limping Savio Vega is in next but walks into a quick backdrop for two. Some clotheslines put him down again but he comes back with a spinwheel kick in the corner to stagger Johnson. Savio's ankle seems perfectly fine and Ross thinks something is up. Vega goes after Johnson's back as the match slows down quite a bit.

Ahmed quickly breaks up a chinlock and hiptosses Savio down, only to miss a middle rope splash. Savio misses the running version though and a belly to back suplex gets two for Johnson. Ahmed calls for the Pearl River Plunge so Vega bails to the outside. Savio grabs a chair and blasts Johnson for the DQ, but the damage is already done.

That leaves Johnson vs. Faarooq with the latter's arm in a sling. The sling lasts about five seconds and Faarooq pounds away even more. JR talks about Faarooq starting out as Ron Simmons and playing college football (JR's obsession) but Johnson comes back with a spinebuster. Ahmed hits the Pearl River Plunge but the delayed cover only gets two, freaking the crowd out. A quick chop block from Faarooq sets up his Dominator finisher for the pin at 13:25.

Rating: D. Johnson is not the kind of guy that you want to wrestle three straight matches like this. The guy had an awesome look and incredible power, but there's only so much you can do with his limited skill set. The crowd died when Johnson got pinned as well, which isn't a good idea given that heels are undefeated on this show.

We recap Vader vs. Ken Shamrock, which is really nothing of note. The match was announced and they stared at each other a lot.

Vader vs. Ken Shamrock

This is submission or knockout only. Feeling out process to start until Shamrock starts firing off some kicks to the legs. A Kimura (standing armbar) sends Vader running to the ropes. More kicks to the legs have Vader in trouble and an attempted suplex sends him out to the floor. Back in and Vader stops trying to be smart and just pounds away at the ribs, only to have Shamrock easily German suplex him down. Some headbutts get Vader nowhere as Shamrock tries an ankle lock, his signature move in the UFC.

More kicks to the legs and a spinning kick to the face have Vader staggered as this is getting repetitive. Vader throws Shamrock around and hits a HARD clothesline to take over. The big man lays on Shamrock's arm but it doesn't work that well since he's probably never used a submission hold other than a bearhug. Shamrock counters into a kind of triangle choke but Vader lifts him up and drops him down to escape. Vader lifts him up and just casually drops him over the top, sending Shamrock down in a great looking crash.

Ken is sent face first into the steps and Vader's nose is bleeding. Back in and Vader pounds away in the corner as this needs to wrap up soon. Vader lays on Shamrock's legs and pulls on the ankle a bit until the fans finally start caring about the match. Shamrock is sent into the corner for a big beatdown and gets the same treatment in another corner.

Vader's moonsault mostly hits even though it wasn't supposed to due to Shamrock not rolling away fast enough. Now it's Shamrock pounding away in the corner but another HARD right hand puts him down. Not that it matters though as Ken trips Vader and wins with a quick ankle lock at 13:21.

Rating: D. This is a hard one to grade because the match itself was horrible but they were trying something very different out there. Shamrock would get WAY better with more ring time but his early days weren't pretty at all. Granted having Vader in there wasn't the best idea in the world given how much of a hothead he could be.

Vader has trouble getting up due to the kicks to his legs being a bit too real and the ankle lock having a bit too much torque.

Austin doesn't care that the Hart Foundation might be here.

WWF Title: Steve Austin vs. Undertaker

Undertaker is defending. The Hart Foundation shows up right before the bell, complete with Bret in a wheelchair (due to Austin's attack). Austin jumps the champ to start but Undertaker fires off right hands of his own and sends Steve into the buckle. Steve bails to the floor and immediately pulls Brian Pillman over the barricade to pound on him a bit, only to have Undertaker punch Pillman back into the crowd. Back in and Undertaker gets two off a nice jumping clothesline before driving his shoulder into Austin's over and over.

Old School connects for two as the fans aren't sure who to cheer for in this one. Austin pulls him down into a headlock on the mat but has to kick out of a few rollup attempts. Undertaker fights up but almost immediately gets taken back down in another headlock. They get up again and Austin actually backflips out of a suplex, which you aren't likely to ever see again. A chop block puts Undertaker down but he pulls himself into the corner and fires off right hands. Austin heads to the floor and trips Undertaker down so he can wrap the leg around the post.

Steve tries to slam the knee into the post again but Undertaker pulls his legs back, sending Austin face first into the post instead. The champion can't follow up though and Austin stomps on the knee even more. He hooks an STF of all things but Undertaker makes it to the rope. Austin tries to cannonball down onto the leg but Undertaker kicks him up and over the ropes to take over for the first time in awhile.

Now Undertaker goes after Austin's heavily braced leg, which really should have happened more often than it did. Off to a half crab from the champion but Austin makes the rope. Undertaker misses a big boot and Austin takes out the leg he was working on earlier to regain control. Undertaker kicks his way out of a leglock so Austin slams the back of the leg down onto the apron. A suplex gets two for Austin and he breaks up another Old School attempt by crotching Undertaker on top.

Taker breaks up a superplex attempt and tries a sleeper but Austin jawbreaks his way to freedom. They slug it out again with Undertaker gaining control again in the corner. Austin kicks him very low and the referee is fine with letting it continue. He yells at Austin though, allowing Undertaker to kick Austin low. A chokeslam puts Austin down but he rolls to the apron. Back in and Austin hits a quick Stunner but Brian Pillman jumps the barricade and rings the bell before the cover. Austin yells at Pillman, allowing Undertaker to get the Tombstone to retain at 20:06.

123

Rating: B. This was one heck of a fight with the ending both advancing stories and giving Austin a way to save face. Notice that he had the title won but shenanigans saved Undertaker. Also, it was Undertaker's own move and nothing physical from Austin that got the pin. Both guys look strong and we get a definitive pin. That's smart, efficient booking.

The Harts immediately jump the railing after the bell and go after the Undertaker, but they leave the wheelchair bound Bret alone. Austin goes after Bret and steals his crutch to clean house in the ring. Undertaker raises the title and gets a Stunner to end the show because that's the kind of guy Austin is.

Overall Rating: C+. The Border War has breathed new life into this company and things are definitely picking up. At this point it's clear that Austin is the future but he's not quite there yet. The handling of Austin and the patience the WWF had with him is very impressive as they could have hotshotted the title to him at any point in 1997 but they held off for the big stage. The rest of the show is certainly acceptable, though the Shamrock vs. Vader match is pretty rough. Things are looking up though for the first time in many, many months.

The next month's pay per view was King of the Ring which was little more than a filler show. The main event saw Undertaker successfully defending the title against Faarooq in a match that almost no one cared to see. However there was a second main event match with the newly crowned Tag Team Champions faced off. It turned out that Shawn Michaels' knee injury was only bad enough to keep him out of Wrestlemania and he came back to win the Tag Team Titles with Steve Austin.

Despite the fact that they were partners and both hated the Hart Foundation, Austin and Michaels did not get along at all. They bickered constantly over who was the leader of the team, resulting in their match at King of the Ring. As is the case in almost all of these matches, the match had no winner and ended in a double disqualification. They would ultimately be stripped of the titles due to Shawn being legitimately suspended for a backstage fight with Bret Hart, leaving Austin alone in his war with the Harts.

The other main match at King of the Ring was the King of the Ring final, featuring Mankind vs. Hunter Hearst Helmsley. Mankind, having split from Paul Bearer, was rapidly turning face and was the polar opposite of Helmsley in every way, shape and form. Helmsley wound up winning, but Mankind wasn't done with him yet as we would see at In Your House #16.

After King of the Ring, the road led to the Saddledome in Calgary, Alberta, Canada, the home city of Bret and Owen Hart, making the show a special night for them. The show's main event was a ten man tag of the Hart Foundation vs. Team America, comprised of Austin, Ken Shamrock, Goldust and the Legion of Doom. This was the grand blowoff for the Border War, with Bret leading the Hart Foundation back to Calgary for his glorious homecoming and a hero's welcome.

For months on end Bret had run down America and preached the greatness of Canada, which was the first time that someone had been a proud Canadian and not a goof. This was a huge moment for Canada, where Bret and the Hart Foundation were the biggest heroes the country had ever seen. It helps that Austin's character is one that is basically a heel in the first place, so being evil is hardly a jump for him.

In Your House #16: Canadian Stampede
Date: July 6, 1997
Location: Saddledome, Calgary, Alberta, Canada
Attendance: 12,151
Commentators: Jim Ross, Jerry Lawler, Vince McMahon

This is a show I've been waiting to get to for a very long time. Canadian Stampede is considered one of the best shows of all time and ran away with the Wrestling Observer Newsletter Award for show of the year. There are only four matches on the card, but even with so few matches the card is nothing short of stacked. Let's get to it.

The opening video talks about how the company has changed to the point where you can't tell who is good or evil anymore. Bret Hart had always been the epitome of a hero, but Steve Austin has driven him to the dark side. Those shades of gray that this story created were excellent.

All three announcers are in cowboy hats which only really works for JR.

Hunter Hearst Helmsley vs. Mankind

Before the match we get a video recapping the feud, including clips of sitdown interviews that Mankind did with JR, screaming about how no one has ever given him the chance to be loved. We also see some of Mankind's home movies where he wanted to be a heartthrob named Dude Love. This was where the character of Mankind became more of a persona of Mick Foley instead of a standalone character, which would be greatly expanded in the future.

Mankind charges at the ring to jump Helmsley and drops him with a double arm DDT. He even throws in a mocking curtsy but walks into Helmsley's facebuster. A backdrop puts Helmsley on the floor and Mankind drops an elbow off the apron for two back in the ring. Back up and a clothesline puts HHH on the floor again but he moves away before Mankind can drop an elbow from the middle rope. Mankind won't let Helmsley leave and suplexes him down onto the ramp. The crowd is red hot here and completely behind Mankind.

Hunter takes his sweet time getting back in the ring and is immediately caught in the Mandible Claw but Chyna blasts Mankind in the head with a forearm. Chyna tells Mankind to bring it on but he's still able to catch HHH diving off the apron. A distraction of the referee though allows Chyna to send Mankind knee first into the steps. HHH blasts the knee with a chair and

Mankind is in trouble. They get back in and a chop block takes the knee out again and HHH hones in on it like a shark.

Some hard kicks to the knee have Mankind in trouble and there's an elbow drop for good measure. A running dropkick to the knee takes Mankind down again and HHH follows it up with a Figure Four leglock. Somehow the referee can't see Helmsley holding the ropes so Mankind punches his way out of the hold. Mankind takes him into the corner but the knee gives out. HHH's Pedigree attempt is countered and Mankind falls head first between HHH's legs to take over again.

Mankind gets two off a pulling piledriver and takes HHH out to the floor with a Cactus Clothesline. He picks up the chair but Chyna makes the save by pulling the chair away. The referee yells at Chyna, allowing HHH to get a chair shot to the knee. Then the referee yells at HHH, allowing Chyna to hit a huge clothesline to give Helmsley control again. Back in and HHH gets crotched on the top rope, allowing Mankind to put on the Claw, only to have Chyna pull him down and crotch him against the steel post. They fight to the floor again but this time go into the crowd for a double countout AT 13:14.

Rating: B. Very solid opener here with the already hot crowd getting even more into the newly face Mankind character. HHH was rapidly rising up the card and becoming more and more hated every time he came to the ring. These two had incredible natural chemistry and would tear the house down almost every time they worked together over the years.

They fight into the crowd with Mankind getting the better of it. It's really hard to see what's going on because of how tight the camera angles are but HHH can be seen getting a running start and diving at Mankind.

We look at the Calgary Stampede parade, an annual event highlighted by Bret's appearance.

The Hart Foundation is in the back for an interview when Austin unsuccessfully tries to interfere.

Taka Michinoku vs. Great Sasuke

This is part of the Junior Heavyweight (soon renamed Light

127

Heavyweight) division which was WWF's answer to WCW's incredibly popular Cruiserweight division. Before the match we see Mankind and HHH still fighting in the audience. Mankind takes over with some hard punches and a clothesline as the referees try in vain to break them up. They fight under a wall and there's the opening bell for the match.

Sasuke throws some kicks to start but Taka backs away to avoid any contact. Instead it's off to a wristlock but Taka grabs a leg to take him down. Lawler references Antonio Inoki vs. Muhammad Ali from back in the 70s for a comparison to this match. That might be pushing it a bit. Sasuke takes Taka down with a headscissors and puts on an early chinlock. Taka counters into an armbar but charges into a BIG spinning kick to the jaw. An elevated half crab has Taka in trouble but he quickly gets to a rope.

Back up and Taka scores with a hard palm shot to the face and a dropkick to the back of the head puts Sasuke down again. Taka misses a charge and falls to the floor, only to sidestep a flying kick from the top rope, sending Sasuke crashing down to the floor. They both get back inside very slowly with Sasuke firing off some very fast paced kicks to the arms and a big one to the face to knock Taka out.

Vince wants the match stopped but Taka counters a kick into a dragon screw leg whip to put Sasuke down again. Sasuke bails to the floor and Taka hits a HUGE running dive out of the corner to knock the Great one out again. Back in and Taka gets two off a standing hurricanrana as the fans are having their minds blown by these big spots.

Sasuke sends him back out to the floor for an Asai moonsault but Taka takes over back inside with a belly to belly suplex for two. Michinoku runs to the corner for a springboard missile dropkick to the back of the head. The Michinoku Driver only gets two on Sasuke but he pops up to dropkick Taka out of the air. A standing Lionsault press gets two and a powerbomb puts Taka down again. Sasuke hooks a tiger suplex for the pin out of nowhere at 10:03.

Rating: B+. This was the WCW formula to the letter: take two guys and let them show off for ten minutes and pop the crowd with high spot after high spot. Really fun match here which introduced this style to the WWF crowd. The division would never reach the Cruiserweight level due to WCW having a far deeper talent pool and the best talent Mexico had to offer, but this was an excellent match.

HHH and Mankind are still fighting in the back, though they've now made it outside with Mankind backdropping his way out of a Pedigree onto some wooden crates. HHH is rammed into the side of a truck and referees finally break it up.

We recap the WWF Title match, which was supposed to be a heel Ahmed Johnson challenging Undertaker but he was hurt before he could have the match. Therefore we have Vader taking Johnson's place.

Paul Bearer is asked how he could accuse Undertaker of murdering his own family by setting a fire at their home as a child. This was the turning point of arguably the biggest storyline of Undertaker's career. We get a clip of Vader pinning Undertaker at the Royal Rumble to give us a reason to think Vader could win.

WWF Title: Vader vs. Undertaker

Undertaker is defending and pounds Vader into the corner to start, followed by a clothesline for two. Old School connects for two more as Vince talks about Bearer's claims of Undertaker's brother still being alive. His name: Kane. Undertaker whips him into the corner but Vader comes back by just running Undertaker over. The champion pops back up and hits a jumping clothesline for two. Vader grabs a huge headlock to slow things down and Undertaker is in trouble.

Back up and Undertaker scores with a big boot to the jaw and clotheslines Vader out to the floor. The champion is sent knees first into the steps and has to endure being called a murderer by Bearer. Undertaker snaps Vader's throat across the top rope and comes back in with a top rope clothesline for another near fall. An uppercut puts Vader back on the floor and Undertaker can go after Bearer, only to be clubbed down by Vader.

They head back inside with Vader pummeling Undertaker down in the corner again and getting two off a middle rope clothesline. A suplex and splash get the same and we hit the nerve hold on

Undertaker. The champ punches his way up but gets poked in the eye to put him back down. Vader pounds him in the corner again as the fans get behind Undertaker again.

Undertaker comes back with rights and lefts of his own but Vader kicks him low to break up a chokeslam attempt. JR wants to know why that wasn't a DQ, which again is a very fair question. Vader powers out of a Tombstone attempt and runs Undertaker over again. Undertaker sits up to avoid the Vader Bomb and hits Vader low as a little payback. A middle rope chokeslam gets two so another chokeslam and the Tombstone retain the title at 12:39.

Rating: B. More good stuff here as Undertaker is on a roll right now. Vader was just a filler but he was still big and strong enough to come off as a threat to the title. There's something awesome about watching a huge man get thrown around like Undertaker was doing to Vader here and the match worked incredibly well.

We get a recap of the recent gang wars in the WWF, which saw Crush and Savio Vega split from Faarooq to form their own street gangs. This is awkwardly transitioned into the main event feud recap. We've been over Austin vs. Bret, the LOD is going after Owen/Bulldog, Pillman has been chasing after Goldust's wife Marlena and Neidhart and Shamrock are both just kind of there. Bret has been promising to destroy these horrible Americans once and for all.

Team America says they're ready to fight but Austin storms off without saying a word.

A Canadian band called Farmer's Daughter sings O Canada.

The Fink (ring announcer Howard Finkel) introduces the Alberta Premiere and the Hart Family. Patriarch Stu gets a HUGE ovation.

Hart Foundation vs. Goldust/Legion of Doom/Ken Shamrock/Steve Austin

Most of the Americans are booed, but Austin is treated like a bunch of ants at a picnic. The Hart Foundation's entrance on the other hand is a sight to behold, with each member getting a louder and louder ovation until Owen's music stops. Bret's reception is louder than everyone's and that's before his music even comes on. The Harts are a unit, all clad in leather jackets and looking like they're ready for war.

The match starts with the only possible combination of Austin vs. Bret. They slug it out with Bret taking over and pounding Austin down into the corner to send the crowd even further into a frenzy. Austin comes back with right hands and might as well be pummeling Santa Claus. Bret hits a headbutt and clothesline before raking Steve's eyes across the top rope. Austin kicks Bret low to slow him down and stomps on him in the corner before slapping on the Million Dollar Dream. Hart climbs the ropes for a rollup for two, which is the same way he beat Austin at Survivor Series.

Bret drags Austin to the corner for a tag off to the raw power of Neidhart. Austin takes him down with a Thesz press and right hands before bringing in Shamrock to easily kick Neidhart down. Pillman comes in to break up an ankle lock attempt so Shamrock takes Neidhart down with ease again. Brian comes in legally now to bite Shamrock's face and fire off chops in the corner. A backbreaker puts Shamrock down again so Pillman grabs his hand and slaps the mat, claiming a submission victory in a funny bit.

Ken comes back with a nice belly to belly suplex and it's off to Goldust vs. Owen. Goldust scores with a backdrop but Owen comes right back with an enziguri to take over again. The fans are all over Austin here, even though it's Hawk in to beat Owen up. A top rope splash gets two but Hawk misses a dropkick, allowing Owen to put on a Sharpshooter. Anvil makes the save, only to have Bulldog come in with the delayed vertical suplex and the powerslam but Goldust makes a save.

Bret comes back in (crowd erupts) to face Animal and gets up a knee in the corner to slow Animal down. Off to Goldust who is immediately tied up in the Tree of Woe and quintuple teamed, drawing in the rest of the Americans for the save. Owen comes in legally but misses a charge into the post, allowing for the tag off to Animal. Owen is fine with that and hits an enziguri followed by a missile dropkick to fire up the crowd even more. Animal will have none of that and counters a hurricanrana into a powerbomb.

131

The Doomsday Device hits Owen but Anvil makes the save, drawing in all ten guys for a huge brawl. In the melee, Austin wraps Owen's knee around the post and hits it with a chair before beating up Bret and Owen's brother Bruce, who is sitting with the rest of the Hart Family in the crowd. Things calm down with Anvil vs. Austin as medics come out to check on Owen. Neidhart sends Austin into the corner for a big beating and Owen is being taken to the back.

Pillman comes in but gets dragged over to the American corner and taken down by a Stunner. Bret makes the save by wrapping Austin's leg around the post and blasting it with a fire extinguisher. He throws on the Figure Four around the post until Hawk makes the save but the damage has been done to the leg. Austin is able to tag in Hawk but Bulldog crotches Hawk on the top rope to take him down again. Austin limps to the back again, leaving us with just four guys per team in the match.

Neidhart and Animal have a test of strength with Jim taking over and driving Animal into the Hart corner for a tag off to Bret. The original Hart Foundation (Bret and Neidhart) take over on Animal to give the crowd a nostalgia pop. Shamrock comes in again and grabs Bret's leg but just stands there, allowing Pillman to sneak in with a clothesline. Shamrock grabs the leg again but Bret gives him a stern lecture from the mat, which actually makes Ken let him up. I wish I could make that up.

Bret sends Shamrock to the floor where Pillman throws him over the French announcers' table. Back inside and it's Bulldog slugging Shamrock down in the corner to send the crowd right back into a frenzy. Ken hits him low, allowing Goldust to come in with a bulldog to the Bulldog, but Pillman breaks up the Curtain Call. Goldust goes up but gets crotched, allowing Bulldog to superplex him down.

Austin stumbles back out to the ring and it's a double tag to bring in Bret vs. Stone Cold. Bret is sent chest first into the buckle and suplexed down for two, only to come back with a DDT. A backbreaker and the middle rope elbow are good for two and it's off to a sleeper hold. Austin jawbreaks his way to freedom but has to have Animal save him from the Sharpshooter.

Now it's Austin putting Bret in the Sharpshooter but Owen comes back out for the save. Owen comes in legally but gets clotheslined out to the floor and stomped against the barricade. Austin goes after the other Hart Brothers at ringside but Bret makes the save and sends Austin back inside so Owen can roll him up for the pin at 24:31, sending the roof into orbit.

Rating: A+. Do I really need to explain this one? Not only is it a great match with everyone working very hard, but it's a great story and the perfect way to blow off the feud. Austin could have been in there with any four guys, but the match ended perfectly and gave Owen a big rub in the process. Excellent match and the best multi-man tag match of all time.

The fight continues post match with the Harts cleaning house thanks to their brothers coming in to help out. The Americans are finally dispatched as the Harts are announced as the winners. Austin eventually tries to charge back in for one last swing at Bret but literally about 15 members of the Hart Family beat him down until security takes him away in handcuffs. Austin, ever the rebel, flips off the Calgary crowd behind his back as he leaves. A huge celebration with all of the Harts, including parents Helen and Stu, ends the show.

Overall Rating: A+. The worst match of the night was above average and continued an awesome feud. The rest of the show ranges from mind blowing to some of the best of all time. What more could you possibly ask for from a show running an hour and forty five minutes? Absolutely amazing show here and definitely worth tracking down if you've never seen it.

It's All Austin

The company was officially on fire now with the Border War carrying it back to respectability. Things weren't quite improving on the ratings front, but the company was no longer spiraling out of control. There was still a lot of work to be done, but things were looking up for the first time in many, many months.

Next up on the pay per view calendar was the second biggest show of the year with Summerslam. After defeating Steve Austin for good, the only thing left for Bret to do was become the WWF Champion again. He had his chance at Summerslam where he would challenge the Undertaker for the title, though it wouldn't be as simple as that. Shawn Michaels, Bret's longtime nemesis, was to be the guest referee.

In the show's main event, Bret pinned Undertaker and won his fifth WWF Title. However, it was not without controversy as referee Shawn swung a chair at Bret but hit Undertaker, giving Bret the WWF Title as a result. If there's one thing we've seen so far in this show's history, it's that a ticked off Undertaker is as dangerous of a monster as you'll ever see in wrestling.

Soon after this, Shawn began showing signs of a heel turn. He didn't seem upset by the fact that he had cost Undertaker the WWF Title and even taunted Undertaker with the same chair. Shawn also started hanging out with HHH and Chyna, as well as his new bodyguard Rick Rude, a former Intercontinental Champion. This group would eventually be called D-Generation X, or DX for short. A few weeks later, Shawn destroyed Undertaker with the chair, setting up the main event of In Your House #17. It was all about revenge for Undertaker which has made for some great matches before.

The other and more important match from Summerslam was Steve Austin challenging Owen Hart for the Intercontinental Title. During the match, Owen tried a piledriver on Austin but dropped him down on the top of his head. Austin was legitimately paralyzed for a few moments, suffering a stinger in his neck. After Owen played to the crowd for a bit, Austin was able to get up and hook a very weak rollup on Owen for the pin and the title.

While Austin was able to move his limbs, he wasn't able to do much more. The neck injury would haunt him for the rest of his career and forced him to change his entire style from the well rounded brawler he was into the wild brawler he's much more famous for being. The injury would put him on the shelf for several months though, meaning there's no Austin until December.

Two final notes: Starting with this show, each edition would be three hours (meaning the multiple dark matches were dropped), and the titles would be switched around, meaning it would be the specific name and then In Your House. For example, #17 will officially be called Ground Zero: In Your House as opposed to In Your House: Ground Zero. The price also changed to $29.95 per show, up $10 from the previous price.

Ground Zero: In Your House #17
Date: September 7, 1997
Location: Louisville Gardens, Louisville, Kentucky
Attendance: 4,963
Commentators: Jerry Lawler, Vince McMahon, Jim Ross

In addition to Undertaker vs. Shawn, the other main event is Bret Hart defending the WWF Title against a masked wrestler named The Patriot. Still playing up the Canada vs. US story, Patriot was a guy who simply loved America very much and was standing up for his country against the evil Canadian champion. In a change of pace, the Patriot was flat out said to be a man named Del Wilkes. His identity wasn't a secret but he just wore a mask. The main event is a pretty simple idea, but the focus is on Shawn vs. Undertaker tonight. Let's get to it.

The opening video focuses on Shawn and his recent change of attitude after costing Undertaker the WWF Title. We hear from some fans who want to see Shawn get destroyed for what he's done.

The announcers welcome us to the show and run down the card. Vince slips up and says Goldust will be facing Marlena.

We recap Brian Pillman vs. Goldust. Pillman has said he's really the father of Goldust's and Marlena's daughter Dakota, making the feud incredibly personal. It was so personal that Goldust removed his face paint and talked to the cameras as Dustin Rhodes, saying that he wasn't about to let Pillman take his child. A match was made where if Goldust won then Pillman would have to leave the WWF forever, but if Pillman won he would get Marlena for 30 days.

Goldust vs. Brian Pillman

Goldust jumps Pillman before he gets in the ring but Brian comes back with chops in the ring. An atomic drop and clothesline put Pillman down and Goldust rains down right hands in the corner. Pillman comes back with an elbow to the face but stops to chase Marlena around, allowing Goldust to catch him in a drop toehold into the steps. Back in and they chop it out again as Jerry implies Marlena has been with half of the locker room. Pillman's bulldog is countered by Goldust crotching him on the top rope, sending Brian up the ramp.

That's not enough for Goldust though so he chases Pillman up the ramp and suplexes him down onto the steel. Pillman gets crotched against the post for good measure before Goldust starts going after the leg. An elbow drop gets two on Brian and Goldust rams him into the buckle. The bulldog is countered again and Lawler is thrilled for some reason. Pillman stomps away and puts on a reverse chinlock to slow things down again. Goldust fights up and drops Brian with an electric chair but both guys are down for a bit.

It's Pillman up first but he's crotched for the third time with this one being on the turnbuckle. Goldust knocks him off the top and into the barricade, allowing Marlena to get in a slap of her own. Back in and Pillman blocks a superplex but misses a missile dropkick. Goldust loads up the Curtain Call but the referee gets knocked out in the process. Instead of staying on Brian, Goldust goes to check on the referee and Marlena gets on the apron with her loaded purse. In an old wrestling cliché, the purse is intercepted by Pillman and he knocks out Goldust for the pin at 11:06.

Rating: C-. This was just ok but the ending was never really in doubt. The story made much more sense if you put Marlena with Pillman for the thirty days and it ended if Goldust won here. Pillman was in bad shape at this point due to a horrible ankle injury but he managed to get by well enough here. More on that later though.

Pillman drags Marlena away with him into a waiting car. Lawler gets the purse and looks inside to find a brick. Goldust chases after the car but winds up destroying his dressing room instead.

Scott Putski vs. Brian Christopher

Putski is the son of WWF Hall of Famer Ivan Putski while Christopher is the son of Jerry Lawler. However Lawler hasn't admitted to this yet, but instead is saying he's a big fan of Christopher while helping him win matches. An immediate Jerry's Kid chant starts us off, which Lawler writes off as a reference to Jerry Lewis' Labor Day marathon. Putski gets in the first shot and drives Christopher into the corner before tossing him out to the floor.

Back in and Brian grabs a headlock before clotheslining him down with ease. Scott comes back with a hurricanrana for two but gets caught in a full nelson leg sweep faceplant (the Skull Crushing Finale or Chris Jericho's Breakdown) gets two. Jerry: "That's my boy!" JR: "What?" Putski falls to the floor and Brian follows with a nice dive to take him out again. The fall seems to have injured Scott's knee and Brian wins by countout at 4:45.

Rating: D. I'm thinking there was something to that knee injury as there was no reason to end the match so soon. It didn't last that long and I have no idea why this was on a pay per view. Putski is a good example of a guy who had a great look but had the big problem of being his father's son. His dad Ivan was a popular wrestler and there was no way Scott could live up to his reputation.

Post match Lawler and Christopher make fun of Putski's knee injury. Scott is taken out on a stretcher.

We recap the triple threat match between the gang leaders. This was a popular feud in the midcard at this point, with Faarooq heading the Nation (now including a recently returned from injury Rocky Maivia), Savio Vega heading Los Boricuas and Crush heading the Disciples of Apocalypse (a biker gang). Tonight is about bragging rights.

Faarooq vs. Savio Vega vs. Crush

Crush gets double teamed to start but he comes back with a double clothesline to put both guys down. He misses a charge into the corner though and Savio grabs a rollup for two. Faarooq takes off his belt for a whipping but Crush takes it from him to give Faarooq the whipping instead. Savio is hiptossed down but

137

Crush and Faarooq argue over who gets two in him. Crush is sent to the floor and Faarooq gets two on Savio off a spinebuster.

Faarooq gets jumped by a returning Crush and taken down with a powerslam for two. All three guys wind up on their knees for a three way slugout until Crush rams the other two's heads together for two on Faarooq. Savio hits a LOUD chop in the corner on Faarooq but runs into Faarooq's boot in the jaw. Crush knocks both guys down again and chokes Faarooq on the ropes until Savio pulls Crush's hair for the break. Faarooq is sent to the floor and Crush hooks a chinlock on Vega.

Rather than easily breaking up the hold, Faarooq comes off the top with a forearm to Crush's back to make him give up the chinlock. Vega pounds on Crush in the corner but Faarooq breaks up another cover and steals a two count of his own. Savio botches a neckbreaker on Faarooq but gets two anyway with Crush breaking it up this time. Now Crush and Faarooq seem fine with teaming up to work on Savio, including a double suplex. They both cover at the same time but the referee says no.

Since that didn't work, Faarooq and Crush fight again and we get probably the sixth backbreaker of the match, giving Crush two on Faarooq. Vega gets knocked to the floor again and Faarooq gets another near fall on Crush via a powerslam. Savio and Crush double team Faarooq in a spike piledriver but Crush turns on Savio and knocks him to the floor. Crush Heart Punches Faarooq but Savio sneaks in with the spinwheel kick, knocking out Crush for the pin at 11:37.

Rating: D. The match wasn't horrible but man alive it wasn't interesting. This just kept going with the same sequences over and over again. The gang wars story never caught on and this is a good example of why. Fans just didn't care about the groups of guys where most of the people didn't stand out in the slightest. Nothing to see here at all.

El Torito vs. Max Mini

This is a minis match, which is another idea that never caught on. Max Mini weighs 83lbs and is billed as the world's smallest athlete. Torito is much bigger and dressed like a bull. Max backflips away from Torito a few times before headscissoring

Torito down. Another big spinning headscissors puts Torito down on the floor and Max hits a nice dive to take him out. Back in and Torito (who is probably a foot taller and 50lbs heavier than Max) runs Max over to a chorus of boos.

A slam puts Max down but he hooks a wristlock on Torito to gain some control. Torito kicks him in the ribs but misses a charge, putting us right back to the wristlock. Torito bites Max on the trunks so Max kicks the referee in the shin and bites him as well for no apparent reason. Now Max runs to the floor and around the ring before sitting on Lawler's lap and putting on his crown. JR: "Pretend it's Brian!"

Max runs back inside but walks into a clothesline and a slam. Torito gores Max's head and a few turnbuckles to waste time but Max pulls himself up into a VERY fast hurricanrana for two. Torito comes back with a nice powerbomb for two more before running Max over yet again. Max armdrags him to the floor and hits an amazing looking Asai moonsault to take Torito down again. Back in and Max scores with a top rope hurricanrana before sunset flipping Torito for the pin at 9:21.

Rating: C. Here's the thing: the wrestling was ok, but probably 97% of fans have no interest in this match or style whatsoever. These guys may be big deals in Mexico, but in America they've viewed as comic acts and nothing more, which is why these things are rarely used in American wrestling. The wrestling was fun, but it had no future in the company and I think everyone knew it.

We recap the recent history of the Tag Team Titles. As mentioned, Austin and Michaels were stripped of the belts so a tournament was held, with Owen and Bulldog winning. However, the tournament was just for a spot in the title match with Owen and Bulldog facing Austin and a surprise partner.

Austin "chose" Mankind's newest personality of a hippie named Dude Love, and by chose I mean Love showed up during the match and declared himself Austin's partner. However, due to Austin's neck injury at Summerslam, the titles have to be stripped tonight, as per the orders of new WWF Commissioner and former WWF Champion Sgt. Slaughter.

Slaughter is in the ring to vacate the titles and here's Dude first to give up his belt. Dude says he's very sad but he knows he couldn't defend the titles on his own, nor would it be fair to do this without Austin. Therefore, with a heavy heart and a pained pancreas, he surrenders the belt. JR brings out Austin to an absolute eruption.

Austin doesn't want to hear from Slaughter and threatens to punch Vince in the face if he shows the video of the neck injury again. He wants Slaughter to give him twenty pushups if he wants the tag belt. Instead Austin throws it to Slaughter's feet and says everyone and everything here makes him sick. JR says the fans would love to see Austin fight tonight but it's not worth him getting paralyzed. That earns JR a Stunner, sending the crowd even further into a frenzy. Again, we'll get back to this later.

Owen and Bulldog are in the back and say they'll win the title back in our next match. Owen also goes on a rant against Austin, saying he should be arrested and stripped of his Intercontinental Title.

Vince calls Austin a jackass, which becomes VERY important later.

Tag Team Titles: Headbangers vs. Godwinns vs. Owen Hart/British Bulldog vs. Legion of Doom

The titles are vacant coming in and this is under elimination rules with the last team surviving being the new champions. The Headbangers, comprised of Mosh and Thrasher, are a rather odd team to say the least. They're obsessed with heavy metal music, pierced in various places and wrestle in skirts. The Godwinns are now evil and look more like something out of Deliverance. Since Bulldog and Owen already got to speak, we get comments from all of the other teams, basically saying they're going to win. The LOD specifically wants to get their hands on the Godwinns.

Thrasher and Henry get things going with the Godwinn pounding away on the Headbanger's back. In an interesting move, Thrasher tags in Phineas to give us the battle of the Godwinns. Henry wants none of that and tags in Mosh to keep things dull. Mosh grabs an armbar until Thrasher comes in with a middle rope clothesline. Thrasher tags in Animal who blasts Phineas out to the floor, giving us another lull in the match.

Back in and Animal throws Henry to the floor before punching him back off the apron. Owen and the Bulldog haven't been a factor at all yet. Henry comes back in and tags Mosh who is clotheslined down by the now legal Hawk. Bulldog doesn't want a tag from Hawk so Hawk punches him in the jaw for a tag. Mosh tags out to Phineas as this match is painfully uninteresting so far. Bulldog cranks on the arm before bringing in Owen, only to have him whipped into the Godwinn corner.

Henry gorilla presses Owen to a big reaction and the slam gets two. Hart comes back with an enziguri for two and tags out to Animal. Henry low bridges Animal out to the floor but the fans still don't react at all. Hawk plays cheerleader from the apron and finally wakes the people up a bit but Henry runs Animal over again. Animal blocks a middle rope splash with a boot though, allowing for the hot tag to Hawk. Everything breaks down but Henry breaks up the Doomsday Device. The Godwinns bring in the slop bucket but Animal takes it away and blasts both of them with it, drawing a DQ and an elimination.

So we're down to three teams now, with none of them doing anything at all for the crowd. Mosh comes in to beat up Henry and a moonsault gets two. Henry is sent to the floor but low bridges Mosh to the floor as well. It's off to Phineas for an elbow drop and a double backdrop as the match just keeps going. They try the backdrop again but Mosh sunset flips Phineas for a quick pin, leaving us with the Headbangers vs. Owen/Bulldog.

Owen comes in immediately to pound away on Thrasher and the fans chant USA. Off to Bulldog for a back elbow and a suplex for two. Owen comes back in (minus a tag) with a missile dropkick for two on Thrasher but Hart gets caught by a crossbody for two. Hart hits a quick neckbreaker as the USA chants continue. Back to Bulldog for what I think was supposed to be a double clothesline between he and Thrasher, but Thrasher was never touched. That looked horrible but it set up the hot tag to Mosh.

Things speed up but Owen pulls Mosh to the floor, only to have his spinwheel kick take Bulldog down by mistake. The Headbangers load up their powerbomb/guillotine legdrop combo but Bulldog crotches Mosh. Cue Austin with a Stunner to the Bulldog though, giving the Headbangers the pin and the titles at 17:15.

Rating: D. Oh sweet goodness this was dull. I get that they had to have the two final teams in there, but man alive there had to be a better way to get there than what they went with. The tag team division was such a mess at this point and it was almost impossible to get interested in what was going on around the belts. Putting Austin in the title scene helped in the short term, but it didn't do anything to help the major problems the titles were having.

The Headbangers celebrate in the concourse.

JR complains to Slaughter about what Austin did while swearing a lot.

We recap Bret vs. Patriot for the title. Patriot beat Bret in a non-title match on Raw and wanted to stand up for America against the evil Canadian champion. This is really a biography of Del Wilkes, including his football career and time in Japan.

Patriot says he can beat Bret again.

Bret says he's going to hit the Patriot once for every fan that has turned their back on him.

WWF Title: Bret Hart vs. The Patriot

Patriot is challenging and comes out to what would become Kurt Angle's theme song. Bret jumps him to start before tying Patriot up in the Tree of Woe for some kicks to the ribs. The fans chant USA to tick Bret off even more so he rakes Patriot's eyes through the mask. The left handed Patriot comes back with a clothesline and a nice dropkick before clotheslining the champion out to the floor. Bret takes his sweet time on the floor before heading back inside to hide in the corner.

Some nice armdrags put Bret down as the pace picks up a good bit. We hit the armbar Patriot sends Bret's shoulder into the buckle before slapping on the armbar again. Hart finally makes it to the corner to break up the hold but Patriot wraps the weak arm around the ropes again. Bret comes back with some kicks to the ribs before focusing in on the knee. He cannonballs down onto the knee a few times before just punching the side of Patriot's leg.

142

Patriot limps around the ring while holding the top rope but Bret kicks his knee out again to take him down. There's a spinning toehold of all things from the champion before he locks on the Figure Four around the post. Back in and Patriot fights up as British Bulldog makes his way out to ringside. Bret takes Patriot down with a Russian legsweep and the fans chant for Austin. Patriot comes back with a kick to the side of Bret's head and gets two off a sunset flip.

The challenger starts coming back with a left hand to the ribs and a legdrop but Bulldog's distraction lets Bret take over again. Bret accidentally hits the Bulldog, allowing Patriot to get a rollup for two and a BIG pop from the crowd. The Uncle Slam (a full nelson slam) gets two for Patriot but Bulldog makes the save. Patriot goes after Bulldog and here's Vader to help deal with Smith. Bret and Vader get in a fight but the match continues.

Vader and Bulldog are taken to the back and Patriot goes up top for his Patriot Missile (top rope shoulder) but Bret gets up at two. There was nowhere near as much of a reaction for that count as the previous ones. A suplex gets two more on Bret but he grabs a quick Stun Gun to put Patriot down again. The bulldog and middle rope elbow get two for Bret but Patriot slugs away at him in the corner.

The referee gets hit in the face with an elbow and as luck would have it, Patriot hits the Uncle Slam again just a few seconds later. It's only good for two when the referee wakes up but it's too late. A double clothesline puts both guys down but it's Patriot up first, sending Bret chest first into the buckle. With nothing left to try, Patriot puts Bret in the Sharpshooter but Bret counters into one of his own and Patriot gives up at 19:20, despite being about a foot from the rope.

Rating: B. The match worked well but the ending hurt it a good bit. Patriot is fighting for America and all that jazz, but he gives up instead of crawling another ten inches? The match took some time to get going but once we got to the interference and all that jazz, things picked up a good bit.

Post match Bret beats up Patriot even more and piledrives him before snapping Patriot's American flag. He chokes Patriot with a rope and beats up the security and officials that come out to pull him off. Bret leaves but when Michael Cole comes up to interview he calls all Americans losers.

We recap the main event. Shawn cost Undertaker the WWF Title and didn't seem to mind all that bothered by it, going so far as to destroy Undertaker with a chair a few weeks later on Raw. At the same time, Paul Bearer has been accusing Undertaker of murdering his brother by lighting their childhood home on fire. Undertaker says it happened, but it was an accident. In other words, Undertaker is furious and tonight is Shawn's punishment.

Shawn says he won't rest in peace and that he'll kick Undertaker's teeth down his throat. Why? Because he can.

Shawn Michaels vs. Undertaker

Michaels' entrance takes so long that his music starts over again. The lights go out, the thunder starts rumbling, and the crowd wakes up. Undertaker turns the lights back on with a big crack and Shawn hides behind the referee in a funny bit. Undertaker stalks him around the ring but Shawn keeps hiding, so Taker punches out the referee. Michaels bails to the floor and tries to walk out but Commissioner Slaughter orders him back to the ring. Undertaker throws the referee onto Shawn to slow him down, and NOW the beating begins.

Shawn tries to run again but this time he can't get through the door to the house set, allowing Undertaker to slam him down on the steel. Michaels is thrown into some shrubbery before being tossed back down the ramp. They get back to ringside with Shawn trying to crawl anywhere he can to escape. Undertaker chokes him by the timekeeper's area with Shawn desperately trying to ring the bell to end the match.

Undertaker punches him onto the announcers' table then punches him right back off of it, knocking Shawn into the barricade. They head back inside for some elbow drops from Undertaker before he rams Shawn into the buckle. Remember that the match hasn't actually started yet. Shawn is whipped into the corner and out to the floor as Slaughter sends out a second referee. Michaels actually begs the new referee to disqualify Undertaker but the referee values his life too much to do that.

Back inside and Shawn gets in a cheap shot to the knee when the bell FINALLY rings. Shawn pounds away in the corner but is easily shoved off. The same sequence happens again but Undertaker grabs Shawn by the throat. A kick to the knee gives Shawn a breather but he goes up top and jumps into a right hand, giving Undertaker control again. Shawn's sunset flip is countered by a lifting choke with Shawn being thrown around again.

Undertaker whips him into the corner and Shawn lands stomach first onto the top rope. Some kicks to the ribs launch Shawn crotch first onto the top rope as the destruction continues. Undertaker cranks on the arm for a bit and drops a leg on it for good measure. Old School is broken up with Undertaker being crotched on the ropes to finally give Shawn a breather. Taker rolls to the floor but he catches Shawn's dive in midair to ram his back into the post.

A backdrop gets two for Undertaker and Shawn is caught trying to escape again. Shawn comes back with a quick neckbreaker but Undertaker casually sits up. Michaels bails to the floor and grabs the chair that started it all, only to have Undertaker kick it back into his face. The referee finally remembers to do his job and takes the chair away, so Undertaker kicks him in the face too.

Shawn pounds Undertaker down and hits a pair of long range elbow drops. Cue Shawn's bodyguard Rick Rude to throw a pair of brass knuckles to Shawn, who knocks Undertaker out cold. A third referee comes in but Undertaker kicks out at two, earning him a beating from Shawn. HHH and Chyna come out to ringside as well with HHH getting in some cheap shots on Undertaker. A whip into the steps bangs up Undertaker's knees as the second referee is woken up again, only to be drilled by Shawn as well.

Michaels makes the huge mistake of letting Undertaker get back up though and they slug it out again. A clothesline puts Undertaker on the floor but he lands on this feet, only to have HHH and Chyna go after him. Shawn drops a top rope ax handle on Undertaker's back and chokes with a cord as HHH gets in some shots.

Back inside and Sweet Chin Music is blocked and Undertaker throws Shawn into the corner for more punishment. A big right hand drops Shawn and Undertaker gets the brass knuckles. Michaels is laid out again and HHH gets a right hand with them as well. Undertaker actually actually covers but Michaels gets up at two. The referee gets a chokeslam and here's referee #4 to FINALLY throw this out at 16:20.

Rating: A. This wasn't a wrestling match in the slightest but it wouldn't have made sense for it to be. It was however probably the best fight you'll ever see, with incredible carnage and a furious Undertaker obsessed with getting his revenge. There wasn't a ton of blood, but we'll get to that later. Excellent brawl though and even more proof of how great these two are at multiple styles.

It's still not over as Undertaker isn't done yet. He throws HHH at Shawn but Michaels is able to score with Sweet Chin Music, knocking Undertaker into the ropes with his arms tied up. The fourth referee is punched out and Shawn gets the chair, but Undertaker kicks it back into his face and loads up a Tombstone, only to have HHH make the save.

Officials come in as HHH is Tombstoned, leaving Shawn alone again. Wrestlers come in to try and break up the fight and Shawn is finally taken to the floor. Undertaker shakes the wrestlers holding him off and DIVES OVER THE TOP ROPE to get at Shawn, which was the debut of said dive. DX bails to the back and the show ends with Undertaker alone in the ring.

Overall Rating: C+. This is a show that would have benefited from being two hours instead of three. The last hour is comprised of the last two matches and it more than holds up. The problem is everything else doesn't work for the most part. It's a bunch of boring matches that no one cared about and makes you less patient to get to the main events. Those two matches more than make up for the rest though, with the brawl definitely being worth checking out.

In between Ground Zero and In Your House #18, there was a pay per view held over in England called One Night Only. The main event saw British Bulldog defend the European Title against Shawn Michaels, with Shawn taking the title and sending the fans into a near riot. The title change only came with a lot of help from DX, officially confirming Shawn's heel turn and making DX an official group.

Two days after One Night Only, the WWF held one of their most famous shows of all time. For the first time ever, Monday Night Raw aired from Madison Square Garden in New York City. This show changed the way the WWF would operate for years to come and was the first time in a very long time where Raw stood up to Nitro. The ratings losing streak didn't end, but the new path was clear.

To begin with, HHH and Dude Love were scheduled to face each other in a falls count anywhere match, but Dude popped up on screen and said that wasn't his thing. Dude brought in Mankind (same guy remember) but Mankind said he wasn't ready either. However, there was one more personality that could fight HHH in this kind of a match, and for the first time ever, Cactus Jack appeared in the WWF. Cactus was Foley's most famous persona at the time and one of the craziest and most violent wrestlers in history. The two had a war with Cactus beating HHH with a piledriver through a table.

However, the real story of this show was Steve Austin. Over the course of the last few months, Austin had claimed that there was a conspiracy throughout the company to hold him back. He had Stunned various officials, ranging from Jim Ross to Sgt. Slaughter, but it was Vince McMahon, the owner of the company, telling Austin to calm down.

Vince said that the company just wanted the best for Austin and asked him to work within the system, meaning not wrestling. Austin said wrestling was what he did for a living and he was the best in the world before Stunning Vince for the first time ever, launching a three and a half year war between the two. The reaction to the Stunner can only be described as an eruption, with the fans cheering on their hero as he did exactly what so many people wanted to do: beat up their horrible boss who tried to stomp on their dreams.

This changed the course of the company entirely, with the focus now being on the Mr. McMahon character as he tried to run the company his way while Austin rebelled against the establishment, to the never ending cheers from the fans. This was the story that would save the company and take them back to the top, but it was still several months away at this point.

As for the main event of the upcoming pay per view, there was no doubt that it would be Shawn vs. Undertaker II, but the question was where did they go now? The problem had been all the interference, so the solution was to lock them inside a cage. Since that had been done before though, the stakes had to be raised. Therefore, a special cage was built which would go around the ring while leaving space on the floor. The new cage was called Hell in a Cell, with Shawn being trapped inside with Undertaker. There was no way this wasn't going to be amazing.

Badd Blood: In Your House #18
Date: October 5, 1997
Location: Kiel Center, St. Louis, Missouri
Attendance: 21,151
Commentators: Jerry Lawler, Vince McMahon, Jim Ross

Other than the main event, the big match was a tag team flag match between Vader/Patriot vs. British Bulldog/Bret Hart. The title wasn't a factor in the feud, but the night was about Shawn and Undertaker, not the WWF Title. Having a match about patriotism is fine as always with all four guys being solid in the ring, meaning we should get a good match. Let's get to it.

Before we get to the show, there is one more thing that has to be addressed. On the day of the show, Brian Pillman was found dead in his hotel room at 35 years old due to heart disease. He had been scheduled to face Dude Love on the show and Love wasn't given a replacement opponent after Pillman was found. It wasn't known that he had the condition and the death came as a complete surprise.

The opening video focuses on Shawn's amazing athleticism and his recent change of attitude, resulting in him starting the war with Undertaker. Tonight, there's no one to save him though as they're locked inside the Cell.

Nation of Domination vs. Legion of Doom

This is a handicap match with Rocky Maivia, Kama Mustafa (a martial artist/street fighter) and D'Lo Brown (a large guy who could move faster than most people his size) representing the Nation. Ken Shamrock was supposed to team up with the Legion of Doom but was injured, leaving them without a partner. Hawk and Brown get us going with D'Lo actually staggering him off a shoulder block.

Back up and a boot to the face sends Brown into the Nation corner for the tag off to Rocky. Animal comes in as well and the Rocky Sucks chants immediately begin. The Nation has a meeting on the floor until Rocky comes back in, only to be taken down by a dropkick. Animal cranks on the arm a bit before tagging out to Hawk for a headlock. Rocky drives him into the corner for the tag off to Kama. The power guys slug it out until a double clothesline is no sold all around.

Hawk actually busts out an enziguri to take Kama down and we hit a chinlock. Back to Animal for a powerslam but Rocky sneaks in with a DDT to put him down. The distraction lets the Nation take Animal to the floor for a triple team before it's off to D'Lo to pound away at the ribs. Animal comes back with a clothesline out of the corner but Brown breaks up another tag attempt. The Nation breaks up another hot tag attempt though and it's off to Rocky for a chinlock.

Maivia draws Hawk in again due to Hawk not being the brightest guy in the world, allowing a low blow to drop Animal for a near fall. Back to Kama for a spinning kick to the ribs but Animal avoids a charge into the corner. The hot tag brings in Hawk but the referee didn't see it, allowing Brown to hit a frog splash on Animal for two.

Animal gets up again and forearms Rocky down, allowing for the seen hot tag to Hawk. Everything breaks down with the LOD taking over. A pair of running clotheslines look to set Rocky up for the Doomsday Device but Faarooq comes out for a distraction, allowing Kama to kick Hawk into the still yet to be named Rock Bottom for the pin at 12:16.

Rating: C+. I liked this much better than I expected to. The LOD was rapidly approaching their expiration date at this point but they looked good enough out there. Rocky clearly had something special, but the character joining the Nation was the best possible option for him, as he got to show some character instead of boring everyone to death as guy who was just happy to be here.

Next up was supposed to be Brian Pillman vs. Dude Love, but

149

Vince tells us of his death. They've come up with the following replacement match though.

Mosaic/Tarantula vs. Max Mini/Nova

The Minis are back and Max gets a nice reception this time. Tarantula, the biggest guy in the match by far, kicks Max to the floor before side stepping a dive by Nova. Nova avoids a charge from both heels and makes them hit each other via some quick dodging. Everyone heads to the floor for a no real action until we get back to Mosaic being armdragged down by Max. A backdrop puts Mosaic down as everything breaks down again.

Max gets two on Tarantula via a hurricanrana but a double big boot drops Max for no cover. Back to Nova who gets slammed down by Tarantula and a top rope splash gets two. Tarantula distracts Max so Mosaic can get in a cheap shot and a slam down onto the announcers' table.

After five minutes of the match, the announcers tell us this is under lucha libre rules, meaning a wrestler going to the floor allows his partner to come in legally. That clears up a lot of issues so far, but couldn't they remember to tell us that earlier? Nova screws up an armdrag on Mosaic but dropkicks him out to the floor instead. Tarantula runs over Max with a clothesline but Max goes up top for a high crossbody. There's no cover, so Max hooks a spinning crucifix for the pin at 6:44, even though Mosaic broke it up at two.

Rating: D+. The idea of the match was fine but the execution didn't work for the most part. There were way too many botches out there and the crowd didn't care for the Mexican rules. This wasn't a good choice for an old school city like St. Louis where tradition means a lot more than in some other towns. Not a terrible match and as good as you could do under the circumstances.

Sunny comes out to be guest announcer.

Tag Team Titles: Godwinns vs. Headbangers

The Headbangers are defending. The Godwinns now have their Uncle Cletus (wrestler Tony Anthony, most famous as the Dirty White Boy in Smoky Mountain Wrestling) as a manager. It's a brawl to start with the champions sending the hog farmers out to the floor. We start with Mosh vs. Phineas after a quick spitting contest. Phineas gets sent back to the floor very quickly, allowing Thrasher to hit something the camera doesn't find important enough to show us. Apparently it was a springboard clothesline to the apron. Good to know.

Back in and we get some miscommunication, as the Headbangers try a double flapjack but Phineas drops his head down like a backdrop, nearly breaking his neck in the process. Things slow down again until we get Thrasher vs. Henry and a rollup gets two for the champion. Henry bails to the floor as the match stalls even more. Back to Phineas who is taken down, allowing Mosh to suplex Thrasher down onto Phineas for two. Thrasher's middle rope clothesline puts Phineas down but Henry comes back in with a clothesline of his own.

Thrasher gets crotched on the top rope and clotheslined to the floor again with Phineas coming in for more stomping. Lawler tries some lame redneck jokes to save this boring match but even his corny one liners have no effect. A bunch of knee drops get two for Phineas but Thrasher comes back with a sunset flip, only to have Henry distract the referee.

Phineas hits a wheelbarrow slam for another near fall on Thrasher but a splash in the corner only hits buckle. The hot tag brings in Mosh to clean house, including powerbombing Thrasher onto Phineas for two. Everything breaks down and Mosh's top rope seated senton is caught in a sloppy powerbomb by Phineas for the pin and the titles at 12:18.

Rating: D-. Not only was this sloppy, but it was really dull stuff. The tag team division is just horrific at this point with nothing interesting and random title changes like this one that don't help anything. Really boring match here with WAY too much stalling and nothing special in the ring at all.

Post match the Godwinns destroy the Headbangers and are threatened with losing the titles if they don't leave. Therefore, they leave.

We get a video on Austin's path of destruction through the corporate structure via Stunning every authority figure in sight. After that, Austin was given the option of either getting doctor's

151

clearance (almost impossible to get), come back after waving the WWF of all responsibilities in case he's injured, or leave the WWF. The decision would come tomorrow night on Raw.

Owen Hart doesn't want to hear about Austin other than when he hands over the Intercontinental Title. He also threatens Austin with a lawsuit if he tries anything tonight.

JR is in the ring to introduce some of the legends of St. Louis wrestling in a very cool moment. Everyone will be getting a video biography, a plaque and a framed letter. First up is Canada's Greatest Athlete, Gene Kiniski, who won the NWA World Title in St. Louis.

Next up is Jack Brisco, who is one of the most talented wrestlers of all time. He's often listed as an all time great, but he's even better than he's talked about being. Jack was a two time NWA Champion.

Dory Funk Jr., who was in the 1995 Royal Rumble, is next. He held the NWA Title for over four years, the second longest reign ever.

Fourth is Harley Race, who was a seven (or eight depending on how many reigns you count) time NWA Champion and perhaps the greatest of all time.

Terry Funk is next and never quite looks right in a suit. Seeing photos of him all professional looking after being famous for his insanity is bizarre. Terry first retired in 1983 and he was active in a match in November of 2013. Let that sink in for a minute.

The final two come out at the same time: Lou Thesz (the longest reigning NWA Champion ever and one of the absolute best in ring technical wrestlers of all time) and Sam Muchnick who ran both the St. Louis Wrestling Club and the NWA for years. It was speculated that if Muchnick had stuck around, the NWA could have survived the WWF and even won the war. Muchnick is also considered one of the only fair promoters ever and almost everyone worked for him at one point.

This was a really classy ceremony and didn't come off as stupid or pointless at all. Very nice moment.

Faarooq says he doesn't need Austin's help to win the Intercontinental Title tonight.

Intercontinental Title: Owen Hart vs. Faarooq

This is a tournament final to crown a new champion since Austin has to forfeit the title. Owen has an Owen 3:16 shirt, with "I Just Broke Your Neck" on the back. Before the match, here's Austin to do commentary. This might not be the best idea given that he and Pillman were best friends. Austin rings the bell as Vince freaks out, so Austin takes his headset.

JR and Jerry can barely get a word in as Austin rants about Owen using the 3:16 shirt for cheap heat. Austin steals Lawler's headset as Faarooq grabs a headlock. The boring match drags on as Austin has a walkie-talkie to mess with security. He knocks JR's hat off as Owen spinwheel kicks Faarooq down and goes after the knee. Austin jumps on Spanish commentary and doesn't like the trash he thinks the commentators are saying about him.

Owen stomps away in the corner and Austin has switched to French. Faarooq kicks Owen shoulder first into the post and gets two off a backbreaker. He misses a middle rope legdrop though and Owen goes after the leg. The Sharpshooter is broken up again and Faarooq gets another near fall off a powerslam. Jim Neidhart comes to ringside but Austin uses the distraction to knock Faarooq out with the title, giving Owen the pin at 5:51.

Rating: D. The match was just a backdrop for Austin's antics and the ending would make more sense after the explanation. The idea was simple: Austin wanted the Intercontinental Title back, but he only wanted to beat Owen for it to prove he was the better man once and for all. Owen and Faarooq weren't great out there, but there was only so much they could do in these circumstances.

We recap the Hart Foundation attacking Vader and the Patriot on Raw before draping Canadian flags over their fallen bodies.

Los Boricuas vs. Disciples of Apocalypse

Los Boricuas are Miguel Perez, Jose Estrada, Jesus Castillo and Savio Vega while the Disciples are Crush, Chainz, Skull and 8-

Ball. Skull starts with Jose with the much bigger Disciple taking over to start. 8-Ball and Skull (identical twins) hit a double big boot to take Jose down and it's off to Miguel who walks into a powerslam for two.

Chainz and Savio come in with the biker scoring with a quick belly to belly for two before it's off to Jesus who is slammed down just as easily. Everything nearly breaks down on the floor before Jesus takes over on Crush back inside. All four of the Boricuas come in for three running clotheslines and a spinwheel kick from Savio to Crush before Miguel hooks a chinlock.

The referee goes to the floor to stop another brawl, allowing the remaining Boricuas to triple team Crush again. A missile dropkick gets two for Jesus and we hit ANOTHER chinlock. Crush finally fights up and everything breaks down with Crush hitting a quick big boot but there's no referee. Jesus gets a close two off a DDT but Chainz grabs a tilt-a-whirl backbreaker to pin Miguel at 8:04.

Rating: F+. This show is really getting bad about having dull matches. As has been the case since the beginning of this feud, no one cares about these teams or anyone on them. None of the guys on the team save for arguably their leaders do anything that sets them apart. I was having trouble remembering which Boricua was which. That's a bad sign in an eight minute match.

Bret says the Hart Foundation will win the flag match.

Bret Hart/British Bulldog vs. Vader/The Patriot

This is a flag match and you can win by pinfall, submission, or capturing your country's flag from the poles in the corners. It's a big brawl on the floor to start with everyone fighting on the floor. Vader pounds on Bret with a Canadian flag pole but Bret sends him into the steps. Now it's Bret hitting Vader with the pole as Bulldog does the same to Patriot in the aisle. We're still waiting for an opening bell. They change positions and the Foundation members are both down.

We finally get a bell as the Americans are alone in the ring. Why they don't go up for the flag is anyone's guess but everyone stands around instead of doing anything. Patriot finally goes up for it but gets pulled down by Bulldog. A snap suplex puts

Bulldog down but Bret distracts Patriot from climbing. Vader comes in and runs Bulldog over before it's off to Bret for the first time. Hart tries to slug it out and is easily punched down into the corner for his efforts.

Bret avoids a charge into the corner and takes Vader down with a Russian legsweep. Vader easily breaks up an attempt at climbing with a low blow before sitting on Bret's chest for two. It's back to Patriot vs. Bulldog with the masked man mostly missing a dropkick for two on Davey. Patriot goes for the flag very slowly and Bret breaks it up again. Vader does the same to the Bulldog as things slow down. Bret sends Patriot's shoulder into the post and puts on the Figure Four around the same post for good measure.

Back in and Bret drops a headbutt to the abdomen before putting on the Sharpshooter, but Patriot easily reverses into one of his own. That's broken up just as easily until all four go into the same corner. Bulldog throws Patriot off and the match slows back down again. Patriot kicks Smith away and finally makes the tag off to Vader to almost no reaction. Bulldog scores with a quick belly to back suplex but Vader runs him over and drops a splash for two.

Vader can't get to the flag either as Bulldog pulls him back down and we hit the chinlock. Back to Bret for a Sharpshooter but Vader is right next to the ropes. Patriot comes in without a tag to break up the hold anyway and Vader takes over. Now it's a Sharpshooter from Vader to Bret as the fans are trying to get into the match. Bulldog breaks up the Sharpshooter so it's Patriot in again with a Figure Four. Smith breaks it up again and comes in for the delayed vertical suplex. Patriot is knocked down again while trying to climb so it's back to Bret.

Hart drops some knees and elbows but Vader easily stops him from getting the flag. Now it's back to Vader vs. Bulldog but the masked man misses his moonsault, only to LAND ON HIS FEET. That's INSANE. Anyway he pounds Bulldog down into the corner but Bret stops an attempt at the flag. Instead Vader clotheslines Bulldog to the floor but gets nailed in the head with the bell.

They head inside again where Bret easily slams Vader and drops a few legs. Vader fights up and clotheslines both Foundation members down, allowing for a lukewarm at best tag to Patriot.

155

House is cleaned and the Uncle Slam gets two on Bret. A fan comes in and is easily taken out by security. The Vader Bomb crushes Bret but Vader isn't legal, so Bret gets a quick rollup on Patriot for the pin at 25:07.

Rating: D+. This wasn't a horrible match but again it just went on WAY too long. This was nearly half an hour long and could have easily been done in about twelve minutes. The flags weren't a factor at all as none of the attempts to get them even came close. It would also be the last major appearance of Patriot who tore his triceps a few weeks later and retired as a result.

Post match Patriot gets all mad and kicks Bret to the floor.

Shawn says the good news is the Cell match isn't for the European Title, but the bad news is Undertaker is locked inside with him.

We recap the main event, which has pretty much been covered already. Shawn claims that he's doing this because everyone blames him for Undertaker's problems instead of taking responsibilities for their own problems. On the other hand, Undertaker wants to kill him.

Slaughter and a referee check underneath the ring to make sure no one can interfere.

Undertaker vs. Shawn Michaels

Inside the Hell in a Cell and the winner gets a shot at Bret next month at Survivor Series. The thunder starts to rumble and the gong goes off, bringing the crowd back to life for the first time in a long while. The entrance takes it sweet time as Shawn is forced to think about what's coming. Undertaker turns the lights back on and Shawn is terrified as reality sets in.

The slow stalking around the cage floor begins before they head back inside, only to have Shawn launched across the ring. A ram into the buckle sends Shawn flying again so he tries some punches, only to be whipped HARD across the ring again. Undertaker rams his shoulder into Shawn's before hitting Old School for no cover. A slam and legdrop get two on Shawn and some big right hands send Shawn down again. Michaels is thrown over the top and out to the floor as the pain begins.

Undertaker continues to walk very slowly around the ring, hitting a single right hand after another. He tries a powerbomb on the floor but Michaels fires off right hands, only to be rammed back first into the cage wall. Now Undertaker picks him up and rams Shawn back first into the post, then the wall, then back to the post and back to the wall again. Shawn manages to escape being rammed in again and sends Undertaker into the wall, but Undertaker shrugs it off and punches Shawn down.

Shawn is sent face first into the steps and choked a bit but he FINALLY sends Undertaker into the post to get a breather. Since the outside doesn't work at all for Shawn, he heads back inside, only to have his neck snapped across the top rope. A dive over the top takes out Undertaker and an elbow off the apron keeps Undertaker down. Michaels slams the steps down onto Undertaker's back a few times before piledriving him onto said steps.

A top rope ax handle sends Undertaker into the cage again and we head back inside. Shawn finds a chair under the ring and the fans are very pleased. Some chair shots to the back put Undertaker down for two so Shawn ties his arms up in the ropes. He doesn't tie up the feet though and Undertaker kicks him down before backdropping Shawn onto the cameraman. Shawn beats up the cameraman because he doesn't have enough problems to deal with already.

Michaels gets in a cheap shot on Undertaker to knock him to the floor before taking a breather. Back inside and the flying forearm and nip up make Shawn a little more cocky. The top rope elbow gets two as Slaughter has the door unlocked to get the cameraman some medical attention. Sweet Chin Music lays Undertaker out but he sits up. Shawn tries to run through the open door but Undertaker grabs him almost immediately. Michaels is catapulted into the cage wall (on the outside), cutting him open. Now the fun begins.

In one of the iconic shots of the match, Undertaker puts Shawn on his shoulder and rams him into the cage wall again. Shawn collapses next to the cage but Undertaker is just warming up. A quick low blow puts Undertaker down and with nowhere else to go, Shawn climbs up the side of the cage. He makes it all the way to the roof but Undertaker follows him. Undertaker counters a piledriver with a backdrop as we go to a wide shot to show how awesome this looks (which is quite awesome as the Cell is quite the structure).

A gorilla press slam puts Shawn down on the roof again and a kick to the ribs sends Shawn to the edge. He tries to climb down, but in the really famous shot of the match, Undertaker stomps on his hands, sending Shawn flying off the cage and through the announcers' table. Undertaker still isn't done and throws Shawn onto the other announcers' table as Shawn's face is just covered in blood.

The stalking continues as the announcers are losing their minds at all this. Michaels crawls back into the Cell but can barely see through the blood. A running clothesline puts Shawn down on the mat before taking him to the top for a SUPER CHOKESLAM. Now we get to the poetic justice portion with Undertaker grabbing the chair. A big chair shot to the head puts Shawn down and Undertaker signals for the Tombstone.....and the lights go out.

Organ music begins to play and Paul Bearer walks a huge man in red down to ringside. Vince: "THAT'S GOT TO BE KANE!" He rips the door off the Cell and climbs into the ring to stare down Undertaker. Undertaker is STUNNED as Kane raises his arms up and pulls them down, causing fire to shoot up from the ring posts. Kane Tombstones Undertaker down and walks out, allowing Shawn to drape an arm over Undertaker for the shocking upset at 29:55.

Rating: A+. This is one of the best matches of all time and the culmination of one of the best put together stories ever. While the brawling is incredible and the violence is off the charts, the storytelling carries this. Undertaker stalking Shawn to start and getting every single bit of punishment in that he could until Shawn used his speed and intelligence to get some control was brilliant. The torment Undertaker put Shawn through was perfect with Michaels being completely destroyed throughout the match and being dead to rites until the ending.

Kane making his debut here was perfect as well, with the story being just far enough in the past that people weren't thinking about it but not far enough that everyone knew who Kane was as soon as he walked out. This set up a feud that went on and off for thirteen years between the brothers, but we'll get to that later. By the way, I told you Fake Diesel would be worth something someday, and all it took was turning him into Kane.

Overall Rating: C-. The main event saves it, but there's no reason to sit through the whole show just to get to the Cell. It's available on several DVDs and is the only worthwhile thing on the entire show. The midcard is a disaster at this point with almost nothing of interest at all. Austin is doing what he can but the fact that he can't get in the ring is really holding him back. His day would come, but it would be a little bit longer.

With Shawn vs. Undertaker out of the way, we headed to Montreal for Survivor Series 1997. This is pretty easily the most infamous wrestling show in history due to the ending alone. Around this time, Bret Hart had made it clear that he was going to be heading to WCW. Though he had signed an unprecedented twenty year contract with the WWF, Vince said he couldn't pay Bret and agreed to let him out of the contract.

Bret's contract expired in November, but he was still the WWF Champion. The idea was to have Bret drop the title to Shawn Michaels at Survivor Series in Montreal, but there was a flaw in the plan. Bret refused to lose the title in Canada to Shawn, but agreed to lose it to anyone else. When that couldn't be agreed to, the plan changed to having the match end via DQ meaning no title change, with Bret forfeiting the title the next night on Raw.

Now hold your place here as we just back to 1991. Around this time, WCW/NWA Champion Ric Flair was in a contract dispute and was eventually released while still holding the title. Long story short, Flair never gave back the NWA World Title belt and brought it with him after signing with the WWF. The title appeared on WWF TV and became a plot point for a WWF storyline, meaning it was hurting WCW business.

Now jump ahead to 1996, when WWF Women's Champion Alundra Blayze's contract expired. Soon after leaving the WWF, she walked onto Monday Nitro with the Women's Title and dropped it in a garbage can. While it wasn't an important title to the WWF, it still came off as a major embarrassment to the company that never should have happened. If it was bad with the Women's Title, it could be a disaster with the WWF Title.

This had Vince scared, so he made a drastic decision. It isn't clear who all knew about this in advance, but it was a very short list. As the match was about to end, Shawn put Bret in a Sharpshooter as had been planned, but Vince demanded that the bell be rung. The title match was over, Shawn was the new champion, and Bret had been legitimately double crossed. Bret realized what happened and spat at Vince before writing WCW with his finger.

The reaction to this was not good at all, with Vince being blamed for a lot of the problems that resulted. British Bulldog and Jim Neidhart demanded and were (eventually) granted releases while Owen was forced to stay. Many big starts including Mankind threatened to quit but were eventually convinced to stay. Soon after this, Vince went on Raw in a sitdown interview and made the infamous statement that "Bret screwed Bret." This line, along with the Austin feud, turned Vince from a commentator into Mr. McMahon, the evil megalomaniac obsessed with running the company as he saw fit.

While all this was going on, the next pay per view still had to take place. The main story going on was the return of Steve Austin, who came back at Survivor Series to win the Intercontinental Title. However he had another feud to deal with due to costing Faarooq the title at Badd Blood. The Rock rose up to fight Austin on the Nation's behalf, including stealing Austin's title belt. This time around, Austin is coming for his belt and revenge.

One last note about Badd Blood: oddly enough there wouldn't be a Kane vs. Undertaker match at Survivor Series. Undertaker swore to never fight his brother, so Kane debuted against Mankind instead. Kane won and continued down his path of destruction through the WWF until he could convince his brother to fight him. We'll get back to these guys eventually.

D-Generation X: In Your House #19
Date: December 7, 1997
Location: Springfield Civic Center, Springfield, Massachusetts
Attendance: 6,358
Commentators: Jim Ross, Jerry Lawler

Since the show is named after DX, it only makes sense that one of their members is in the main event. In this case it's WWF Champion Shawn Michaels defending the title against Ken Shamrock who is being given the first title shot because...well someone has to do it. Seriously there's nothing more to it than that. One night it was just announced that he would challenge for the title and that was it. Let's get to it.

Light Heavyweight Title: Brian Christopher vs. Taka Michinoku

This is a tournament final to determine the new champion. The title had actually been around for years but was only defended in Mexico and Japan while never being mentioned in America. Christopher plays to the crowd before we get going but scores with a quick slam to take over. An armdrag puts Taka down again as the Jerry's Kid chant starts up again. Taka flips out of a German suplex and takes Brian down with a pair of kicks to the face and a clothesline to send him out to the floor. A HUGE springboard dive off the top takes Christopher out again and fires up the crowd a bit.

Brian crotches Taka on the top rope as they come back in and a dropkick sends Michinoku back to the floor. Taka avoids a dive off the apron to send Brian into the barricade but misses a crossbody back inside to give Christopher control again. Now it's Brian's turn to miss a charge, allowing Taka to hit a tornado DDT for two. A hurricanrana sends Brian to the floor again and a top rope moonsault takes him out. Lawler goes to help his son back inside but Taka dropkicks Christopher right back down.

Back inside and a pair of dropkicks put Brian down again but Taka gets caught in a full nelson legsweep. There's a sitout powerbomb by Christopher but he poses too much, allowing Taka to grab a rollup for two. A missile dropkick to the back of Taka's head puts him down again and a backbreaker gets two.

Brian stays cocky by slapping Taka in the face over and over (Jerry: "Just like I slapped Andy Kaufman!") before clotheslining him down for two. Now the release German suplex connects but Brian takes forever to cover. Instead it's a powerslam to put Taka down but Christopher misses the top rope legdrop, allowing Taka to hit the Michinoku Driver for the pin and the title at 12:02.

Rating: C. Really basic match here but it made sense to put the belt on Taka at first. Christopher was just a guy who happened to be in the weight division and never fight the style at all. The match wasn't bad or anything but the division never worked nearly as well as the company hoped it to.

Los Boricuas vs. Disciples of Apocalypse

Remember the match they had on the last show? Well here it is again but in a six man match with Savio and Crush sitting this one out. Crush isn't here due to an injury and Savio is ejected to really make it three on three. Miguel and Chainz get us going with the biker cleaning house and sending Miguel into the corner for a tag off to Jesus. 8-Ball comes in as well to send Jesus face first into the mat.

Off to Jose who is powerslammed down, followed by a knee drop from Skull for two. A side slam and swinging neckbreaker put Jose down again but the other Boricuas interfere to take over. Miguel hits something off the top but hurts his leg so it's off to

Jesus for a chinlock. A jumping back elbow from Jose puts Skull down again as Savio tries to come out and replace Miguel. Skull avoids a charge into the post and makes a hot tag off to Chainz. House is cleaned with Chainz hitting a Death Valley Driver but the referee is distracted by Savio, allowing a perfectly fine Miguel to sneak in and blast Chainz to give Jose the pin at 7:58.

Rating: D+. Not only was the match boring but it couldn't have been more uninteresting if it tried. There's just no reason to care about these guys and there's no real story other than they're both gangs. Savio and Crush were the only people in the match people would have cared about and they weren't even around. Horrible idea here.

Butterbean, a professional boxer, says he's ready for Marc Mero.

We look at a recap of Mero vs. Butterbean, which is about Mero being obsessed with people looking at Sable. Therefore, he challenged Butterbean to a fight which was eventually called a Toughman contest to avoid issues with the state athletic commission.

Marc Mero vs. Butterbean

Butterbean is a legitimate boxer who weighed over 300lbs so this is fixed to prevent Mero from being killed. There are four two minute rounds and Mero runs a lot to start round one. He hides in the ropes and Butterbean gets annoyed so he knocks Mero off the apron with a big right hand. Back in and they keep feeling each other out with nothing of note until the end of the round. A brawl breaks out between the rounds but again it goes nowhere.

Round two starts with Mero choking away before firing off rights and lefts. Nothing of note happens until the end of the round when Mero dropkicks Butterbean into the corner. Round three is all Butterbean with Mero getting pounded into the corner and being knocked silly by a huge right hand to end the round. Butterbean doesn't want it to end that way though so he pours water on Mero to wake him up. Round four begins with another huge right hand to drop Mero so he hits Butterbean low for the DQ at 10:20 total, counting time in between the rounds.

Rating: F. Considering the fans were chanting boring before the match started and were almost silent other than for the big punches, what else would you expect from this mess? This kind of stuff has never worked and almost never will because of one simple reason: wrestling fans want to watch wrestling, not boxing. If they wanted to watch boxing, they'd buy a boxing show. It really is that simple.

Post match Mero breaks a stool over Butterbean's back and runs off before Butterbean eats him.

Here are Goldust and his new valet Luna Vachon. The idea here is that Goldust is starving for attention so he's in, I kid you not, pink leather with a pink wig and a Mardi Gras mask while being lead around on a chain by Luna. He reads Green Eggs and Ham by Dr. Seuss in various voices and is dragged off by Luna, who calls him scum.

We recap the New Age Outlaws shocking the world by beating the LOD (who beat the Godwinns a day after the last show) for the tag team titles with the help of a chair. The New Age Outlaws are the newly formed team of Jesse James (now called Road Dogg) and Billy Gunn who said they were tired of fighting each other and formed a team.

LOD promises to get their belts back.

Tag Team Titles: Legion of Doom vs. New Age Outlaws

The Outlaws are defending and have their signature entrance in place but they're not quite perfected yet. The LOD chases them up the aisle when the Outlaws want to stretch a bit beforehand. Road Dogg continues to run his mouth before getting in the ring until some officials force them back towards ringside where the LOD tosses them back inside. Animal beats on Road Dogg to start and clotheslines him down. Off to Hawk for some right hands and a dropkick, sending Road Dogg out to the floor.

Back in and Hawk hits a neckbreaker to send Dogg back to the floor for a meeting with Billy. Hawk clotheslines both guys down from the apron and kicks Dogg in the face for good measure. A rake to the face sends Dogg to the floor for the third time where he is sent face first into the announcers' table. It's all LOD so far with Animal coming back in to counter Dogg's leapfrog into a powerbomb for two.

They head outside for the fifth time where Billy gets dropped face first onto the steps, putting him in just as much pain as his partner. The champions try to leave but the LOD will have none of that and drag the Outlaws back to the ring. With the referee distracted, Billy hits Hawk low and Road Dogg finds a cooler of soft drinks to crack him over the back. Back in and the Outlaws actually get to take over with Road Dogg getting two off a dropkick.

Billy comes in legally for the first time and distracts the referee, allowing Dogg to get in a cheap shot from the apron. Gunn hooks a neck crank but Hawk fights up, only to have a double clothesline put both guys down. A double tag brings in Animal to powerslam Dogg before crushing him with a shoulder block. LOD loads up the Doomsday Device but the referee is with Billy, allowing the Godwinns to come in with their buckets. Hawk takes it away and wears out the Outlaws for the DQ at 10:32.

Rating: D+. The match wasn't much but it got the LOD away from the title picture for awhile. The Outlaws were the breath of air that the division had been starving for since about 1995 and the impact was quickly felt. Their matches never were all that great but they were eventually so ridiculously over that it didn't matter.

We recap Sgt. Slaughter vs. HHH. There isn't much to this one: Slaughter is authority, DX is anti-authority. Tonight they're having a boot camp match (a street fight) which was Slaughter's signature match back during his career.

HHH has a Sgt. Slaughter survivor kit: a comb (Slaughter is mostly bald), prunes and Depends. He says this isn't Slaughter's generation but rather D-Generation, so it's time to take care of the old guys.

Sgt. Slaughter vs. HHH

Anything goes. Slaughter comes out to the same music that Patriot came out to for his earlier appearances. Slaughter pounds on HHH with his riding crop to start and pounds him down before stomping away at the ribs. HHH is thrown out to the floor and dropped throat first across the barricade as the match continues its slow start. Slaughter covers for no count, establishing that the fall has to occur in the ring.

HHH goes into the steps and gets kicked into the aisle with Slaughter still in full control. Back inside and Slaughter drops him with the riding crop to the throat before choking away. A clothesline gets two and Slaughter calls for his Cobra Clutch but HHH rolls out of it. Slaughter is whipped into the corner and out to the floor (a signature spot) to give HHH a breather.

HHH whips him into the barricade for a little payback before throwing him into the crowd. Back to ringside and HHH chokes away, only to have to duck the Slaughter Cannon (running clothesline), which takes out the timekeeper instead. Slaughter is cracked in the back by a belt and we head back inside. A chain to the jaw puts Slaughter down for two as the timekeeper is taken to the back.

HHH drops the chain for some reason, allowing Slaughter to pick it up and give him a chance. Not that it lasts long or anything though as he is almost immediately backdropped to the floor to keep HHH in control. Back in and HHH goes up, only to dive into a boot to the jaw. Slaughter can't slam HHH but can hit a suplex to put both guys down. For some reason Slaughter thinks it's a good idea to go up top, allowing HHH to slam him down without much trouble.

HHH grabs a sleeper for a good while until Slaughter escapes and puts on the Cobra Clutch, only to have Chyna come in for the save. Chyna gets yelled at so she blasts the referee and pulls in a chair. Slaughter sees her coming through and throws powder in her eyes, only to be blasted in the face by HHH's boot. Another boot shot misses though and Slaughter grabs the Clutch again. The referee wakes up to check HHH's arm but Chyna kicks Slaughter low to break up the hold. A Pedigree onto the chair is finally enough to end Slaughter at 17:39.

Rating: D. This just went WAY too long, running nearly eighteen minutes. They easily could have accomplished the same goals with about half the time and that's a problem when you have a retired guy pushing 50 out there. Slaughter wasn't really worth much here though, especially with Vince as the real boss of the company now.

The returning Jeff Jarrett is ready for his in ring return. He promises the cream will rise to the top tonight and become the

#1 contender. He's in a white outfit with big shoulder pads that looks like something you would see in a low budget sci-fi movie.

Jeff Jarrett vs. Undertaker

Undertaker stalks him to start and no sells some right hands. A bunch of right hands in the corner just make Undertaker mad, so he grabs Jarrett and launches him into the corner for a beating. There's a hard clothesline to put Jarrett down for two and Taker cranks on the arm a bit. Old School connects but Jarrett tries some kicks to the knee for a breather. A chop block takes Undertaker down but he fights back and pounds away. There's a legdrop for two and a big boot keeps Jarrett in trouble....until the lights go out. Cue Kane to the ring, only to chokeslam Jarrett for the DQ at 6:54.

Rating: D-. This was a waste of time and nothing more than a way to run an angle. Amazingly enough, this didn't launch Jarrett up the card and almost no one remembered him because of the story going on. The match was a glorified squash for Undertaker as Jarrett couldn't get anything going at all.

Kane slaps Undertaker in the face and Undertaker is tempted to fight but instead just stands still as Kane launched fire out of the corners of the ring. Kane leaves so Jarrett goes after Undertaker's knee again, earning himself a horrible looking chokeslam. Jarrett is named the winner and you would think he won the WWF Title.

Mark Henry is in the Milton Bradley (yes as in the board game company) cheering section.

We recap Rock (yes it's officially his name) vs. Steve Austin. Rock has proclaimed his greatness and let all of his early success go to his head. On the other hand, Austin is a rebel who will fight anyone and everyone, including the Nation who has come after Austin due to his attack on Faarooq at Badd Blood. Rock then stole the belt (Austin is still champion) and dared Austin to come get it back. This led to an awesome series of promos and segments with Austin encouraging the ROCKY SUCKS chants.

The biggest segment of all though was Austin saying that Rock was going to be walking through the airport when his beeper goes off and it says Austin 3:16, meaning Austin owns him. Rock was in the ring for a promo when his beeper went off and read 3:16. Austin popped up and pounded the tar out of Rock, sending the crowd through the roof. It was clear that these two were the future and that Rock had just needed the right feud to bring him up to the next level.

Intercontinental Title: The Rock vs. Steve Austin

The Rock is defending and brings the Nation with him. That's fine with Austin, who drives a Stone Cold truck down the aisle. The brawl is on immediately and the bell hasn't even rung yet. The Nation gets in the ring and beats Austin down four on one. Austin gets up and backdrops D'Lo onto the hood of the car before Stunning him on the top. The bell rings and Austin slugs it out with Rock before taking him down with a Thesz press and more right hands.

Rock throws him to the floor and the Nation gets in a few extra cheap shots to the back. They fight into the aisle but Kama's chair shot hits Faarooq in the head, allowing Austin to ram Kama head first through the window. The fans are just nuts for Austin here. Austin hasn't even been able to take his vest off as Rock pounds away at him and chokes on the ropes. Rock stomps Austin down in the corner before dropping the yet to be named People's Elbow.

We hit a chinlock to give them a breather but Rocky misses another elbow attempt. Now it's Austin stomping Rock down in the corner but has to punch Kama instead of Stunning Rock. Austin backs up and blindly Stuns the referee. Rock finds some brass knuckles but gets caught in the Stunner as another referee comes in to count the pin at 5:28.

Rating: B-. This one depends on your taste but the match is very important from an historical perspective. This match paved the way for what would become the Attitude Era style with no semblance of order or rules and the two guys just beating the tar out of each other. The style had to be implemented to protect Austin's neck and give him a way to still compete while not risking further injuries. These two would have several more matches and we'll get to see one of the better ones later.

We recap Ken Shamrock vs. Shawn Michaels. Shamrock has been destroying everyone in his path so far and making everyone from Rock to Bret to Austin tap out. On Raw, Shawn put a fake leg in a wheelchair and had HHH twist the ankle around to show how much pain he could withstand in a funny bit.

Shamrock says he's ready.

WWF Title: Shawn Michaels vs. Ken Shamrock

Shawn is defending here and also has the European Title for reasons of selfishness. Shawn throws some right hands to start but gets his head kicked off, sending Michaels out to the floor. Back in and Shawn stalls a lot before being launched hard into the corner. A backdrop puts Shawn down and another whip sends him out to the floor. Chyna tries to distract Ken but he catches Shawn sneaking in with a right hand, sending Shawn's water flying out of his mouth.

Shawn gets him into the corner and pounds away but Shamrock will have none of it and sends Shawn to the floor again. This match still hasn't had a chance to get going and it's getting a bit annoying. Shawn rakes Shamrock's eyes and pounds away, only to have his sunset flip blocked. Shamrock sends him into the corner to crotch Shawn on the top rope. The champ escapes the belly to belly suplex and sends Shamrock to the floor for some punishment from HHH.

A plancha from the ring takes Shamrock down again but a baseball slide misses, allowing Shamrock to pound away with lefts and rights. HHH takes a shot as well but Chyna sends Ken into the post to put him down. Shawn distracts the referee so DX can pound away even more before sending Shamrock back inside. Michaels goes after Ken's back with a series of elbows, including one from the middle rope. A dropkick gets two and Shawn chokes away in the corner. The admonishment allows HHH to get in even more cheap shots.

Shamrock rolls through a Shawn crossbody for two and Michaels is scared. A rake to the eyes puts Shamrock down again and we hit the chinlock. It's off to a sleeper instead as Shawn calls some very loud spots. The hold stays on for a good while until Shamrock powers his way back up. Ken pounds away and scores with a powerslam, putting Michaels in big trouble. A standing hurricanrana allows Shamrock to pound away even more before countering a sunset flip into a rollup for two.

Shawn comes back with a quick hot shot to slow Ken down but his hurricanrana is countered into a powerbomb for a very close two. HHH and Chyna pull Shamrock to the floor again and beat him down (the referee didn't think anything of Shamrock being down when Shawn never touched him), setting up Shawn's top rope elbow for no cover. Sweet Chin Music is countered into into the belly to belly suplex but DX comes in for the disqualification at 18:27 before the ankle lock can go on.

Rating: C+. The match got better once they got down to business but the ending hurt it a lot. Shamrock never even got to put on the ankle lock to give the fans a sweat which should have been the most obvious spot of the match. This wasn't terrible, but it could have been better if they planned the match better.

Post match DX destroys Shamrock until a man in a black sweatshirt comes out to destroy Shawn. It's Owen Hart, making his first appearance since the Survivor Series. He pounds away on Shawn before running away through the crowd. DX poses a lot to end the show.

Overall Rating: D. The main event is just ok and the only good match on the show only runs about six minutes so there's really no reason to see the show. This was a weird time for the company as they were trying to figure out where to go next. The end result at Wrestlemania was obvious, but they didn't exactly know how to get there. This show wasn't the right way though and it was a horrible show as a result. Not worth seeing at all with the exception of Rock vs. Austin which is always worth a look.

This brings us to the road to Wrestlemania XIV, meaning everything is about to change. First and foremost, the next night on Raw, Austin literally handed the Rock the Intercontinental Title because he was ready to go after the WWF Title. The best way for him to get there would be winning the Royal Rumble, which he immediately entered. It was very hard to believe that anyone other than Austin was going to win the Rumble, but that didn't necessarily mean it was a bad thing. People were ready to see Austin win the title and get there in the most traditional way.

However before we get there, we have to touch on WCW again for a few seconds. On December 27, WCW held its biggest event of the year: Starrcade. The main event was Sting challenging Hulk Hogan for the WCW WWF Title in a match built up for over a year. Due to a variety of reasons, including the newly signed Bret Hart being involved in a Survivor Series style angle, the show was considered a disaster and there was an opening for the WWF that hadn't been there in years.

The Royal Rumble came around and the WWF kicked the door in. Austin won the Rumble to the shock of almost no one, guaranteeing him a WWF Title match at Wrestlemania in Boston. The question though was who would he be facing. Based on the ending to In Your House #19, the seemingly obvious match was Owen Hart vs. Shawn Michaels for the title.

However, Michaels refused to work with Owen for reasons that aren't really clear. It might have been fear of Owen trying to get revenge for Bret due to the events in Montreal or Shawn not wanting to potentially drop the title for a one month Owen reign, or perhaps something else entirely. Either way, there wasn't going to be a Shawn vs. Owen title match, so Shawn needed another opponent.

The solution was the Undertaker, who picked up his feud with Shawn again for one more match, in this case a casket match. The match wasn't bad, but there was a specific spot in the match that changed everything. Undertaker backdropped Shawn over the top rope and Shawn landed spine first on the edge of the casket. Shawn's back was basically broken, basically ending his active career on the spot. Somehow Shawn finished the match and won with the help of an interfering Kane. More on Shawn in a bit.

After the match, Kane locked his brother inside the casket and lit it on fire to end the show. I don't think I can make it much clearer than that: Kane lit his set brother on fire. Undertaker disappeared from the casket though and wasn't seen for months, because Undertaker is cool like that. This allowed

Kane to go on another path of rage for the next few months, including a match with Vader at the next In Your House.

We're still not there yet though, as everything was cranked up again the next night on Raw. After the Rumble, a major celebrity was announced for Wrestlemania: Mike Tyson was going to be appearing at the show and refereeing the main event. However, Steve Austin came to the ring and got in Tyson's face before the announcement could be completed. A brawl broke out and Vince screamed that Austin ruined it. This would be the real catalyst for their feud but we'll get to that later. For now we've got In Your House #20, which is really a glorified pit stop on the way to Wrestlemania XIV.

No Way Out of Texas: In Your House #20
Date: February 15, 1998
Location: Compaq Center, Houston, Texas
Attendance: 16,110
Commentators: Jim Ross, Jerry Lawler

Since we have the main event already set for Wrestlemania, tonight's main event is a way to develop the WWF Title feud while also tying in the other main feuds. The main event is an eight man tag between Austin/Owen Hart/Cactus Jack/Chainsaw Charlie (Terry Funk) vs. Shawn Michaels/HHH/New Age Outlaws. However since Shawn is injured, a replacement will be announced during the show. Let's get to it.

They don't even bother with an opening video this time around. That's how unimportant this show really is.

Marc Mero/The Artist Formerly Known As Goldust vs. Headbangers

Goldust is still desperate for attention and is in this tag team which won't bring him much attention whatsoever. Mero's entrance gets a huge pop due to Sable coming with him. Goldust's manager Luna hates Sable so we might get a catfight sometime tonight. Mero tells Sable to get out of the ring and the arena because there's only room for one beautiful lady. Goldust is dressed (I think) like Marilyn Manson tonight to keep the levels of strange up high.

Mosh and Mero get us going with Marc pounding away in the corner and dropping Mosh with a back elbow to the jaw. More

172

body shots put Mosh down but he comes back with a hard clothesline to put Mero on the floor. Back in and Thrasher scores with a middle rope clothesline before it's off to Goldust who is loudly booed. Thrasher stomps away at Goldust and brings in Mosh for a backdrop. In a nice double team, Thrasher goes to the middle rope to lift Mosh up and drop him down on Goldust for two.

Mero comes in off a blind tag and scores with a knee lift to take over on Thrasher. The fans chant for Sable to tick Marc off and it's back to Thrasher for some running shoulder blocks. Goldust pulls Thrasher to the floor though and sends him into the steps to put the Headbangers on defense again. Back to Goldust for some slow fist drops and a running clothesline for two. Thrasher is bleeding from the back of his head but it doesn't look that bad.

Mero pounds away and puts on a chinlock as the blood starts flowing much worse. The fans get all over Mero to mess with his head again so it's back to Goldust. Thrasher comes back with a quick crossbody for two but Goldust makes a tag to Mero who takes Thrasher down again. A choke with some wrist tape makes Thrasher scream even more and a sitout powerbomb gets two for Marc.

The TKO (Mero's fireman's carry into a spinning Diamond Cutter) is countered into a DDT and it's finally off to Mosh. Everything breaks down and Luna crotches Mosh to break up the powerbomb/legdrop combo. This brings out Sable (in less clothing than earlier) to go after Luna, but the distraction lets the Headbangers switch places, allowing Thrasher to roll up Mero for the pin at 13:27.

Rating: D+. The match was pretty dull stuff but opening with Sable was a good idea. The fans absolutely loved her and she would get the crowd fired up every time she was on screen. Sable was probably the most financially successful Diva of all time as she drew insane money and ratings for the company around this time, which is unheard of for a woman in wrestling.

Luna tries to go after Sable but the guys break it up. Sable yells at Mero and slaps him down, furthering the split between the pair.

Jackyl, a semi-religious prophet character who did interviews and occasional commentary at this time, predicts that the mystery partner will lead DX and the Outlaws to victory tonight. This guy had potential but never got off the ground.

Owen doesn't care who the mystery partner is but thinks things will be fine if Austin stays out of his way.

Light Heavyweight Title: Pantera vs. Taka Michinoku

Sunny is the guest ring announcer. Pantera, the challenger, is another guy who has had success in Mexico but isn't known by about 99% of the American audience at any point in history. Brian Christopher comes out to do commentary as both guys speed things up to start. Taka slides to the floor and Pantera hits a nice dive but the camera is on Lawler and Christopher. Back inside and Pantera gets taken down by a nice headscissors to the floor, allowing Taka to hit his signature huge dive to wipe Pantera out.

Back in and Pantera is sent to the apron but he comes back with a top rope headscissors to the floor. The camera misses a suicide dive because of Lawler and Christopher again but thankfully replay shows us what we missed. Back in again and Pantera hits a butterfly backbreaker to set up a camel clutch. Off to a surfboard submission, complete with Pantera pulling on Taka's neck for added leverage. Taka gets out and fires back with some strikes to the face but gets backdropped out to the floor.

Pantera hits a great looking dive over the top, landing head first on Taka's back to keep the pressure on. A backbreaker sets up a top rope elbow to the back as Christopher talks about eating tacos with chopsticks. Taka gets in a shot to the ribs and goes up top, only to be caught in a top rope hurricanrana. Pantera gets two off a moonsault but misses a second attempt, allowing Taka to hit a top rope knee to the back of the head. Pantera comes back with a quick majistral cradle and a powerbomb for two each but misses a missile dropkick. The Michinoku Driver retains the title at 10:09.

Rating: C+. Nice match here even though the fans didn't care at all. The WWF was trying with this division but it never clicked with the audience. Taka was fine for what he was but he never became a big deal at all for the most part. Pantera was fine out there but the WWF never had a Mike Tenay (WCW commentator and lucha historian) to fill us in on the details and history of all these guys.

Post match Christopher tries to go after Taka but Lawler stops him, allowing Taka to dive on both of them to show them up.

Cactus Jack and Chainsaw Charlie don't care who the mystery partner is. Tonight is all about revenge for them though so they've been coming up with some evil ways to hurt the Outlaws.

Godwinns vs. Quebecers

The Quebecers (Jacques and Pierre) were a glorified comedy tag team from 1993 who came back for a few weeks in 1998. No one is really sure why as they were nothing special and a very random team to bring back. It didn't help that they lost their signature Mountie outfits and are now just generic guys. Henry and Jacques get us going with the fans booing both heel teams. After a minute of stalling it's Henry grabbing a headlock but Jacques suplexes him down.

Off to Pierre to trade some wristlocks until Henry grabs an armbar. Back to Jacques who gets clotheslined down and screams a lot during a wristlock. This match is already boring and it doesn't help after the fans haven't been interested in anything tonight. The Godwinns double team Jacques as Lawler implies he wants Bill Clinton shot. Jacques gets a quick two off a sunset flip to Phineas but it's back to Henry to keep control with a chinlock.

Phineas comes in to headbutt Jacques in the ribs but Jacques comes back with an elbow to the jaw. The ice cold tag brings in Pierre as things break down. A bad looking piledriver puts Phineas down and the Cannonball (assisted top rope flip splash from Pierre) gets two with Henry making the save. Not that it matters as Henry clotheslines Pierre from the apron to give Phineas the pin at 11:15.

Rating: D-. It was long, it was boring, and the fans didn't react to anything in the entire match. I'm not sure why the Quebecers were hired again but it never worked for the most part. The tag division still isn't great from top to bottom but the Outlaws have definitely helped things out a lot.

The Godwinns lay out the Quebecers with the buckets post match.

The Outlaws say they don't know who their partner will be.

Jim Cornette and Jeff Jarrett say they're ready for Bradshaw. This is part of the NWA storyline, where the WWF brought in some old guys to be the NWA representatives and basically humiliate the NWA/southern wrestling as a whole. Jarrett is going to go after Bradshaw's injured leg which the NWA guys hurt recently.

NWA North American Title: Bradshaw vs. Jeff Jarrett

Bradshaw, the native Texan and challenger, chases the NWA (Cornette, Jarrett, Rock N Roll Express and Barry Windham, Bradshaw's former tag partner) to the floor to start. The NWA save for Cornette is quickly ejected to make this as fair as possible. Bradshaw throws Jarrett back inside and whips him with his chaps to start before chopping Jarrett down over and over. A big boot to the face staggers Jarrett and a clothesline sends him to the floor.

Bradshaw makes the mistake of going after Cornette though and Jeff gets in some kicks to the chest to take over. There's a middle rope dropkick from Jeff for two and Cornette gets in some choking of his own. The choking only ticks Bradshaw off and he rolls up Jarrett for two. The referee yells at Jarrett though, allowing Cornette to blast Bradshaw in the bad knee with his tennis racket.

Jeff goes after the knee but gets crotched on the top rope. Bradshaw's superplex is blocked but he catches Jeff in a fall away slam to put both guys down. There's the powerbomb to Jeff but Bradshaw pulls Cornette into the ring, allowing Jeff to hit Bradshaw in the chest with the tennis racket for the DQ at 8:33.

Rating: D+. Not as bad of a match as some of them and the Texas man helped get the fans interested but this still didn't do much for me. The NWA angle was little more than a way for Vince to make fun of the organization and make them look like nitwits. The match was nothing special either with a basic knee story which went nowhere.

Post match the NWA jumps Bradshaw until the LOD makes the save.

HHH and Chyna won't say who the mystery partner is either but there's a long list of people wanting the spot with DX because they're the new train in wrestling. However, there's no one that can replace Shawn so tonight it's a handicap match.

Faarooq says the Nation is ready for war while Rock makes funny faces.

Nation of Domination vs. Ken Shamrock/Ahmed Johnson/Disciples of Apocalypse

This is a ten man tag with the Nation comprised of Faarooq, Rock, Kama, D'Lo Brown and the now heel Mark Henry. The match has been billed as a war of attrition which would imply survival and elimination rules, but this is one fall to a finish. Skull starts with D'Lo and Brown goes to the eyes for an early advantage. An atomic drop slows D'Lo down though and it's off to Shamrock for a back elbow to the jaw. A double tag brings in Kama and Chainz with Mustafa pounding away in the corner.

Some quick elbows have Kama in trouble so he tags off to Mark for some raw power. Henry wants Ahmed though and the fans till care about Johnson at this point. Johnson wins a slugout and slams Henry down, only to have the Nation come in with some cheap shots to take over. D'Lo hits a spinebuster to put Ahmed down and a long distance frog splash gets no cover. Instead it's off to Faarooq who walks into a spinebuster from Ahmed but Rock breaks up the Pearl River Plunge.

8-Ball gets the tag and powerslams Faarooq down for two as the good guys start speeding things up. It's off to Rock vs. Shamrock which is one of the matchups that people have wanted to see. Rock scores with a quick DDT and stomps away in the corner before bringing in Kama to miss a charge. Skull and 8-Ball take turns on Kama as we get some o the original twin magic. Kama will have none of that though and takes Skull into the Nation corner for a beating.

Rock comes in with the yet to be named People's Elbow for two and it's back to Faarooq to punch Skull in the jaw a few times.

Skull comes back with a faceplant but Rock breaks up a hot tag attempt. Henry comes in to pound on Skull for about ten seconds before it's back to Kama for a chinlock. D'Lo gets a tag but misses a moonsault, finally allowing for the hot tag off to Shamrock. Everything breaks down and the ring is cleared except for Shamrock to ankle lock the Rock for the win at 13:44.

Rating: C-. It's not a great match or anything and the elimination rules would have helped things a lot, but it was certainly better than some of the other stuff tonight. Above all else though the fans CARED about this. It wasn't some dull filler match that was there to make sure a card was complete but rather a match with characters and a story we've been given reason to care about. That's a big step up from a lot of this show.

Post match Rock and Faarooq are about to fight but eventually make up.

Austin doesn't care who the mystery partner is.

We recap Kane vs. Vader. There isn't much here other than Kane attacking Vader because Kane is evil and Vader wanting a fight as a result.

Kane vs. Vader

JR says Vader has won titles on more continents than he can count. That says a lot about the Oklahoma school system. Kane gets a BIG pop during his entrance as the monster is cool. The brawl is on to start with Kane taking Vader down via a clothesline. They head outside with Kane still in control, even though the fans chant for Vader. Back in and Vader kicks away at the leg before dumping Kane out to the floor for a whip into the post.

They head back inside again with Kane hitting his top rope clothesline and pounding Vader down into the corner. A nice looking suplex puts Vader down and a top rope forearm to the back does the same. The slow pace continues until Kane clotheslines Vader down yet again. We hit the nerve hold for a bit until Kane slugs Vader down to stop another comeback bid.

Vader finally scores with some right hands in the corner and a low blow to break up a chokeslam attempt. The moonsault mostly connects but Kane pops up, only to be clotheslined out to the floor. Vader is sent into the steps but comes back with a fire extinguisher to blind Kane. Vader's powerbomb is no sold and it's a chokeslam and Tombstone to give Kane the win at 10:57.

Rating: C-. This wasn't terrible but it's another case where the ending was obvious. Everyone knew that Kane was destined to face Undertaker and that Undertaker was the only person capable of defeating him. Vader was nothing more than a jobber to the stars at this point and his time in the company was dwindling.

Post match Kane grabs a wrench from under the ring and blasts Vader in the face with it to put him on the shelf for a few months.

We recap the main event which is really three feuds combined into one. The Outlaws put Cactus and Chainsaw into a dumpster and dumped them off the stage a few weeks back. Owen is feuding with HHH since Michaels wouldn't do it. Austin would be feuding with Michaels but he's injured, necessitating the mystery partner.

New Age Outlaws/HHH/??? vs. Steve Austin/Chainsaw Charlie/Cactus Jack/Owen Hart

This is one fall to a finish and anything goes. Billy Gunn brings a table with him just in case. The mystery partner is.....Savio Vega, who is a pretty big disappointment, but to be fair there was no one who wouldn't have been a downgrade. At least he does have a history with Austin, but Rock would have been a much better choice. Cactus brings a small dumpster full of weapons to make sure this is as violent as possible. Austin comes out to a roar and the fight is on fast.

Austin blasts Billy in the head with a trashcan lid but Billy bails from a Stunner attempt. The bad guys all bail to the floor as Austin and Charlie rule the ring. Everyone heads to the floor now with Austin choking HHH with I think a broom. Back in the ring and it's Cactus working over Road Dogg while Austin pounds on the back of HHH's head. The table is brought in as Charlie hits Dogg in the head with something in a bag. Dogg is sent into but not through a table in the corner as the carnage continues. This is one of those matches where it's practically impossible to call most of the stuff as there is so much going on.

Gunn is powerslammed through the table and Vega is sent knees first into the steps. HHH has to break up a Sharpshooter on Gunn and DX actually makes a comeback. Austin gets pounded down with a trashcan lid and HHH powerbombs Owen for two. HHH blasts Charlie in the head five or six times with a trashcan but it takes a DDT to put him down for two. Owen comes back with a spinebuster to HHH and a quick Sharpshooter but Road Dogg breaks it up.

The referee actually tries to get people on the aprons for a tag match but they'll have none of it. Road Dogg hits Charlie low and the Outlaws double powerbomb him through a pair of chairs. We actually get some of the people on the apron and start (seven minutes after the bell) with Billy pounding Charlie down until it's off to HHH for more of the same. Dogg suplexes Charlie onto a trashcan lid for two as Cactus makes the save.

Austin comes in without a tag and throws a trashcan at Gunn's head but it's HHH with an atomic drop on Charlie before Austin can do any more damage. Owen gets the tag but the referee was busy with Road Dogg so it doesn't count. You know for a match where anything goes, it certainly seems like there are a lot of rules being enforced. Charlie runs Road Dogg over and makes the hot tag off to Cactus to clean house. He puts Road Dogg under part of a table in the corner and throws Gunn into the same corner to crush Dogg even worse.

A double Mandible Claw slows the Outlaws down but HHH hits Cactus low to break up the hold. The fans demand Austin but get Cactus and Billy fighting to the floor instead. Gunn crushes Cactus with the steps and we head back inside for a two count from HHH. Savio comes in to wrap barbed wire around Cactus' head before kicking him in the ribs. Owen FINALLY comes in to break it up despite the lack of a tag but Vega blasts Cactus in the head (still wrapped in wire) with a chair.

Cactus ducks a Gunn chair shot which blasts Dogg in the head and Jack has an opening. The hot tag brings in Austin to the pop of the night and house is cleaned. Austin destroys everything in sight and sends Road Dogg to the floor. He stomps away on Gunn in the corner before Dogg comes back in for the Stunner from Austin and the pin at 17:37.

Rating: B. This was a nice tag match with the wild carnage part at the beginning and the perfect ending. There was no way this didn't end with Austin getting the pin and standing tall which is exactly what we got. The fans went NUTS for Austin and he's got all the momentum rolling into Wrestlemania. It's the exactly right ending and it was done very well.

Post match Chyna gets in Austin's face and gets a Stunner for her troubles to end the show.

Overall Rating: C-. The main event was exactly what it should have been but the rest of the show wasn't much to look at. This was nothing more than a breather before the biggest show of the year which is all it was supposed to be. Austin is on top of the world at this point but he still needs to make it official next month in Boston.

And Now, Everyone Else

That's exactly what he did too. There was nothing tricky, out of nowhere or surprising about it. At Wrestlemania XIV, Austin blocked the superkick, Stunned Shawn Michaels and took his official place on top of the wrestling world once and for all. JR got the famous call by saying "The Austin Era has begun." That sums it up perfectly: Austin was the undisputed king and there was nothing that could stop him.

However, one person tried and that was Vince McMahon. After Austin won the title, Vince wanted him to become more of a corporate champion but Austin would have none of that. This ignited the war between the two and made Vince obsessed with taking the WWF Title off of Austin. His first idea was to face Austin himself in a one on one match on Raw.

It turned out that's what the WWF was looking for all along. After nearly two years of losing literally every week, Monday Night Raw FINALLY beat Monday Nitro in the ratings, giving them the first proof that everything they had been done was actually paying off. While WCW would get a few wins here and there, but for the most part Monday Night Raw was on top to stay.

The match went about as you would expect it to have gone. Austin destroyed Vince for a bit but then someone came out for a save. That man would be Vince's new man to challenge Austin for the title: Dude Love. At Wrestlemania, Cactus Jack and Chainsaw Charlie won the Tag Team Titles in a dumpster match, which is just like a casket match but with a dumpster.

However it was said they didn't put the Outlaws in the correct dumpster so there was a rematch the next night. The Outlaws won the titles again in a cage match with the help of DX, joining the group (now headed up by HHH) in the process. During the attack on Cactus and Chainsaw, the fans chanted for Austin to make the save.

This didn't sit well with Cactus, who said he'd spent months sacrificing his body for the sake of the fans, only to have them cheer for someone else. Cactus said that it would be a long time before anyone saw Cactus Jack again, but the next week Dude Love made his return as Vince's corporate enforcer. That's your main event for In Your House #21: Austin defending the title against Dude Love.

The other big match at Wrestlemania was Undertaker finally fighting his brother. If you're a fan of wrestling at all, you likely know that Undertaker didn't lose at Wrestlemania back then and he didn't lose to Kane either. A feud that many months in the making couldn't end with just one match though, so the rematch was made for In Your House. The gimmick was something new though, as it would be an Inferno match. The ring would be surrounded by fire and the first person to light the other one on fire wins. That's a bit more intense.

Unforgiven: In Your House #21
Date: April 26, 1998
Location: Greensboro Coliseum, Greensboro, North Carolina
Attendance: 21,427
Commentators: Jim Ross, Jerry Lawler

As mentioned, this is in a new era for the WWF as they're back on top of the mountain for the first time since about In Your House #10. The company is on fire with Austin at the helm and the most evil man in company history going after him. This made for some very entertaining shows and hopefully this is one of them. Let's get to it.

The opening video focuses on Undertaker vs. Kane, which may not be the bigger story but it's about setting someone on fire.

Nation of Domination vs. Faarooq/Ken Shamrock/Steve Blackman

Rock has officially taken over the Nation (Rock/Henry/Brown here) after kicking Faarooq off the team. The non-Nation team does the Nation salute just to tick them off. The fans are already all over Rock about five seconds after the bell. Brown grabs Blackman's (a rather dull yet intense martial artist) arm to start things off and they trade shoulder blocks until Brown hooks a snap suplex. Blackman comes right back with a dropkick and an armdrag into an armbar.

It's off to Shamrock to stay on the arm but the ankle lock is escaped via the ropes. Faarooq hesitantly comes in but Brown asks for mercy. Instead he gets a whipping with Faarooq's belt and a snap suplex from Blackman. Back to the armbar but Brown gets away to tag Henry. That lasts about five seconds before it's back to Brown who walks into a crossbody for two. Back to Faarooq who is easily taken down before it's back to Rock for the cheap shots he's been looking for.

Henry comes back in and drops some elbows for a somewhat delayed two count, allowing Faarooq to pound away and make a tag off to Blackman. Henry runs Steve over but takes his time covering again. Back to Brown for a middle rope elbow and a standing one to the jaw for two. Rock comes in and stomps away in the corner while talking a lot of trash.

The still yet to be named People's Elbow gets two and you can see the crowd really starting to react to it. Rock hooks a chinlock and it's back to Brown for some trash talk and a backbreaker. D'Lo misses a moonsault and Steve makes the hot tag off to Faarooq. The Nation's house is cleaned and everything breaks down with Faarooq hitting the Dominator out of nowhere to pin Rock at 13:32.

Rating: D+. This didn't do much for me. The match wasn't horrible but the crowd didn't really react to it very strongly and the ending didn't work nearly as well as it was supposed to. Faarooq getting some revenge on Rock is a good idea but when the fans seem to like Rock more than Faarooq, it's not the best move.

Before we get anywhere else, here's Austin to really fire the place up. He calls the timekeeper into the ring due to him ringing the bell on Vince's orders last week during a match. If that happens again tonight and Austin gets screwed, the timekeeper will be beaten out of the company. It's fine if Dude Love beats him for the title, but if Austin gets screwed, the timekeeper is going to feel some pain.

European Title: Owen Hart vs. Hunter Hearst Helmsley

HHH is defending. Owen had won the title by dressing up as Goldust and surprising HHH but then HHH went after a bad leg injury that Owen had suffered to get it back. Chyna cost Owen his rematch at Wrestlemania, so tonight Chyna is trapped inside a one person cage suspended above the ring. Slaughter forces Chyna into the cage as a lot of time is killed. HHH spends too much time talking to Chyna and Owen gets in a cheap shot to take over. They fight up the aisle and the bell hasn't rung yet.

Owen pounds on HHH in the aisle and sends him face first into Chyna's cage while it's still on the ground. They finally get inside and the bell rings as Chyna's cage rises into the air. It's all Owen

184

still as he chops away in the corner until HHH drops him face first onto the top turnbuckle to get himself a breather. The jumping knee to the face puts Hart down and HHH chokes away with his boot in the corner. The knee drop to the head gets two and HHH hooks a dragon sleeper of all things.

Back up and Owen is sent chest first into the corner ala his brother to give the champion another two count. Chyna drops what appears to be a small saw from the cage but neither guy in the ring noticed it. Owen gets two off a sunset flip but HHH grabs a swinging neckbreaker for the same result and it's back to the dragon sleeper. Hart fights up again but gets sent into the post to put him right back down. A facebuster gets two more for HHH as the match stays slow.

We hit the dragon sleeper again but Owen fights up and flips over HHH to suplex him down. Chyna has bent the cage bars open as Hart gets two off an enziguri. The spinwheel kick gets the same and there's a piledriver on HHH for good measure. A top rope elbow hits HHH but Chyna is out of the cage. She can't get down though so it doesn't matter much.

HHH gets his leg caught in the ropes for a bit as Owen goes over to look at Chyna. That gets boring though so Hart DDTs HHH and puts on the Sharpshooter. The cage is lowered though and Chyna gets to the ground so Owen breaks the hold. Slaughter holds Chyna back as X-Pac (new DX member) comes in to blast Owen with a fire extinguisher to keep the title on HHH at 12:26.

Rating: D+. So to clarify, Owen stuck around after his brother got screwed, doesn't get the WWF Title shot, and gets to lose to HHH on back to back PPVs (not counting HHH eliminating Owen from the Royal Rumble). HHH on the other hand gets to lead DX and win the European Title. Funny how that works. The match was dull stuff though with the majority being spent on HHH putting the same hold on Owen. It's hard to not feel sorry for him here, and things would only get worse.

Post match Owen says enough is enough, which meant a heel turn for him.

Here's Jim Cornette to introduce the next match, which is going to be....interesting.

NWA World Tag Team Titles: Rock N Roll Express vs. New Midnight Express

The New Midnight Express (defending here) is comprised of Bombastic Bob (Bob Holly) and Bodacious Bart (Bart Gunn). The original version was managed by Cornette and feuded with the Rock N Roll Express for most of the 80s in a feud that revolutionized tag team wrestling. The Rock N Roll Express comes out to the Rockers' (a WWF tag team) music. Bob and Robert Gibson start things off with Gibson shoulder blocking Bob out to the floor.

Back in and the formerly very fast Rock N Roll Express are just kind of quick here with their signature double leg snap into a rolling double punch to the Midnight on the apron. The fans just do not care here and it's rather sad to see. Ricky Morton comes in and works on Bob before sending him into Bart, starting an argument between the champions. Bart comes in and puts on an abdominal stretch as they attempt to replicate the original feud but it's just not working at all.

Cornette gets in an argument with the referee and comes into the ring for a boxing match which is an old signature spot of the feud. The referee is ready to go and Cornette runs away to wake up the crowd a bit. Cornette drops back to the floor and trips Morton, allowing Bart to hit a knee to the back, sending Ricky to the floor. The Midnights double team Ricky for two and Bart's powerslam gets the same.

Bob misses a top rope legdrop though and it's off to Gibson with no one reacting at all. Everything breaks down with the Rock N Roll in control and hitting their double dropkick on Bart. Gibson has to avoid a Cornette elbow drop but the distraction lets Bart bulldog Gibson down for the pin to retain at 7:12.

Rating: F. This match wasn't so much bad as it was pitiful. This was a tag team trying to get back to its old level of glory and just not being able to do it anymore. The match wasn't horrid, but the idea of the match just didn't work at all. The NWA angle never worked and had to have been a way to humiliate Cornette instead of help the company at all.

Luna says she'll win the evening gown match.

Sable vs. Luna Vachon

This is the first evening gown match, meaning they start in gowns and the first to be stripped to their underwear loses. They walk around very slowly with both girls losing a sleeve each. Luna, an actual wrestler, drives in some shoulders in the corner before ripping off Sable's skirt. Lawler is thrilled and Sable charges at Luna to take over. Mero comes out to yell at Sable, allowing Luna to strip the rest of Sable's dress off for the win at 2:50. There wasn't enough to rate here but this wasn't wrestling anyway.

Post match, Sable powerbombs Luna and rips off most of her dress anyway. They head under the ring and Sable comes out with Luna's underwear in hand. Goldust covers Luna with a robe to get her out.

Here's Vince, flanked by his Stooges Pat Patterson and Gerald Brisco. Vince addresses the rumors that he's here to screw Steve Austin out of the WWF Championship. However, he's really here because he was born here in North Carolina but stops to listen to the Vince sucks chant. He won't be responsible for the main event tonight and Austin will screw himself.

Tag Team Titles: New Age Outlaws vs. LOD 2000

The Outlaws are defending and LOD 2000 is nothing all that different. It's still Hawk and Animal but with helmets on the way to the ring and Sunny as a manager. Road Dogg says they've brought University of North Carolina basketball coach Dean Smith out of retirement for one night only but it's actually a blowup doll. Billy starts with Animal but is quickly taken down by a shoulder block. Gunn misses a crossbody and gets taken down by another flying tackle.

Road Dogg comes in and has his arm cranked on before it's off to Hawk for an ax handle to the shoulder. A powerslam puts Dogg down and a jumping fist to the face sends him crawling into the corner. Gunn is literally pulled into the ring for a botched slam and a shoulder breaker for two. Animal comes back in for a chinlock as this has been one sided so far. Another powerslam gets another two on Gunn before it's back to Road Dogg. The LOD immediately loads up the Doomsday Device but Gunn comes in with a chop block to break it up.

187

Dogg puts Animal in a spinning toehold and drags the bad leg into the corner so Billy can wrap it around the post a few times. Back in and Dogg puts on a leglock before driving his own knees into Animal's knee. Billy drives a knee in as well before cranking on a leglock of his own.

It's back to Dogg for some punches in the corner and some choking from Billy. Gunn comes in but can't piledrive Animal, getting caught in a leg drag instead. The hot tag brings in Hawk to clean house as everything breaks down. Hawk hits a top rope splash on Dogg but Billy hits him in the back with a tag belt....for two. Dogg hits Gunn in the face with a belt and a German suplex by Hawk gives the LOD the titles back at 12:13.

Rating: D. So basically it was the same match as last time but with the LOD regaining the belts instead of losing again? That doesn't really make me want to see more from the LOD as they're just too far gone in years at this point. It's not as bad as the Rock N Roll Express but it's still not working in the slightest. What else were they expecting?

Or not as the referee says Hawk's shoulders were down and Dogg's were up, meaning the Outlaws keep the belts. The LOD beats up the referee as a result. The replay shows that Dogg never raised his shoulders at all and the referee screwed up.

Here's Jeff Jarrett to sing with Sawyer Brown (a country band). There isn't really anything to say here other than Jeff sings and the band has the real talent. This goes on for the better part of seven minutes until Steve Blackman comes out to break it up. He gets a guitar to the head and the Figure Four for his troubles, though that might be better than feuding with Jarrett.

Lawler gets out some marshmallows and hot dogs to roast during the inferno match.

We recap Undertake vs. Kane which we've pretty much covered already. It's a rematch from Wrestlemania where Undertaker beat Kane, but Paul Bearer wants more revenge. Tonight it's about lighting the other person on fire. Various caskets with various remains of Undertaker's relatives were burned to further the feud as well.

Kane vs. Undertaker

They get in the ring and the flames come up around the ring in a cool visual. They slug it out in the corner and Undertaker actually busts out Old School, giving us the other feature of the match: the flames go WAY higher when anyone lands hard on the mat. Kane gets back up and sends him into the corner before choking away on the ropes. Lawler wants Undertaker's face lit on fire. Undertaker rips at Kane's mask to blind him for a second and fights back up.

Kane powerslams him down, sending the flames higher into the air. Paul throws in a chair which goes upside Undertaker's head to give Kane the first significant advantage. Undertaker pops back up though because that's the kind of guy he is. They slug it out in the middle of the ring with Kane taking over but not being able to put Undertaker in the fire. Kane pounds away in the corner but charges into a boot to the face. A Russian legsweep puts Kane down and a legdrop sends the flames flying up again.

Both guys grab the other by the throat but it's Kane chokeslamming his brother down. Undertaker slips out of a Tombstone and chokeslams Kane down this time. Kane is up in just a few seconds so both guys kick the other in the face at the same time. Undertaker misses his jumping clothesline and Kane goes up, only to have Taker crotch him down onto the top rope. A superplex takes Kane down and sends the flames even higher than they were before.

With little else to do to each other in the ring, Undertaker throws Kane over the top rope and over the flames. Kane tries to walk out so Bearer bullies the guy in charge of the flames into turning them up even higher. Before Kane can get away though, Vader returns to fight Kane back to ringside. Undertaker dives over the top rope to take them both out in a great visual.

To sum up what just happened: a possibly undead 7'0 demonic man just dove over a wall of flames to get his hands on his possibly even more demonic, pyromaniac brother who is trying to light his on fire as well as a man known as the Rocky Mountain Monster. That sounds AWESOME among many other things. Vader leaves and Undertaker caves in his brother's head with a pair of chair shots. That leaves Undertaker alone with Paul Bearer and Paul is chased up to the band set where a drum is wrapped around Bearer's head. Back to ringside and a big boot puts Kane's (covered) arm into the fire for the win at 16:04.

Rating: D+. This is a good example of a match where a bunch of still shots and audio clips of the match would have done much better than the match itself. There were some AMAZING moments in there like the dive over the top and that superplex, but that's not enough to carry a fifteen minute plus match. It's fun, but would be better with just a highlight package.

We recap the main event with Austin becoming WWF Champion and Vince declaring it a public relations nightmare. Cactus Jack wasn't pleased with the fans' universal love for Austin and became corporate Dude Love to fight Austin for Vince. Austin is convinced there's a conspiracy and Vince sitting at ringside for the match ala Montreal isn't helping things.

WWF Title: Steve Austin vs. Dude Love

Austin is defending and Dude jumps him from behind. That's fine with Austin, who comes back with right hands in the corner. An elbow sends Dude to the floor before a Thesz press takes Love down back inside. Austin hits a snapless spinebuster and an elbow drop for two before having to chase Dude up the aisle. They head back to the music stage with Austin slamming Foley down and hiptossing him off the stage and down onto the floor in a big crash.

Back and ringside and a clothesline puts Love down again before they get back in the ring. Love avoids a running hip attack to the ropes and bulldogs Austin down for two. Steve explodes out of the corner with a clothesline but Dude gets in a shot to the ribs to put him down again. Dude puts on a bodyscissors with a choke as Vince and the Stooges come out to watch. Austin fights out of the hold with a bunch of elbows to the face but stops to look at Vince, giving Dude a rollup for two.

Steve wraps both legs around the post and does the same to the arm for good measure. They head back to the floor with Love backdropping out of a piledriver attempt on the concrete. Austin is sent into the barricade so Vince can go laugh at him like the evil monster he is. Steve gets up but Dude saves his boss from probably death. Dude knocks Austin off the apron and Vince tells Austin to be a man and get back in.

Back inside and Dude puts on an abdominal stretch with Vince nearly calling for the bell as fast as he could. They head outside for the fifth or so time with Austin suplexing Dude legs first onto the steps. Now they head into the crowd with Austin in full control but once they're back inside, Dude is able to score with a swinging neckbreaker to put the champion down.

Sweet Shin Music (exactly what it sounds like) is blocked but Dude clotheslines the referee down. The Stunner is countered and Dude gets the Mandible Claw. Austin goes out but there's no referee to call the win. Dude lets go of the hold and gets backdropped out to the floor. Austin and Vince fight over a chair but Dude saves his boss again. The chair is knocked into Love's face but Austin misses Dude and knocks Vince out cold with a chair shot to the head. Back inside and the Stunner puts Dude down for Austin's own three count to end the match at 18:49.

Rating: B+. This is another solid brawl with both guys knowing exactly how to work this style. Vince being out there was a sword of Damocles over Austin's head and the chair shot to him sent the crowd into delirium. Love would be back but this was a solid way to have Austin's first title defense. The pin didn't count of course but it kept Austin looking strong, which is what you needed here.

A long stretcher job by Vince ends the show.

Overall Rating: D+. This is another example of the main event being the only thing worth seeing on the show, but unlike the older shows it's not enough to save things. That's the problem with having a three hour show: you need more than a great twenty minute match to make it work. The main event scene was on fire at this point but everything else was pretty dreadful. However, that would soon change and things would get a lot better in a hurry. Not a good show here, though the main event is worth seeing.

The next In Your House was just a month later so there wasn't a lot of change. The main event was Dude Love vs. Steve Austin II with Vince as the special guest referee, Brisco as guest timekeeper and Patterson as guest ring announcer. We'll get to more details during and after the match, but the rematch is considered some of the finest work of the Attitude Era style and there's a lot of substance to that theory.

The rest of the card was about what you would expect: Vader vs. Kane, Jarrett vs. Blackman, Rock vs. Faarooq and the Nation vs. DX. The last one may sound a bit strange, but it was the best thing that could have happened. DX turned face soon after Unforgiven due to the massive crowd support they were receiving. This launched a feud with the Nation which would run for the entire summer and was really more of a massive backdrop for HHH vs. The Rock, which would catapult both guys to the main event scene.

Over the Edge: In Your House #22

Date: May 31, 1998
Location: Bradley Center, Milwaukee, Wisconsin
Attendance: 9,822
Commentators: Jim Ross, Jerry Lawler

The idea of this show is simple: how can Austin possibly overcome the odds that are being placed in front of him? This is Vince's first major assault on Austin where he's stacked the deck so heavily against the champion that there's no way he could walk out with the title. The match is similar to the one last time, though with the odds even higher against Austin. That's what happened with Undertaker vs. Michaels and the second match was a masterpiece, so hopefully it's the same time time. Let's get to it.

The opening video talks about how Austin must conform to authority and lists off all the people against him tonight. The shots of a military in lock step is a nice touch.

The set is designed like a junkyard with a bunch of broken down cars piled on top of each other.

LOD 2000 vs. Disciples of Apocalypse

It's Skull and 8-Ball accompanied by Chainz here with Sunny and Darren Drozdov (an LOD associate) in the LOD's corner. It's a six man brawl to start until we get down to Animal pounding on 8-Ball, only to be taken down by a swinging neckbreaker. Animal leg drags 8-Ball down and drops a somewhat low headbutt to keep control. It's off to Hawk vs. Skull with the fans completely behind the LOD.

They test the power game here until Skull sends him into the corner and comes out with a side slam for two. Skull's piledriver is no sold, as is Hawk's custom, allowing Hawk to powerslam Skull down. Animal comes back in for a chinlock on Skull before it's quickly back to Hawk with a clothesline for two. The top rope version misses though, allowing Chainz to pull him to the floor for some extra punishment. Drozdov comes in to make the save but it just makes things worse for Hawk as the DOA hits a double big boot for two.

Hawk gets in a quick running clothesline to 8-Ball but it's quickly back to Skull before Hawk can follow up. Skull chokes away for two before losing a slugout in the corner. Hawk tries to make a comeback but runs into a boot in the corner to stop him cold again. Back to 8-Ball for a chinlock as this match is starting to drag. Skull comes back in to kick Hawk in the side of the head for two but misses a middle rope elbow.

Animal FINALLY gets the tag and the fans really don't seem all that impressed. A double clothesline puts the DOA down and everything breaks down. Animal suplexes Skull down but the DOA (identical remember) switch behind the referee's back. Not that it matters though as Drozdov knocks the cheater into Animal's powerslam for the pin at 9:57.

Rating: D+. This wasn't terrible but it dragged a lot and the fans just didn't care. The LOD was too far past their primes here and the big muscleheaded offense wasn't what it used to be. It was a glorified retirement tour at this point but they needed something much different from the DOA to have a decent match here.

Here's Rock for a chat before his Intercontinental Title defense later tonight. Rock isn't pleased with being in Milwaukee because you don't become a blue chipper by sucking down beers and filling your mouth with bratwursts. However, he'd have to be drunk to date one of the women in this town.

Before he can run down the city even more, here's Faarooq to pound Rock down but Rock gets a chair. His shot completely misses Faarooq though and hits the rope, knocking the chair back into Rock's head. Faarooq loads up a piledriver onto the chair but completely misses as well. Rock sells it like his head hit the chair but it looked really bad. Faarooq runs before the Nation can kill him. Rock is taken out on a stretcher with his neck in a brace.

Austin knows no one is going to have his back tonight because Vince scares everyone but him to death. He'll be ready for his fight tonight though.

Jeff Jarrett vs. Steve Blackman

Jarrett is the only person to be able to beat Blackman though it took the help of a guitar to the head. Blackman has his martial arts sticks with him to scare Jarrett off before the bell. There isn't much to Steve other than he knows a lot of martial arts so this could be a rather dull match. Jarrett gets jumped in the aisle but takes over back inside by sending Blackman throat first onto the middle rope. We stop for some posing by Jeff, allowing Blackman to come back with some kicks and a German suplex for two.

Steve ties him up in the Tree of Woe and pulls at Jeff's throat like any honorable martial artist would do. Jarrett's manager/promoter Tennessee Lee (Colonel Robert Parker from WCW) breaks it up before tripping up Blackman, allowing Jarrett to clothesline him down. Blackman is sent into the barricade as we see slightly crazy wrestler Al Snow on Spanish commentary. Back inside and Steve misses a middle rope splash but catches Jarrett in a backslide for two. Snow is taken away by security as Jarrett hits a clothesline and hooks a sleeper.

Blackman's arm only drops twice before he fights out but a double clothesline puts both guys down. Back up and Steve suplexes Jarrett down but a middle rope splash hits knees. A kick to the chest puts Jarrett down and Blackman pounds away with a variety of strikes. Tennessee Lee distracts Blackman but Jeff's running punch misses Blackman. Steve grabs one of his sticks to blast Jarrett behind the referee's back but Jeff gets his foot on the ropes. Blackman goes up top again but Lee hits him in the back with the stick, giving Jarrett the pin at 10:15.

Rating: D. The match was rather boring but what's even worse was Blackman. He's not the worst wrestler ever or anything but man alive he was so boring. It just wasn't worth caring about and felt like a very long ten minute match. Jarrett wasn't working at all in this country music gimmick and it would take awhile to get to something better.

We recap Marc Mero vs. Sable. She's tired of him treating her like dirt so Sable has agreed to find a surrogate to fight Mero. If the surrogate wins, she's out of her contract with Mero but if he wins, she's out of the WWF forever.

Marc Mero vs. ???

JR suggests that Sable has gotten Undertaker to fight, even though she's in her wrestling gear. Sable says she doesn't need a man fighting her battles for her so indeed, it's Mero vs. Sable. Mero says that she really must hate him (JR: "Duh.") if she's willing to risk her safety to get out of her contract. He offers to lay down for her but as Sable covers, Mero rolls him up for a fast pin at 0:18. Mero celebrates like he won the WWF Title as JR is disgusted. Sable's "forever" sabbatical lasted about two weeks and she was even on the poster for next month's PPV.

In the back Sable thanks her fans while holding back tears.

Rock is in a neck brace but has to defend the title against Faarooq or have it stripped.

Kaientai vs. Taka Michinoku/Justin Bradshaw

Kaientai is a three man team (Dick Togo, Sho Funaki and Mens Teioh) who has been attacking Taka for reasons not quite clear. Bradshaw has befriended the much smaller Taka and is backing him up tonight. The good guys (the two) jump Kaientai to start, sending them out to the floor. Bradshaw launches Taka over the top to take them all out until we get down to Taka vs. Funaki. A clothesline puts Taka down but it's quickly off to Bradshaw, sending Funaki running to the floor for a conference.

Bradshaw gets tired of waiting and chases everyone around until we get down to Taka vs. Togo. Taka hits a tornado DDT for two but everyone else come in, leading to Bradshaw and Michinoku cleaning house again. Back in and Togo gets a sitout wheelbarrow slam to take over ad it's off to Teioh. A big boot to the face and a release butterfly suplex gets two on Taka and a cannonball attack off the top puts Taka down again.

We hit the chinlock on Michinoku before a powerslam gets two more. Togo comes in off the top with something resembling a Swanton Bomb before it's back to Funaki for a sleeper. Kaientai starts cheating again with Teioh distracting the referee so Funaki can put on a camel clutch and Togo can hit a quick dropkick to Taka's face.

Michinoku finally avoids a charge and makes the hot tag to Bradshaw with the big man cleaning house. Togo hits him low though and Kaientai literally uses Bradshaw as a pedestal to pose. Bradshaw throws them all off and cleans house again but Taka's Michinoku Driver only gets two on Togo. Teioh and Bradshaw head to the floor, allowing Togo to hit a top rope senton backsplash for the pin on Taka at 9:52.

Rating: C. This is one of those matches that was better than the crowd reaction would suggest. The fans didn't quite get this style yet and in an old school town like Milwaukee, the reaction really isn't surprising. Bradshaw wasn't much of a factor here but Kaientai bouncing off of him was fun stuff.

Sable, still in ring gear, leaves the arena in shame.

Intercontinental Title: Faarooq vs. The Rock

Rock is in a neck brace and defending. He doesn't come out despite Finkel introducing him three times in a row. Instead we get Commissioner Slaughter who says if Rock doesn't get out here right now, the title is awarded to Faarooq. Rock finally comes out and gets jumped on the way as the bell rings. Faarooq rips off the neck brace and blasts Rock in the face with it for two before clotheslining Rock down a few times. Rock bails to the floor a bit but gets in a cheap shot when Faarooq comes after him.

A back elbow to the jaw puts Faarooq down and the more and more popular People's Elbow (still not named) gets two. Faarooq comes back with a slam and a falling headbutt for two of his own. Rock grabs a quick DDT for a pair of near falls and the frustration is setting in. We get an awkward looking sequence with Faarooq hitting a bad spinebuster and looking like he's not sure if he should cover Rock or not. He finally does and gets the three but the foot was on the rope. The referee says we keep going, allowing Rock to trip Faarooq into a rollup for the pin at 5:07 with his feet on the ropes.

Rating: D+. The match wasn't terrible but the ending really messed things up. I'm assuming Faarooq didn't have Rock in the right position to get his feet on the ropes but it really stood out as a bad looking moment. The match was short though and the neck injury didn't mean anything at all for the most part.

Faarooq piledrives Rock two more times post match until the Nation (including Owen Hart, who joined the Nation in a bizarre choice) makes the save. DX comes out to clear the ring as the Nation drags Rock away.

Kane vs. Vader

The loser has to unmask, even though Vader's mask is smaller than the Lone Ranger's and he's taken it off before. This is Vader's revenge match after the wrench attack at No Way Out. They slug it out to start with Kane pounding him into the corner and punching him down with ease. A clothesline puts Vader down but he comes back with a pair of running body attacks to put Kane down for a few seconds. Kane counters a suplex into one of his own but misses an elbow drop. Basic stuff so far.

Another clothesline puts Vader down again and a nice slam does the same. Kane hits his top rope clothesline for no cover before a big boot drops Vader again. Back up and they start slugging at each other with Kane taking over again. We hit a chinlock as the crowd is somehow getting even more bored than they already were. There's the chokeslam to send Vader to the floor where he finds a very fake looking wrench for some shots to Kane's back. They head inside again but the Vadersault misses, allowing Kane to hit the Tombstone for the pin at 7:20.

Rating: D-. This was a glorified squash and the ending was never in doubt at all. Vader's only real advantage came from a wrench shot and Kane was only in trouble for about thirty seconds. It's never a good sign when the best part of a match is how short it was but that's about all I've got here. Kane would get better but it would take time.

Post match Kane takes off Vader's mask to reveal a face we've seen many times before. Bearer gets the mask and puts it on to rub salt in the wounds.

Vader starts to leave and declares himself "just a big piece of s***." He even teases retirement, which isn't a good sign.

We get another mini legends ceremony with Maurice "Mad Dog" Vachon and The Crusher, with the latter known as the Man Who Made Milwaukee Famous. Both guys get plaques with Vachon thanking his wife and niece Luna. He thanks Vince too but isn't crazy about everything he's done lately. Lawler keeps shouting boring and eventually gets in the ring to ask these guys who they think they are. He makes fun of both legends and tries to steal Vachon's leg, only to get punched out by Crusher. Lawler bails to the floor, goes back in, and gets punched out again. I have no issues with any of this.

D-Generation X vs. Nation of Domination

It's HHH/New Age Outlaws vs. Kama Mustafa/D'Lo Brown/Owen Hart here. Chyna, X-Pac and Mark Henry are the seconds/thirds for the respective teams. The fans start an Owen sucks chant before we get D'Lo vs. Dogg to start. They trade hammerlocks to start until Brown runs him over with some shoulder blocks. Dogg comes back with a hiptoss and sits on Brown's chest to block a sunset flip.

It's off to Billy vs. Owen with the latter being clotheslined down almost immediately. A gorilla press puts Owen down again and it's off to HHH for the jumping knee to the face. HHH gets two off a tilt-a-whirl backbreaker and it's back to Dogg for some hard kicks to the ribs. Owen gets sent into the corner by HHH but comes out with a low blow, allowing for the tag off to Kama. A facebuster puts Mustafa down again so it's back to Billy. Kama pounds away on Gunn and takes him into the Nation corner for a triple teaming.

Billy fights out of the corner pretty quickly and tags off to Dogg for a front facelock on Brown. DX keeps tagging quickly by bringing in Billy for a delayed suplex before it's back to HHH to keep firing off right hands. Dogg comes in again but gives up the tag to Owen who kicks Road Dogg's head off. Back to Kama for another kick to the face as the Nation takes over. Owen piledrives Dogg for two before it's back to D'Lo who gets two off a rollup.

Brown scores with his lifting powerbomb (eventually named the Sky High) for two before it's back to Owen (sans tag) for the enziguri. Kama comes in again with a chinlock to kill some time before Brown comes in with a moonsault for two. A middle rope backsplash doesn't work as well though and it's hot tag to Gunn, though the fans still don't react for it. Everything breaks down and Billy hits the yet to be named Fameasser on Brown. Billy and HHH hit a spike piledriver to send Brown's head into a title belt but Owen breaks up the pin and Pedigrees HHH onto the belt to give D'Lo a pin at 18:33

Rating: C+. This was longer than it was good but it's certainly not bad. These guys would feud for most of the year though and it would launch the leaders into the stratosphere by the end of the feud. It wasn't a great match or anything but it had the time to develop which is more than can be said for a lot of matches tonight.

We recap the main event with clips of the match at Unforgiven and Vince stacking the deck against Austin. There was also a sequence where Austin got Vince arrested for assault and humiliated him into an apology. Vince then said that he's not afraid of anyone that might try to keep things straight at the show, which brought out Undertaker to choke Vince down.

Vince says if Austin attacks him at any point during the match, he's stripped of the title and Dude is champion. Also, the fall has to come at Vince's hand and his hand only. Remember that.

WWF Title: Steve Austin vs. Mankind

Austin is defending, Vince is guest referee, Patterson is ring announcer and Brisco is timekeeper. Fink gives Patterson a LONG intro, including a mention of Patterson's tournament victory to become the first Intercontinental Champion (JR: "Wink wink." For those of you unfamiliar, the tournament is the worst kept secret in wrestling history as there is zero evidence that it ever existed. It's since become a running joke in wrestling with WWE even getting in on it at times.).

Brisco gets a similar introduction and takes time to point out the Brisco Brothers Body Shop sign painted on one of the cars, which gets a full ad from Patterson, complete with address and phone number. Vince gets a speech fitting of a president as this is hilarious stuff. Love is called "the cat that makes the kittens purr." Patterson refuses to introduce a bum like the champion. Vince tells Austin to hand him the belt but Undertaker comes out to keep watch on everything. The entrances are literally over twelve minutes long.

They fight into the corner to start and Vince breaks it up, earning a double bird from Austin. Love shoulder blocks him down for a fast two count and Undertaker gets up onto the steps. The place is LOUDLY chanting for Austin here. Austin grabs a headlock as a loud Vince is dead chant starts up. Steve punches Dude's false teeth out and throws them into the crowd for one heck of a souvenir.

The Thesz press puts Love down again and a clothesline puts Dude on the floor. Austin is whipped into the steps and Vince declares there are no countouts. We head back inside for a Russian legsweep for two on Austin. A knee to Austin's back gives Dude a target and a running knee in the corner gets two. Austin comes back with a swinging neckbreaker and three clotheslines in a row before stomping a mudhole in the corner. Love counters a whip into the corner and grabs the Mandible Claw but gets his head tied in the ropes

They head outside again with Love throwing Austin over the announcers' table. Patterson reminds us that this is No DQ as the rule changes continue. They fight into the crowd with Austin clotheslining Love over the barricade. JR is in his element here, shouting about how Love is nearly dead. Austin misses a charge into the ropes and crotches himself, allowing Love to baseball slide him to the floor. A bad looking swinging neckbreaker on the concrete is enough for Patterson to remind us that this is also falls count anywhere. JR: "SINCE WHEN???"

Austin comes back with some hard right hands but charges into a backdrop, sending him through the windshield of one of the cars. That only gets two for Love as the fans are WAY into this. Now it's Love charging into a hot shot onto the roof of a Gremlin for two as Undertaker keeps watch. Austin takes Love on top of a car but his Stunner is countered with Austin being shoved onto the hood of a Mercury. Love sunset flips him off the roof of a car for two in a cool visual.

Dude picks up what appears to be a tail pipe but Austin elbows him in the ribs to break it up. Austin is BADLY busted open and gets backdropped on the concrete for another near fall. Love's elbow drop off a car misses and Austin gets a two count. They head back to the ring where Patterson trips Austin, allowing Love to pound away more right hands. A buckle pad is pulled off but Love hits a running knee to Austin in the corner.

Austin is sent face first into the exposed buckle but Love puts on a reverse chinlock instead of covering. Austin fights up again and the fans are right there with him but Love sends him into the buckle again for two. Patterson hands Dude a chair and a double arm DDT onto the chair gets two. Love charges at Austin with the chair but gets it kicked into his face. Now it's a ticked off Austin with the chair and he caves in Love's head but Vince refuses to count. Austin yells at Vince so Love gets the chair but hits Vince by mistake.

The Stunner puts Love down and another referee comes in for the count but Patterson punches him out. Love gets the Mandible Claw and Patterson tries to call for the bell but Undertaker chokeslams him through a table. Brisco tries to count a pin but gets a chokeslam as well.

Undertaker is awesome when he just starts breaking stuff, usually people. Austin counters the Mandible Claw into the Stunner but there's no referee. It's time to get smart though so he grabs Vince's hand and raises it three times for a count, giving Austin the pin in the only way Vince would count to retain the title at 22:27. The crowd goes NUTS on the pin, as they should have after that kind of a performance.

Rating: A+. There might not be a better match that sums up the Attitude Era in one match. This was a FIGHT with Austin and Love just beating the tar out of each other for over twenty minutes. The ending is nothing short of brilliant with everything being timed perfectly. The idea was used by writer Vince Russo over and over again but it was never anything close to this. Even without the Vince stuff it's still a great fight and both guys looked awesome out there. The crowd reaction puts it over the top as well.

Overall Rating: C-. The fact that the main event runs nearly 45 minutes counting intros and recap video helps this show out a lot. Other than that though, there's nothing worth seeing here at all. The midcard is getting better but it's still miles away from what it needed to be. Austin vs. Vince was just getting going though and would be a highlight for years to come. Undertaker being added to the mix was a good idea as Love is defeated and we now have someone new for Austin to focus on. Outstanding main event, lame everything else.

Following the two match series with Dude Love, Austin needed a new challenger. Vince decided that he needed a new monster to challenge Austin, so he put the two biggest monsters in a match for the title shot. On June 1, Kane defeated Undertaker to earn the title shot at King of the Ring. Mankind returned that night after Dude Love had been fired earlier in the show and cost Undertaker the match. As we've learned over the course of this series, ticking off Undertaker is the worst thing you can do.

The match at King of the Ring was inside the Hell in a Cell, but the levels of violence far exceeded those from Badd Blood. In one of the most famous matches in company history, Undertaker threw Mankind off the Cell and through the announcers' table as well as chokeslamming him through the top of the Cell. The match shortened Mick Foley's career by years but reestablished Undertaker the resident monster of the WWF.

The other main event on the show was Austin defending the title against Kane in a first blood match, which stacked the deck against the champion even more since Kane had very little visible skin. With an unintended assist from Undertaker, Kane won the match and the title in a shocking upset. Not that it mattered though as Austin pinned Kane in a rematch the next night on Raw to get the title back.

Soon after this, Undertaker was named #1 contender for Summerslam, setting up arguably the biggest match of the year. However, around this time Austin began to believe that there was a massive conspiracy with Undertaker, Kane, Mankind and Paul Bearer in league with Vince to take him down. There was no hard evidence of this, but Austin never was the most trusting guy in the world.

In a commonly used booking decision, the main event for Fully Loaded was a combination of the two main feuds from King of the Ring: Steve Austin teaming with Undertaker to face Mankind and Kane. Mankind and Kane also won the Tag Team Titles on Raw, making the match a Tag Team Title match, just to sweeten the deal a bit.

Fully Loaded: In Your House #23
Date: July 26, 1998
Location: Selland Arena, Fresno, California
Attendance: 9,855
Commentators: Jim Ross, Jerry Lawler

In addition to the main event match, the other top match was

HHH vs. the Rock in a 2/3 falls match for the Rock's Intercontinental Title. The Nation vs. DX feud had refocused into a feud between the two leaders which was the best move for everyone involved. Other than that there isn't much of note to see so let's get to it.

We open in the back with Jerry Lawler trying to find out what Sable is wearing in her bikini contest against Marc Mero's new valet Jacqueline. She goes behind a privacy screen and lets Jerry see, sending him into euphoria.

The opening video focuses on the conspiracy theory which might be against Austin while bringing up the possibility of Austin and Undertaker teaming up to go after Vince.

Val Venis vs. Jeff Jarrett

Venis is a newcomer and an adult film star who is trying his hand at wrestling. Jarrett now has Southern Justice (the Godwinns, now known as Mark Canterbury (Henry) and Dennis Knight (Phineas), their real names) in his corner along with Tennessee Lee but the referee sends them to the back. Before they're gone though, here's Kaientai who has been feuding with Val due to Val sleeping with the wife of Kaientai's manager Mr. Yamaguchi-San (on commentary. Kaientai is sent to the back.

Val takes Jeff down with ease and gyrates his hips a lot before elbowing Jarrett in the face. A hot shot gets two for Val and a Russian legsweep puts Jarrett down. Val ducks his head and gets caught by a powerbomb while Yamaguchi-San gets mad at Lawler for jokes about his wife. Jarrett sends him to the floor for a baseball slide before coming back inside for a chop off. Jeff takes over again and puts on a sleeper as this is still a very basic match. Val counters into a sleeper of his own but Jarrett suplexes out of the hold.

It's Venis up first with a fisherman's suplex for two before Jeff goes up top for a crossbody, getting the same result. Another suplex puts Jeff down again but he breaks up the Money Shot (Val's top rope splash). The referee goes down, allowing Tennessee to crotch Venis on the top. A superplex puts Val down again but he counters the figure four into a small package for two. Tennessee gets on the apron but Val rams Jeff into him for a rollup and a pin at 7:45.

Rating: C. This could have been on any given episode of Raw but that doesn't mean it was bad. Venis was always a good hand in the ring and could have good matches with just about anyone. The fact that Jarrett was one of the other great hands in the company almost ensured that this was going to be solid. That doesn't mean it was interesting though, as the match was mainly about Yamaguchi-San's commentary.

We see the Hart House, where there's a Dungeon Match later between Owen Hart and Ken Shamrock (the King of the Ring winner). The Dungeon is the name of Stu Hart's (Bret and Owen's father) basement where he's trained dozens of wrestlers over the years.

D'Lo Brown vs. X-Pac

Brown is the new European Champion, having stolen the title from HHH recently on Raw, but this is non-title. He also has Kama Mustafa with him, though Kama is now known as the Godfather of the Nation. Brown also has a chest protector due to a very long running "injury" at the hands of new guy Dan Severn. Feeling out process to start with Brown grabbing a headlock but being countered into a wristlock.

A hiptoss puts Brown down again and X-Pac fires off some right hands. Brown's leg lariat gets two but X-Pac comes back with a spinwheel kick of his own to get a breather. D'Lo avoids a charge into the corner and gets two as control changes again. X-Pac gets caught in a chinlock as the fans chant for Chyna. A legdrop gets two for Brown and they slug it out in the corner until X-Pac kicks him down again.

Brown whips him hard into the corner and drops a middle rope elbow for two. Back to the chinlock for a bit before a hard clothesline puts X-Pac down again. Brown misses a moonsault though and X-Pac starts fighting back with another kick and the Bronco Buster in the corner. Godfather gets up on the apron for a distraction though, allowing Brown to hit the Sky High for the pin at 8:26.

Rating: D. This didn't work for me for the most part. These teams feuded for so long that we would see almost every possible combination between them over the summer. Most of the matches worked and this wasn't horrible, but it didn't have anything of interest to it at all and just came and went.

A newcomer named Edge is watching from the crowd.

Undertaker isn't here yet and Austin might have to go it alone.

Faarooq/Scorpio vs. Terry Funk/Justin Bradshaw

There's nothing to this one either as they're just two thrown together team having a match. Before the match, Funk says this is his last match in the WWF for awhile, ticking off his partner. Bradshaw starts with Scorpio and gets caught with a quick dropkick and clothesline to limited effect. A hurricanrana takes him down though and Scorpio pounds away with some quick right hands to the head.

Faarooq comes in and gets caught by a hard clothesline in the corner followed by a top rope shoulder block to give Bradshaw two. It's off to Terry who pounds away with left hands and a neckbreaker for two. Bradshaw gets the tag and tries to come off the top, only to dive into a powerslam for two. Back to Scorpio for some kicks in the corner but Funk breaks up whatever Scorpio was loading up off the top. Bradshaw comes in again for a powerslam but Funk gets another tag and takes it to the floor.

Terry can't hit his springboard moonsault but pounds Scorpio down and takes it back into the ring. A rollup gets two for Funk but Faarooq blasts him in the face to put change momentum again. Scorpio hits his Tumbleweed for two and a middle rope legdrop gets the same. Everything breaks down and the fans aren't thrilled to say the least. The power guys go to the floor and Scorpio ends Funk with a 450 splash at 6:49.

Rating: D+. The match wasn't bad with Scorpio's high spots helping things a lot but there's only so much you can do when the match is there for the post match stuff and little more. This is what happens when the Tag Team Titles are tied up in the main event scene and there's little to do until those guys are done with the belts and they can go back to the Outlaws.

Post match Bradshaw beats up Funk, leaving Faarooq and Scorpio to make a failed save attempt.

Lawler is still freaking out over the sneak peak of Sable.

Mark Henry vs. Vader

This is part of Vader's attempted career turnaround and a rematch from Vader losing on Raw. They ram into each other to start with no one moving at all. Henry easily slams Vader down and drops an elbow, sending Vader to the floor. Back in and an ax handle to the back puts Vader down for two but Vader sits on Henry's chest for the same.

A splash gets two more for Vader and he pounds away in the corner. They head to the floor with Henry going into the step, followed by a middle rope splash from Vader back inside. That's about it though as Henry catches a charging Vader in a falling powerslam and a big splash gets the pin at 5:03.

Rating: D. Another lame match here but at least it was short. Having two monsters pound on each other is a tradition in wrestling, though that doesn't mean it's the most interesting thing in the world. Henry still wasn't anything to see and Vader's time in the company was measured in days at this point.

Undertaker still isn't here but Kane and Mankind are in the arena. Paul Bearer says it's clear that Undertaker is hiding from Kane so he'll be in one piece at Summerslam. Here are the Outlaws to interfere and get rid of Kane's annoying red lights. Road Dogg says that if Kane and Mankind are so sure they'll keep the titles, they'll be ok with defending against the Outlaws tomorrow night. A brawl breaks out before there's a chance to answer but referees break it up.

We look back at Raw where Hawk didn't show up for a tag match and the DOA jumped Animal. These teams were feuding after LOD's longtime manager Paul Ellering had turned on them to join the DOA.

LOD 2000 vs. Disciples of Apocalypse

The idea here is that Hawk is having "personal problems" which means he's having bad drug addiction issues. Animal (in the shorts again) starts with Skull but 8-Ball quickly pulls him into the corner for a double team. Both Disciples drop elbows on

Animal but it's quickly off to Hawk who takes it to the floor. Skull takes a beating against the barricade before it's back to Animal with the LOD hitting a Hart Attack of all things for a pair of two counts. Hawk hits his neckbreaker and brings in Animal again as Skull stays in trouble.

Skull finally low bridges Hawk to the floor where 8-Ball and Ellering can double team him. Ellering chokes away and gets in some stomps of his own, showing more aggression than he has in years. Back inside and 8-Ball hooks a chinlock before clotheslining Hawk into the DOA corner.

Ellering gets in even more shots and we hit the chinlock again to kill a bit more time. A backbreaker gets two for 8-Ball but Hawk comes back with a double clothesline to put both guys down. The hot tag brings in Animal to clean house and the Doomsday Device lays out Skull, only to have Ellering distract the referee. DOA switches, allowing 8-Ball to DDT Animal for the pin at 8:50.

Rating: D. Egads these matches are getting harder and harder to sit through. This was similar to the Vader vs. Henry match with the similar styles being very hard to work around given the LOD's advanced age. Ellering is a character that was also hard to use in the WWF as he barely worked there other than a few months in 1992, meaning the fans weren't as invested in him. Another boring match though.

Vince and company come out as everyone is leaving. Vince talks about Austin accidentally hitting Undertaker with a chair on Raw and how many times Austin has provoked Undertaker over the last few weeks. That was all Austin and Vince had nothing to do with it, so blame Austin if Undertaker doesn't show up tonight.

Vince reads from tonight's official program, which mentions replacements being used in the event of talent not being at the show. The promoter, meaning Vince, gets to make that selection and Undertaker's suitable replacement would be......The Brooklyn Brawler, who might have won five matches in his 15 year career.

Ken Shamrock vs. Owen Hart

This is a submission match in Stu Hart's basement, more commonly known as the Dungeon. There isn't much of a backstory here other than they've both won King of the Ring and

Owen challenged Shamrock to a fight. Dan Severn, former UFC Champion and rival of Shamrock (though he doesn't like Owen either) is referee. Shamrock's entrance is through a door from what looks like the kitchen, giving this a very low rent feel but in a good way.

Owen takes him down to start but Shamrock reverses and pounds away with right hands. Shamrock throws him around and slams Owen against the wall, only to be kicked low and then in the face. Owen rams him head first into the wooden wall before suplexing him down. Ken reverses and slams Owen's head into the wall but Hart grabs a water pipe to pull himself up for a hurricanrana. Owen swings a dumbbell at Ken's head but gets kicked back into the corner. Ken Irish whips him into the wall and tries the same hurricanrana using the water pipe but Owen powerbombs him down.

In a spot you don't see that often, Owen lifts him and rams Shamrock's head through the ceiling to set up the Sharpshooter. Ken rolls through but can't hook the ankle lock. Instead he fires off a kick which accidentally takes out Severn, allowing Owen to hit Shamrock with a dumbbell to knock him cold. Owen puts on a kind of armbar and slaps Shamrock's hand on the mat for a submission with Severn waking up in time to see it, giving Hart the win at 4:46.

Rating: C+. This was different to put it best and in this case it worked. The match was kind of a hybrid between MMA and a stiff wrestling match and it came off pretty well. MMA hadn't hit the mainstream yet so this wasn't something most people had seen before. It was very clear that this was pre-taped and edited due to the people being in slightly different places after some camera cuts but that's not the worst thing in the world.

Owen celebrates and walks up the stairs like he's probably done a thousand times. That's cool in a unique way.

Intercontinental Title: HHH vs. The Rock

Rock is defending and this is 2/3 falls. All the people on the outside other than Chyna are sent to the back before we get going. JR makes sure to tell us that there is a thirty minute time limit which will likely come into play at the end. Also the third fall has to be decided by pin or submission. Rock punches HHH up against the ropes to start before a clothesline gets two. The fans think Rocky Sucks but he's still in full control early on.

The champ takes too much time yelling at Chyna though, allowing HHH to clothesline him out of the corner. Chyna gets in a cheap shot in retaliation but Rock backdrops out of the Pedigree. HHH throws him to the floor and they fight up the aisle with HHH getting the better of it. Back to ringside with Rock dropping him throat first over the barricade to take over before sending HHH into the steps. They get back inside where Rock clotheslines HHH down again and stomps him in the corner.

HHH explodes out of the corner with a knee to the face and a knee drop to the head for a two count. They trade chops in the corner until Rock whips him over the corner and back outside. A snap suplex puts HHH down again and Rock heads inside for a breather. The referee keeps him inside, allowing Mark Henry to sneak down and splash HHH on the floor. Billy Gunn chases him off and Chyna tries to tell the referee what happened, but the distraction lets Rock hit HHH in the head with the belt for a very near fall.

A swinging neckbreaker gives Rock the same near fall and we hit the chinlock. Rock stomps HHH to the floor again and we're about fifteen minutes into the thirty minute time limit. Back in and Rock can't quite hit the floatover DDT but the regular version is good for another two count. We continue the chinlockery by Rock as JR tells Jerry to just go to the back since he's a lot more interested in the bikini contest. Back up and Helmsley shoves Rock down to send the back of his head into the mat.

HHH's jumping knee to the face puts Rock down again but the followup takes awhile. Rock comes back by throwing HHH into a hot shot as Godfather comes back out. The Outlaws cut him off immediately but Rock is stomping HHH in the corner. The referee gets in an argument with the referee, allowing D'Lo Brown to sneak in for a cheap shot. HHH is ready for him and knocks Brown to the floor, only to walk into the Rock Bottom for the pin and the first fall.

After a one minute rest period between falls, Rock clotheslines HHH down and we head to the floor. HHH gets whipped into the barricade but comes right back with a clothesline of his own to put Rock down. Rock comes back with a catapult onto the

Spanish announcers' table but HHH just bounces off of it in a painful looking spot. Back in and the People's Elbow finally has a name but only gets a two count. Brown tries to interfere again but Chyna lays him out. The distraction lets X-Pac sneak in with the X Factor on Rock, giving HHH a VERY close two.

Another Chyna distraction lets HHH bring in a chair but Rock kicks it out of his hands. It's Rock swinging the chair instead but he hits the referee, allowing Chyna to hit Rock low and DDT him on the chair. The referee wakes up just in time to see HHH get the second fall, tying us up and sending us into another rest period.

HHH immediately covers again but Rock kicks out and rolls to the floor. We've only got two minutes left in the time limit so things start picking up again. A second referee comes out as HHH clotheslines Rock down on the floor. Back in and HHH hits the facebuster and a clothesline for two with a minute left. Rock comes back with a Samoan drop for a close two. Back up again and HHH hits the Pedigree as time expires to end the match in a draw.

Rating: C-. The match wasn't terrible but the amount of interference and the worthless ending doesn't work that well. The constant filler like the rest periods and chinlocks became obvious quickly and made the match drag on longer than it should have. Also they were getting repetitive with stuff like the clotheslines. The match isn't a disaster but it felt like a big waste of time.

DX and the Nation come out to brawl with DX clearing the ring.

Undertaker has arrived, ending any drama about the Brooklyn Brawler.

We recap Sable vs. Jacqueline. This is a simple story: Sable left Mero who replaced Sable with Jackie. The girls called each other some rather catty names, leading to a bikini contest to see who looks better.

Before the contest, Dustin Runnels (Goldust), who is now a Christian preacher character, leads the audience in a prayer for forgiveness for what they're about to look at. Lawler, the emcee, basically throws Dustin out. Jackie comes out in a robe and

Sable in a t-shirt before disrobing. Jackie goes first and is in a very small red one piece, which is basically V-shaped and wraps around her chest. Sable on the other hand has on a thong and a half shirt, but the half shirt comes off to reveal only paint in the shapes of hand prints. Lawler loses his mind and declares her the winner. Vince comes out and puts a coat around Sable.

We recap the main event, which centers around one idea: can Austin trust anyone, or is he in a three on one handicap match? Undertaker cost Austin the title by mistake at King of the Ring so Austin stunned Undertaker after winning the title back the next night. Undertaker went on a path of destruction and beat up everyone in sight until Vince made the tag match for tonight to let them blow off some steam. Things got even more complicated just before the PPV as Undertaker swung a chair and hit Kane, but he might have been aiming for Austin. Austin hit everyone with a chair because that's just how he is.

Tag Team Titles: Undertaker/Steve Austin vs. Mankind/Kane

Mankind and Kane are defending. Undertaker stares Austin down in the aisle but the champions jump them from behind to get us going. They finally get inside with Austin flipping off Undertaker and pounding away on Mankind to start. A thumb to the eye breaks up Mankind's wristlock but Mankind rams Austin into the buckle and makes the tag out to Kane. The Thesz press puts Kane down but Kane bails to the floor to avoid a Stunner.

The fight goes back outside where Austin rams the champions' heads together. Back in and it's off to Undertaker to crank on his brother's arm. Undertaker gets two off a Russian legsweep and flips Austin off which makes Austin laugh. Back to Mankind who gets an elbow up to stop a charging Undertaker in the corner to take over. Undertaker pounds away in the corner but it's quickly back to Kane to slug his brother down. A running clothesline in the corner staggers Undertaker and it's back to Mankind to pound away with right hands in the corner.

Mankind gets two off a double arm DDT and a Cactus Clothesline takes the two of them out to the floor. Kane clotheslines Undertaker down as well but Austin knocks Mankind off the apron and onto the announcers' table which still doesn't break. Back in and Undertaker hits a nice running DDT to take Mankind down. Kane knocks Undertaker into the corner for the tag off to Austin and house is quickly cleaned. Everything breaks down with Mankind sending in a chair but Austin cracks Kane in the head with it for two.

Kane comes back with a big boot to the face and sends Austin over the top to the floor. After some choking with a boot it's back inside so Mankind can rip away at Austin's face. Back to Kane who whips Austin hard into the corner before dropping an elbow to the chest. Mankind comes in again for a long chinlock before Austin fights up, only to have a double clothesline put both guys down.

Kane gets the tag first but Austin escapes the Tombstone and Stuns him. Mankind comes in and gets the same but Austin is too spent to tag. Undertaker finally puts his hand out for the tag and comes in to clean house again. A pair of chokeslams put the champions down and a Tombstone to Kane is enough for the pin and the titles at 18:08.

Rating: C+. The match was ok and the ending could have gone either way which is a good thing. Unfortunately the problem here is the Tag Team Titles are clearly just there to advance the Austin vs. Undertaker feud to Summerslam. Things would however get more interesting as the lines would become more and more blurred, and that's when things got better.

Undertaker leaves with both belts to end the show.

Overall Rating: D. This show was billed as a warmup show to Summerslam and that's exactly what it was. There's no real reason to care about a lot of this stuff since it would either change or be erased in just a few weeks. On top of that, the best match is just slightly above average and most of them could have been on any given episode of Monday Night Raw. This is a show that didn't need to exist and could have been done over a few weeks on TV instead.

The following show was one of if not the biggest show of the year: Summerslam 1998 from Madison Square Garden in New York City. The main event saw Undertaker challenging Austin for the WWF Title with the question being whether or not Undertaker was in league with Vince McMahon. During the main event, Kane attempted to come to Undertaker's aid but Undertaker sent him to the back, saying he wanted to beat Austin on his own. This wound up being a bad move, as Austin beat Undertaker with the Stunner to retain the title.

This was all Vince could take so he played the last card he had against Austin: a triple threat match with Undertaker and Kane both challenging Austin for the title. The match was officially not a handicap match but Undertaker and Kane weren't allowed to pin each other. At this point, there was almost no way Austin could keep the belt, which is something we'll get into later.

Other than Austin vs. Undertaker, the big match at Summerslam was HHH challenging Rock for the Intercontinental Title in a ladder match to blow off the Nation vs. DX feud (for the most part). HHH won the title despite destroying his knee in the process. This was the match that made both guys and sent them up to the next level in the WWF after being big deals already. With HHH on the shelf, Rock would be entered into a triple threat cage match against Mankind and Ken Shamrock for a shot at the WWF Title at some point in the future.

Breakdown: In Your House #24
Date: September 27, 1998
Location: Copps Coliseum, Hamilton, Ontario, Canada
Attendance: 17,405
Commentators: Jim Ross, Jerry Lawler

This is an interesting time for the company as they're just off the big event in Summerslam and things need to start pointing towards Wrestlemania, but it's hard to see what we'll get there. Austin vs. McMahon is clearly the top story in the company, but at the end of the day Vince is an executive rather than a wrestler. It's going to be interesting to see how they work around that. Let's get to it.

The opening video talks about Vince's master plan to get the title off of Austin. By this point Vince had given up any pretense that he was being fair and was full fledged evil.

Owen Hart vs. Edge

Edge had debuted a few months earlier and this is his PPV singles debut (he was in a mixed tag with Sable at Summerslam). Owen wears a Toronto Argonauts jersey to the ring to try to get the fans to hate him. Hart grabs a top wristlock to start but Edge grabs the ropes and flips backwards to escape. A suplex puts Edge to the mat and Owen stays on the arm. Back up and Edge rolls out of a monkey flip and dropkicks Owen down before putting on an armbar of his own.

Edge takes Owen down with a hurricanrana to send Hart outside, allowing Edge to baseball slide him down. Owen catches Edge diving off the apron in a powerslam before hitting a missile dropkick back inside for two. A backbreaker and neckbreaker combing for two for Owen and a belly to belly suplex gets the same. We hit the chinlock for a bit until Edge fights up, only to get caught in a victory roll out of the corner for two.

Owen chops him into the corner and fires off some shoulders into the ribs, only to get caught by a quick crossbody for two. The enziguri puts Edge down but he still catches Owen on the top with a front faceplant. Edge gets two off a flapjack and a DDT but Owen comes back with a German suplex to put Edge down again. Edge gets his feet up to block Hart coming off the middle rope, but Owen tries the Sharpshooter to a BIG pop. He can't get it all the way on, but a fan jumps the railing to stare down Edge. Apparently Edge knows him because he stops cold, allowing Owen to roll him up for the pin at 9:16.

Rating: B-. Nice opener here with both guys looking good and giving the crowd something to cheer for. Edge was still a rookie here but would get much better when his personality started to change. The man that came through the crowd would be either Edge's brother or best friend depending on the current year: Christian.

Too Much vs. Scorpio/Al Snow

Snow is completely insane and carries a mannequin head with him. Too Much is Brian Christopher and a newcomer named Scott Taylor. The fans get all over Too Much, sending Taylor into a fit before he starts with Scorpio. Feeling out process to start with Scorpio cranking on a wristlock before dropping him with a spinwheel kick. Taylor flips around and takes Scorpio down with a dropkick, only to have Scorpio in his face by the time Taylor nips up.

It's off to Snow vs. Christopher with Snow hitting a bunch of headbutts to gain the early advantage. Things start to break down a bit with Scorpio bringing a chair into the ring but Snow uses it as a launching pad to dive at Taylor in the corner. Taylor falls face first into Christopher's crotch to make the crowd wince. Christopher misses a charge at Snow on the floor and Scorpio hits a top rope splash on Taylor for two.

Snow moonsaults Christopher off the apron before heading back inside to slam Taylor. Scorpio goes up top but takes too long, allowing Brian to crotch him down to the floor. Taylor hits a nice springboard dive to take Scorpio down again. Things settle down with Too Much hitting a double backdrop on Scorpio but Christopher stops to dance.

Snow comes in sans tag with Head to clean house, only to hit Scorpio by mistake. The referee checks on Scorpio, allowing Al to hit Taylor low for a close two. The save is botched a bit with Christopher coming off the top late and the referee just stopping his count. Scorpio makes a save of his own (also a bit late) but Snow pops up and Snowplows (scoop brainbuster) Taylor for the pin at 8:03.

Rating: C. The ending was pretty messy but the rest of the match wasn't bad at all. Scorpio had some incredible talent and Snow was one of the most underrated guys on the roster. Too Much would get far better when they stopped being goofy heels and became dancers. If nothing else it was probably better than the original idea for them: the first openly gay (and in love) tag team.

Undertaker and Kane aren't worried about fighting each other until they're done with Austin.

Marc Mero vs. Droz

That's Darren Drozdov of course. Mero pounds him into the corner to start but Droz comes back with some nice clotheslines. Marc heads to the floor and tries to leave but Droz will have none of that. Back in and Mero pounds away before sending Droz back

216

to the floor for a flip dive over the top. They head in again so Mero can choke away with some wrist tape. Jackie adds a top rope high heel to the head, setting up Marveolcity (Shooting Star Press) for the pin at 5:12.

Rating: D. The ending looked good but there wasn't much to see here. Droz was still a rookie at this point but he was showing some promise in his matches. This is another match that could have been on Raw though and that's only going to help Droz so much this early in his career.

Vader vs. Bradshaw

This is falls count anywhere and no holds barred for no apparent reason. Bradshaw pounds him down into the corner to start and takes him down with a clothesline. A slam and an elbow drop get two for Bradshaw but Vader runs him over and works on the leg. Vader gets two on a splash but Bradshaw kicks him in the face and clotheslines him over the top. The ring bell goes upside Vader's head and Bradshaw adds an elbow drop for two. Bradshaw accidentally punches the post a few times though and Vader slugs him down.

Some shots to the back with the steps would look to have Bradshaw in trouble but he shrugs them off and fires off right hands back inside. Bradshaw misses a clothesline and falls out to the floor where Vader rams him into various metal objects. Back in and the middle rope splash gets no cover for Vader but the Vader Bomb gets two. Bradshaw comes back with two hard clotheslines and a neckbreaker for the pin at 7:56.

Rating: D-. This would be better as a regular match but as an anything goes match this was nearly a disaster. Vader was done at this point and it was very clear in this match. Just two years ago that Vader Bomb was beating Shawn Michaels and now a midcarder is kicking out at two. This was Vader's last PPV appearance, which is the best thing for everyone, but especially for him.

We get a WWF.com ad with a comedian named Jason Sensation. His regular voice was annoying but he does the best WWF impressions I've ever heard with Undertaker and Owen Hart being exceptional.

D'Lo Brown vs. Gangrel

Brown had lost the European Title to X-Pac just a week before this while Gangrel is a vampire who hasn't been around all that long. He charges at D'Lo to start and hits a running back elbow to the jaw to take over. An overhead belly to belly gets two on Brown as JR rants about Brown still wearing the chest protector. D'Lo hits a leg lariat and tells Gangrel that he needs to recognize.

Brown misses a middle rope elbow as the fans don't seem to care that much. Not that it matters as Brown comes back with a running powerbomb for a very delayed two count. Gangrel comes back with an attempted inverted DDT but Brown grabs the rope and suplexes Gangrel down for two. A superplex is blocked as Gangrel shoves D'Lo down for two, only to be taken down by a quick clothesline for two.

We hit the chinlock on Gangrel for about two seconds before Gangrel fights up and mostly botches a hot shot attempt. Here's Mark Henry for a closer look as Gangrel gets two via a high crossbody. Henry low bridges Gangrel to the floor which the referee somehow misses despite Gangrel going into the ropes near Henry and then being down on the floor. Henry throws him back inside for the Sky High and the pin at 7:46.

Rating: D. This was longer than it needed to be and again could have been on any given episode of Monday Night Raw. That's the problem with a lot of these recent shows but at least the midcard is looking a lot more solid than it was before. Things are still developing but there's something there to develop and that's the important thing.

Post match Gangrel spits the red liquid he drinks (implied to be blood) into Henry's eyes and hits his Impaler DDT on Brown.

We recap Mankind vs. Rock vs. Shamrock. They were fighting in a triple threat on Raw for the title shot when Undertaker and Kane beat up both guys. Vince made another match for tonight with the same shot on the line but inside a cage.

The cage is lowered.

Shamrock says he's frustrated with getting burned so tonight he's taking those out on Mankind and Rock.

Rock says he'll lay the smackdown on Mankind and Shamrock, raise the People's Eyebrow, drop the People's Elbow, climb out of the cage and then become the People's Champion. You can see the mega star in him already.

Mankind talks about having a history of stupid things and throws in a Monica Lewinsky joke to really date this show. However, he's never seen anything as stupid as the People's Elbow and thinks Shamrock is a breakfast cereal.

Mankind vs. The Rock vs. Ken Shamrock

In a cage and you can win by pinfall, submission or escape. Rock gets a HUGE reaction when his music hits. Mankind sits in the corner while the old rivals slug it out, only to try to sneak out the door in a smart move. Rock makes the save but Mankind punches both guys down into corners. A clothesline from Rock puts Mankind down but Shamrock keeps him from escaping and takes over for the first time. He pounds Rock down with forearms before putting Mankind in an abdominal stretch, only to have Rock sneak up and put Shamrock in an abdominal stretch at the same time.

Shamrock flips Rock out of the hold but gets flipped down by Mankind to get us to a standoff. Rock suggests to team up with Mankind to take out Shamrock but jumps the gullible Mankind to take over. Shamrock and Rock get in a fight and Mankind tries to escape again, only to be pulled down and sent into the cage. Shamrock can't get out either despite trying twice in a row. Now it's Rock and Mankind stomping Ken down at the same time and choking him on the middle rope.

Ken is sent face first into the cage as the double beating continues. Mankind is very excited that the two of them work well together so Rock punches him in the face and stomps him down in the corner. Now it's Rock and Shamrock double teaming Mankind as JR says this is a preview of Undertaker and Kane double teaming Austin. Shamrock puts the ankle lock on Mankind, earning him a right hand to the back of the head. We get the only remaining combination for a mini alliance as Rock is double teamed, much to the annoyance of the crowd.

A double suplex and a double backdrop put Rock down but he

sends Shamrock into the cage and clotheslines Mankind down. Rock DDTs Mankind and hits the floatover DDT to set up the People's Elbow on Shamrock, but plants Mankind next to him for a double People's Elbow. The place goes NUTS and starts a Rock chant, only to have Shamrock stop an escape attempt. Rock comes back with a low blow on Ken and the Rock Bottom to Mankind for two as Shamrock makes the save.

The fans are all over Ken now as Lawler calls Canada a strange place. Rock punches Shamrock down into the corner but walks into the belly to belly suplex which sets up the ankle lock. This time it's Mankind making a save and going up the cage, only to have Rock make the save. Mankind's body is out of the cage but Rock grabs him by the head to make a save.

They're both sitting on top of the cage but Shamrock pulls the Rock back inside. Mankind is left alone up there but climbs to the top to try a flying elbow, only to have Rock move and send Mankind crashing down to the mat. Everyone is down with Shamrock crawling to the door but Mankind makes the save. Shamrock finds a chair while his arms are outside though and drags it inside. He misses Mankind though and gets caught in a double arm DDT for no cover. Mankind blasts Ken in the head with the chair before climbing the cage, but Rock crawls over and pins Shamrock to win the match and title shot at 18:49.

Rating: B+. Really fun match here with the match having a little bit of everything to go around. Mankind diving off the cage was expected but still looked great. That double People's Elbow was awesome and the fans are clearly loving Rock right now. It was entertaining and violent while still being fun. Everything works.

Mankind is shocked at what happened. Shamrock goes nuts and beats on a variety of things with a chair.

We recap Dustin Runnels vs. Val Venis. Dustin has become a Christian and preaches a lot, which apparently has ticked off his wife Terri (Marlena). She starred in one of Val Venis' films, basically splitting up their marriage. Dustin has promised to make Venis repent.

Val Venis vs. Dustin Runnels

Val has Terri come out with him, basically wearing underwear and a dress with one button holding it together. A quick spinebuster puts Dustin down but Val gets his face slammed into the mat to put him down. Dustin powerbombs Val down and pounds away but Venis rakes his eyes. They head outside where Val clotheslines him inside out and the match goes back inside.

Dustin scores with a backdrop and fires off more right hands in the corner but gets caught by some knees to the ribs and a Russian legsweep. Venis gyrates his hips (with Terri doing the same) before punching Dustin in the face over and over. We hit a camel clutch for a bit with Dustin screaming for Terri. Back outside and Runnels is dropped face first onto the announcers' table. They head inside where Dustin gets two off a belly to back suplex, only to get distracted by Terri and put in a chinlock.

The announcers try to figure out who to blame for the marriage falling apart with JR reminding us that Dustin walked out on his family just a few months ago. Dustin fights up and hits a quick DDT for two, only to get caught on the top rope. Val looks to set up a superplex but instead dumps Dustin over the top and out to the floor, sending him face first into the apron.

Val heads to the floor as well but gets distracted by Terri's leg right in front of Dustin. Venis teases leaving but sneaks back in for a rollup for two. Dustin hits his bulldog for another near fall, despite Venis screwing up by not moving an inch. The crowd is confused but Val comes back with a powerslam and some elbow drops, followed by the Money Shot for the pin at 9:09.

Rating: D. This wasn't very good at all with a lot of boring non-action and a really bad botch with that two count. Dustin continues to fall even further into his black hole as Venis is on the rise so to speak. The solution of course was to bring Goldust back for the ultimate revenge, which was probably the best idea for everyone concerned.

We recap Jeff Jarrett and Southern Justice jumping DX on Heat, the show that aired before PPVs at this point.

Jeff Jarrett/Southern Justice vs. DX

Jarrett has changed his gimmick around, now basically just a jerk with an attitude. He's also cut his hair and dropped Tennessee Lee which is definitely the best thing that's happened to him since he's been back. It's the Outlaws (Tag Team Champions again) and X-Pac here with the champs jumping them from behind for an early advantage. X-Pac officially starts with Jeff and powerbombs him down for two before bringing in Road Dogg. An atomic drop sets up the shaky knee drop on Jarrett but Jeff tags off to Mark Canterbury to take over.

Canterbury slams Road Dogg down and drops an elbow for two before bringing Jarrett back inside. They hit heads in the corner though and both guys go down to give Dogg a breather. The tag brings in X-Pac for a spinning clothesline but Canterbury gets a blind tag and catches him in a powerslam. Off to Dennis Knight for a delayed vertical suplex for two. Jarrett comes back and gets two off a powerslam before avoiding a charge in the corner to put X-Pac down again.

Back to Canterbury as Billy keeps trying to come in but getting held back by the referee. Jeff hooks a chinlock but X-Pac fights back to his feet and suplexes Jarrett down. Billy gets the hot tag and cleans house, allowing X-Pac to hit the Bronco Buster on Jeff. Canterbury takes X-Pac's head off with a clothesline but Billy steals Jeff's guitar. The referee takes it from him but drops it, allowing Jarrett to shatter the guitar over X-Pac's head. Gunn hits a quick Fameasser on Canterbury for the pin at 11:17.

Rating: D. This was another slow and rather dull match with the finish being less polished than it should have been. X-Pac can take a good beating and it was the right choice to have Gunn clean house. The guy may not have been the best in the world but he could speed things up when he needed to.

Post match X-Pac is having eye troubles from the guitar shot.

We recap the main event. Vince is obsessed with getting the title off of Austin so he's sending both Undertaker and Kane to get it at the same time. The question is whether the brothers can work together.

WWF Title: Steve Austin vs. Kane vs. Undertaker

Austin is defending, Undertaker can't pin Kane and Kane can't pin Undertaker. Austin gets smart here and blasts Undertaker with a chair during Undertaker's slow entrance. Kane gets hit with one as well and they head into the ring for the bell. Undertaker is down in the aisle as Austin and Kane fight in the ring. The top rope clothesline misses Austin but Undertaker is on his feet. Kane throws Austin out to the floor where Undertaker is waiting.

Austin fights back again, sending Undertaker through the steps and sending Kane crotch first into the post. Back in the ring and Austin hits a fast Stunner on Kane but Undertaker breaks up the count. Undertaker throws him back inside and chokes away, only to charge into an elbow to the face. Austin's comeback is stopped almost immediately though by a jumping clothesline, getting two for Undertaker. The Thesz press takes Undertaker back down and a neckbreaker gets two.

Kane heads to the floor for a breather as Austin hopes to divide and conquer. That only lasts for a bit though as Kane pulls Austin to the floor for a double beating. Undertaker misses a big right hand though, knocking Kane down by mistake. Austin uses the distraction to ram the giants' heads together but Taker gets in a shot to the back to take over. The brothers pound on Austin together before heading back inside.

Patterson, Brisco and fellow crony Sgt. Slaughter are now at the arena entrance watching the beating. Undertaker rams Austin into the ring apron before choking away on the floor for a bit. Austin is beaten up the aisle but gets in a quick comeback with right hands, only to be backdropped down onto the concrete. Austin gets away from the monsters for a bit and takes out Brisco, only to be stomped by Slaughter.

The challengers get their hands on Austin though and carry him back to the ring for more punishment. Taker cranks on Austin's leg while Kane chokes him down for a few moments. Austin fights back AGAIN but is knocked to the floor, but he's able to grab a chair. A big shot to the head puts Kane down but Undertaker blasts Austin for two, as Kane breaks it up. Undertaker chokes Austin to allow Kane to hit a top rope sledge to the back. Kane covers, but Undertaker breaks it up this time.

Now the brothers start going at it which gives Austin a breather. Austin, ever the fighter though, wants to try to win instead of take a break. The brothers get back on the same page now though but Undertaker breaks up a pinfall attempt by Kane. The brawl between the tall people is back on again and Austin jumps them both with his 19th burst of energy. Undertaker is knocked to the floor but Kane hits a quick powerslam to slow Austin down. Taker tries to go up but gets crotched down, only to get back in the ring to break up a Stunner. A double chokeslam and a double cover takes the title away from Austin at 22:18.

Rating: D+. The problem here is that the match ran too long while doing the same stuff. The opening was good with Austin being full of energy and fighting for his life, but once the beatdown started it kept going on and on for twenty minutes. The ending was also kind of boring as the monsters just hit their big double move on Austin to take the title.

The important thing to remember here is that Austin didn't overcome the odds, which happened a lot more often than not. That was a necessary key to keeping Austin as popular as he was. If someone keeps overcoming the odds every single time, it doesn't work in the fans' eyes. It's fine to have the hero win in the end, but it's also ok to have the hero stumble along the way.

It's the same thing from earlier this year when Austin lost the title at King of the Ring against impossible odds but came back to win it again just the next night. That's a much better way to tell a story than having Austin overcome everything and Kane gets a nice win too. That's smart storytelling all around and it was the same thing here. It would have been really hard to buy Austin surviving here and even more damaging to both Undertaker and Kane. Go with what makes sense and Austin can get the title back later. It's not a great match, but it's a properly booked one.

Before the announcement of who the new champion is, Vince runs out and takes the belt before running to the back. He shouts that Austin doesn't have the title anymore and speeds away in a limo to end the show.

Overall Rating: D+. This wasn't all that great of a show but the cage match is really solid stuff which luckily takes up about twenty five minutes. The majority of the rest of the show is full of matches that could have been on Raw but like I said, at least there's a decent midcard to fill in the rest of the show for a change. The ending leaves us on a cliffhanger which is a good idea for the following night. Not the worst show in the world but like most of the Vince Russo booked shows, it's more about getting people to tune in next time instead of giving them much tonight.

Everything Gets A Little Nuts

So obviously the big problem now is the lack of a WWF Champion. Given the way the previous show ended though, the next main event was obvious: Undertaker vs. Kane for the vacant title. However since Vince is kind of a jerk, he made Austin the guest referee so that he has to count the fall to crown a new champion. Also if Austin doesn't do his job, he's fired. If you can't see the controversy from here, you're clearly not paying close enough attention. One other note: Undertaker and Kane weren't pleased with having to fight each other and broke Vince's leg as retaliation.

Other than that, there isn't much to talk about on this show. There are only two other significant matches here: Mark Henry vs. the freshly face rock Rock due to the Nation splitting up and Goldust vs. Val Venis as Dustin needs a way to finish things off. There just isn't much to see on this one but maybe it's better than it sounds.

Judgment Day: In Your House #25
Date: October 18, 1998
Location: Rosemont Horizon, Chicago, Illinois
Attendance: 18,153
Commentators: Jim Ross, Jerry Lawler

There were only three weeks between the two shows so there hasn't been time to get much set up for tonight. Things are really going well for the WWF at this point though as they've been crushing WCW for most of the summer and fall in the TV ratings, save for a month of Nitro wins due to the Ultimate Warrior's return. Eight days after this show would be Nitro's final victory ever. Let's get to it.

The opening video focuses on Vince being assaulted by Undertaker, Kane and Austin over the last few weeks but thinking it was all worth it for the sake of getting the title off of Austin.

Al Snow vs. Marc Mero

Al, still crazy, says this is the Pack and Save so everybody wants head. Before the match here's Jeff Jarrett who has been feuding with Snow lately. He says he's wrestling instead of Mero but that's not cool with Marc. Either way he uses the distraction to jump Snow for an early advantage as the bell rings. Snow comes back with a quick belly to back suplex followed by a clothesline for two. Mero hits a jumping back elbow and a hard clothesline of his own to take over.

They fight into the corner where Snow comes out with a DDT to set up a moonsault for no cover. Instead Snow goes after Jacqueline, allowing Mero to hit him low. A DDT by Mero gets two for him and a top rope moonsault press gets the same. Snow grabs Mero for a series of headbutts but yet another clothesline puts him down.

Mero catches a kick to the ribs but Snow scores with an enziguri and a sitout spinebuster. Again he won't cover because he'd rather talk to Head. A second moonsault attempt only hits mat thanks to Jackie but Mero misses Marvelocity, giving Snow a two count. Mero loads up the TKO but gets countered into the Snowplow for the pin at 7:12.

Rating: C. This was a nice back and forth match but the lack of any meaning whatsoever hurts it a bit. Mero was still good at this point but he wasn't as crisp as he used to be. Snow was starting to get over as the crazy man but it was still a few more months away. Fun little match here though.

Austin wasn't allowed to go into the wrestlers' locker room and was sent to the referee's room, which is basically a closet.

Disciples of Apocalypse vs. LOD 2000

This is a six man tag with Droz and Paul Ellering joining the regular teams. The LOD are the hometown boys and therefore more over than usual. This is Hawk's return match after suffering from "personal problems", meaning he's the official alternate for the team at the moment. Animal starts with Skull but an 8-Ball distraction lets Skull get in some cheap shots to take over. Animal comes back with a clothesline and a forearm to 8-Ball to clear the DOA out of the ring.

It's off to Hawk vs. 8-Ball with the biker pounding away until he gets caught in a neckbreaker for two. Droz gets the tag but is taken down almost immediately and stomped on in the corner. A series of elbows to the head puts Droz down and it's off to Skull who is caught by a jumping clothesline. 8-Ball breaks up the tag and Ellering is able to come in for some cheap shots. Droz finally catches Skull with a DDT and makes the hot tag off to Hawk as everything breaks down. 8-Ball takes the Doomsday Device but Droz comes in to steal the pin at 5:04, much to Hawk's annoyance.

Rating: D. These teams need to stop feuding already as the matches aren't working most of the time and the storyline with LOD splitting up isn't interesting. They're one of those teams that just don't work apart and splitting them up wasn't going to work. DOA was decent as a team but were never going to be anything important.

Light Heavyweight Title: Christian vs. Taka Michinoku

Taka is defending. This is Christian's in ring debut and he's accompanied by Gangrel. He's also been confirmed as Edge's brother (since retconned because you can do that in wrestling) but they don't see eye to eye at the moment. Taka is still champion but has since turned heel and joined Kaientai because Yamaguchi-San was revealed to be his brother in law. Feeling out process to start until Taka hits a spinwheel kick and clothesline to put Christian on the floor. Taka follows it up with his signature springboard dive as we see Edge watching from the crowd.

Back in and Taka drops a top rope knee but misses a charge in the corner, allowing Christian to take control with a reverse DDT. Two rolling snap suplexes set up a sitout front suplex for two on Michinoku. Taka misses a charge and is low bridged to the floor, setting up a nice springboard dive from the challenger. Back in again and Christian chokes away but misses a top rope splash to put both guys down.

Taka sends him to the floor for an Asai moonsault before going back inside for a high crossbody but Christian rolls through for two. A low dropkick gets two for Michinoku but Christian gets the same off a Russian legsweep. Taka comes back with a tornado DDT to set up the Michinoku Driver but Christian rolls through for the pin and the title at 8:34, plus a big pop from the crowd.

Rating: C+. This was a long overdue title change but Taka wasn't a failure with the title. He would soon be shifted into the tag team division though, which was the best move for him.

Christian would go on to have a huge career and win virtually every title in the company which makes his first win here all the more interesting.

We recap Goldust vs. Val Venis, most of which was covered last month. Even the recap video has a lot of the same clips. However, the night after Breakdown, Venis and Terri were in the ring together when Goldust appeared on the screen. Later he would debut his new signature move on Val: Shattered Dreams, a running low blow in the corner.

Val Venis vs. Goldust

Earlier tonight, Goldust sent Val a golden cup, as in the protective kind. Venis isn't sure what to do to start so he takes Goldust down and pounds away with right hands to the head. Goldust takes it to the floor and sends Val into the barricade before dropping him face first onto the steps. Back in and Val scores with a quick right hand to take over again and it's out to the floor again for the second time in fifteen seconds.

Val comes off the top with a crossbody to the floor before heading back inside where Goldust takes over again with a clothesline. Goldust stomps away and snaps a seated Val's neck forward for no cover. Val gets back up and avoids a charge into the post before going to the floor to ram Goldust's shoulder into the post again. Back in and Venis slams Goldust down on the arm before putting on a short armscissors to keep Goldust on the mat.

Back up and they trade forearms with Venis getting the better of it and a near fall. Goldust goes back to the armbar for a bit before Val scores with a Russian legsweep and powerslam. He goes up top, only to have Goldust pop up and catch him with a superplex for two. Val gets up again and grabs a quick sleeper, only to have Goldust reverse into one of his own.

A belly to back suplex gets Val free and both guys are down. Goldust's glove comes off and he's still wearing his wedding ring, which apparently Terri does as well. The bulldog puts Val down but Terri gets up on the apron for a distraction. Val almost clotheslines her down by mistake, allowing Goldust to kick him low for the pin at 12:05.

228

Rating: C. Not a bad match here but the story was the focal point here. There's nothing wrong with that at all mind you as this was a basic but pretty well done story. The fact that both guys are solid in the ring and can have good matches helped a lot, making this about as good as it could have been all around.

We recap the new Intercontinental Champion Ken Shamrock (HHH had to forfeit the title and Ken won a tournament to become the new champion) attacking HHH's bad knee by crushing it with a car door. X-Pac says he'll deal with Shamrock tomorrow.

European Title: X-Pac vs. D'Lo Brown

X-Pac is challenging. They've been trading the title back and forth for a while and Brown is defending tonight. They talk trash to each other to start until Brown takes him down with a shoulder block. It's off to a wristlock by the champion to take X-Pac down to the mat but he fights up and hits some quick kicks to take over. Brown comes right back with a clothesline (popular move tonight) for two before dropping some elbows.

X-Pac gets taken to the corner for some chops but he avoids a splash and hiptosses Brown to the mat. Some kicks in the corner put D'Lo down but he blocks the Bronco Buster with a well placed boot. We hit the chinlock by the champion for a good while before D'Lo kicks him in the face for two more. A running powerbomb puts X-Pac down again but just like last time, D'Lo takes too long to cover and only gets two. X-Pac blocks a superplex and hits a high crossbody but Brown rolls through for another near fall.

Back to the chinlock for a good while before X-Pac fights up again. Brown sidesteps a charge into the corner though and drops a middle rope elbow for two. A backbreaker sets up a Texas cloverleaf on the challenger but X-Pac slips through D'Lo's legs to escape. The fans are all over D'Lo here as he goes up, only to miss a front flip legdrop. X-Pac makes his comeback with a kick to the face and a flipping clothesline to set up the Bronco Buster.

Chyna gets in a cheap shot to Brown's head for two but the referee is taken out a few seconds later. Here's Mark Henry, who has recently filed a sexual harassment lawsuit against Chyna.

Brown uses the distraction to hit X-Pac in the face with the title belt as Henry throws the referee in for a two count. Another powerbomb puts X-Pac down for two but Brown goes up top and dives into the X-Factor to give X-Pac the title back at 13:50.

Rating: C-. This wasn't too bad but it wasn't as good as the previous match. The ending didn't work for the most part as it was too overbooked and there was no reason for D'Lo to dive forward like he did other than to dive into the X-Factor. It's not bad but these guys have feuded long enough now. Hopefully this wraps it up.

Paul Bearer might have been seen going into the Undertaker's locker room.

The Headbangers think the Outlaws suck and make gay sex jokes. They're also mad at Road Dogg for breaking their boom box with his face on Raw.

Tag Team Titles: Headbangers vs. New Age Outlaws

The Outlaws are defending and get jumped during their entrance. The champions quickly take over and it's Billy pounding on Mosh to start. A shoulder block gets two on Mosh and it's off to Road Dogg for a hiptoss, only to be pounded in the back to change momentum. Thrasher comes in but gets dropkicked down and punched in the face for two. Mosh comes back in off a blind tag and dropkicks Dogg down for two.

The Headbangers double team Road Dogg in the corner with some fast tags as the fans start a SUCK IT chant. Dogg comes back with a belly to back suplex to put Thrasher down and it's a double tag off to Billy and Mosh. Billy starts cleaning house but gets low bridged out to the floor by Thrasher, sending Billy crashing down onto his head. That's not enough though so Thrasher sends him into the steps for good measure. Back in and Thrasher suplexes Mosh from the middle rope onto Gunn.

Billy comes back with a quick clothesline but Thrasher breaks up the hot tag attempt. A catapult sends Gunn's throat into the bottom rope and it's back to Mosh for an armbar. Even JR points out that the move doesn't make a lot of sense at this point. The Headbangers trade places sans tagging for some double stomping and it's back to Thrasher for a chinlock.

Gunn fights up and hooks a chinlock of his own but Thrasher suplexes him down. Mosh comes back in and charges into the corner, only to get caught in a belly to back suplex to put both guys down. Thrasher runs in and breaks up the tag before the Headbangers hit Billy with a double flapjack. Road Dogg is tired of waiting and hits Mosh in the head with a boom box for the DQ at 14:01.

Rating: D. The match was very boring and the ending didn't help it at all. The Headbangers clearly weren't a threat to the belts here but to be fair no one really threatened the Outlaws at this point. It felt like they realized they were out of time and had to wrap things up really fast here which isn't a good thing.

Paul Bearer in Undertaker's locker room can't be confirmed, but Bearer being in Kane's locker room can be.

Mr. Socko (a sock on Mankind's hand) talks about Shamrock giving brutal interviews, which apparently have been leading to teen suicides. Mankind wants to know what kind of underwear Socko is wearing before ripping the sock off to reveal taped fingers for the Mandible Claw.

Intercontinental Title: Mankind vs. Ken Shamrock

Shamrock is defending and is mostly a heel now while Mankind had his ankle attacked on Raw. Mankind takes him into the corner to start but gets kicked in the thigh to put Mankind down. After some quick ankle work Shamrock tries an armbar of all things to take Mankind down again. Mankind comes back by raking the eyes and drops a leg for two, only to be countered into a hammerlock.

Back up and Shamrock fires off some knees and forearms to the face, which wouldn't seem to have much effect due to Mankind's mask. Instead Shamrock takes Mankind down and just rains down right hands to the head before hooking a front facelock. Mankind fights up but loses a slugout and gets taken down by a hurricanrana. A quick Mandible Claw changes things around though and Shamrock bails to the floor. Shamrock gets back in but loses the slugout rematch, allowing Mankind to grab a bodyscissors to try the Claw again.

231

Shamrock will have none of that though and pounds on Mankind's head again. They fight outside with Mankind sending Ken into the steps but having his chair taken away by the referee. Ken takes it away from the referee and blasts Mankind in the head right in front of the referee. The match keeps going for some reason though with Shamrock taking him back inside. A clothesline gets two for the champion and it's back to the arm work. Mankind fights up by biting Shamrock's ear but misses a charge into the corner to keep Shamrock in control.

Mankind gets in a quick shot to the ribs followed by the double arm DDT but he can't cover. Instead he sits up and pulls out his own hair like the good old days. Shamrock gets pounded down into the corner and tied up in the Tree of Woe for a running ax handle to the face. A legdrop across the middle rope puts Shamrock down again but the fans don't seem to care at all.

The Cactus Clothesline puts both guys on the floor one more time and Mankind drops an elbow off the apron. He goes inside to rock back and forth a bit but as he heads outside, Shamrock catches him in a powerslam to send Mankind's knees into the steps. Back inside and Shamrock gets the ankle lock but Mankind makes it to the ropes. The hold goes right back on though and Mankind hits himself in the head to keep from tapping out. When that stops working, he puts the Mandible Claw on himself, knocking himself out to retain Shamrock's title at 14:35.

Rating: C+. Nice brawl here though the fans didn't care for the most part. This was a good first win for Shamrock's title reign though as Mankind was certainly still a big deal. Shamrock was much better suited as the heel gladiator that just destroyed people left and right. Not a great match but it did its job.

Post match Shamrock is mad (shocking) because it wasn't the ankle lock that won the match. He beats up the referee but gets dispatched by the Mandible Claw.

Big Boss Man, Vince's new bodyguard, says no interviews, though in much angrier terms.

Mark Henry vs. The Rock

D'Lo is with Henry and this is a revenge match after Henry beat up Rock on Raw for bailing on the Nation. Henry dedicates a poem to Chyna, saying he loved her long before the implants and wants to father her children. The place FINALLY wakes up for Rock's music as he's the most popular guy in this company not named Austin right now. Rock pounds away on Henry to start and knocks him down with right hands. Rock actually suplexes Henry down for two in an impressive power display.

They head outside with Henry getting in an elbow to the ribs and slamming Rock face first into the announcers' table. Back in and Rock clotheslines Henry down but Mark comes back with a pair of elbows for two. Rock fights out of the corner with right hands but gets clotheslined down and legdropped for two. We hit the chinlock for a bit but Rock comes back with, what else, right hands to the jaw. A DDT gets two on Mark and Rock easily slams him down. There's the People's Elbow but D'Lo distracts Rock from covering. Henry hits a clothesline from behind and a splash for the shocking upset at 5:07.

Rating: D+. Rock's power displays were impressive but I have no idea why Henry gets to pin the fastest rising star in the company. No it wasn't clean but it didn't need to happen in the first place. Henry never really went anywhere off this win, which makes the whole thing all the stranger. Just an odd decision here.

We recap the main event. Austin was robbed of the title in the three way last time and has to count the fall tonight or be fired. Vince is absolutely loving this and has reached new levels of maniacal by this point.

WWF Title: Kane vs. Undertaker

Vince and Bearer are nowhere in sight and the title is vacant coming in. Austin, in jean shorts and his latest t-shirt, flips off both guys and calls for the bell. Undertaker pounds away on Kane to start but Kane comes back with a clothesline. The fans of course chant for Austin. Kane sends Undertaker face first into the buckle but charges into a boot and a clothesline. Austin refuses to count despite being down in position, ticking Undertaker off. Kane takes Undertaker down and Austin counts a very fast two to mess with everyone's minds.

They head to the floor with Undertaker ramming Kane into the barricade, steps and post in succession. Undertaker misses a big chair shot by hitting the post instead of Kane, allowing the younger brother to get in a shot to the face as we head back inside. Undertaker comes right back with a suplex but Kane is on his feet first. A clothesline puts Undertaker down but he sits up just as quickly.

Undertaker gets the better of a slugout and starts kicking at Kane's knee. The fans are still cheering for Austin and don't seem to care about the match at all. Kane gets caught in a leglock for a few seconds before Undertaker drives elbows into Kane's knee. The match slows way down as Undertaker hooks another leglock for a few moments. Kane fights up but misses a big boot, allowing Undertaker to take the leg out again. Now the fans think this is boring and I can't say I disagree all that much.

We get leglock number three before undertaker kicks Kane down into the corner. The fans are getting restless as this match has slowed way too far down. Kane gets tied up in the Tree of Woe so Undertaker can choke away. That goes nowhere so for a change of pace, Undertaker chokes in a different corner. The boring chants are getting louder and louder. More choking ensues and Undertaker gets mad at Austin for asking if Kane submits.

Undertaker charges (a stretch if there's ever been one) into the corner and gets caught in a spinebuster. Kane fires off right hands in the corner....and chokeslams Austin. That means a double beatdown until Undertaker chop blocks Kane's knee. Kane no sells it and chokeslams Undertaker but there's no referee.

Here's Paul Bearer with a chair to swing at Undertaker but he hits Kane instead, breaking a bond that lasted almost a full hour. Kane doesn't move an inch so Undertaker cracks him in the head with the chair but Austin glares at both of them. A Stunner and chair shot put Undertaker down and Austin counts three on both of them. Austin calls for the be.ll and declares himself the winner at 17:35

Rating: D-. This was HORRIBLE with way too much laying around and resting despite there being almost nothing done to require resting. Austin was doing what he could but he's kind of limited when Undertaker wants to lay on the mat for half of the match. The ending clearly keeps the story going but that's not a good idea more often than not. People want champions, though I can understand the fans not being pleased with either of these options. This was the worst match in this series in a very long time.

Austin tells Vince to come out and fire him but goes to the back when no one shows up. Vince is nowhere in sight so Austin comes back to the ring. Vince's voice comes over the PA system and says to raise the screen. The Titantron rises up and Vince is behind it with Big Boss Man. The fans aren't pleased to see him, but Vince fires Austin to shock the crowd. Austin admits he was wrong about being fired but says he'll start hunting tomorrow, meaning Vince hasn't seen the last of him. Austin asks for his music to be played and a lot of beer is consumed to end the show. JR of course misses the fact that Austin said he'll be back.

Overall Rating: C-. The show wasn't terrible for the most part but that main event was horrible. Austin vs. Vince is above the title and there's nothing wrong with that, but the title could elevate someone else right now. Things will of course change soon, but this wasn't a good way to end the show. Austin being fired won't last of course, but it's a good way to get the fans to hate Vince even more. This was the opposite of most In Your House shows: instead of the main event bailing out a horrible show, the main event nearly sinks a good show.

With the ending to the show, it was clear that there was a need for a new champion and that a one off match wasn't going to do it. The solution was a 14 man tournament to be held at the Survivor Series known as the Deadly Game. Why the Rock, the #1 contender, wasn't given a one on one chance to become champion wasn't clearly explained. The majority of the tournament doesn't matter, but the final four came down to Rock vs. Undertaker and Mankind vs. Steve Austin for quite the field of choices.

The story of the night up to this point had been Vince telling Mankind that he was the corporate pick to win the title and would have their help throughout the night. This seemed to be the case when the Corporation interfered and hit Austin with a chair, allowing Vince's son Shane to count the pin, sending Mankind to the finals. The other semi-final went a bit faster, with Kane interfering and attacking Rock to send him to the finals in an act of revenge for Undertaker eliminating Kane earlier in the night.

That set up the finals with Mankind vs. the Rock, with the latter being the huge crowd favorite. After a long match, Rock countered the Mandible Claw into the Rock Bottom before putting on the Sharpshooter. Just like the previous year, Vince rang the bell before Mankind had a chance to do anything, revealing that Rock had been the corporate pick all along and making him the new WWF Champion.

If you had been paying attention throughout the night, this wasn't a huge surprise. Rock's first round match had been against Vince's bodyguard Big Boss Man who Rock literally beat in three seconds with a rollup. Rock's quarter final match had been against Shamrock with Boss Man throwing in his nightstick, presumably to Shamrock, but in the perfect spot for Rock to intercept it for the win. Other than the Undertaker match which Rock won thanks to interference, the Corporation was involved in every match Rock wrestled in during the tournament.

This led us to In Your House #26, where the main event was a rematch from the tournament final with the now Corporate Rock defending his title against Mankind. The other main event of the night was Undertaker vs. Steve Austin in a Buried Alive match. Undertaker cost Austin his shot at the WWF Title the night after Survivor Series and has been trying to attack Austin at any opportunity since. He even tried to embalm Austin until Kane made the save. The winner of the match gets a spot in the Royal Rumble.

Rock Bottom: In Your House #26

Date: December 13, 1998
Location: General Motors Place, Vancouver, British Columbia, Canada
Attendance: 20,042
Commentators: Michael Cole, Jerry Lawler

We're closing out 1998 with this and we're once again in the death slot to end the year. December has almost always been a bad month for pay per views as the holidays usually mean people have less money to spend on wrestling. It also doesn't help that the main event is a rematch where a new champion would be a major surprise. Let's get to it.

We open with a video of the grave being set up for later tonight.

Rock was at Planet Hollywood yesterday and introduces us to his PPV because we need to get used to all the rock themed PPVs: Rock Solid, Rock and Roll, and Laying the Smacketh Down. The fans just need to sit back and enjoy his pay per view, if you smell what he's cooking.

The opening video shows Undertaker talking about taking Austin's soul and giving it to the Ministry of Darkness (Undertaker's new stable). He promises to take Austin mind, body and soul.

Rock is injured coming into the show but Vince has guaranteed that he will defend the title tonight.

Supply and Demand vs. Mark Henry/D'Lo Brown

Supply and Demand is Val Venis and the Godfather who is now a pimp and brings his ladies to the ring with him. I think you can figure out the joke yourself. Godfather says the holiday season is upon us and Val will be hanging some mistletoe, so tonight the girls have the night off and get Val as a present. Val says he has the yule log if they have the fireplace. Henry and Brown have the Pretty Mean Sisters (Terri and Jacqueline) with them here in the start of a story that went on way too long and didn't work. In short, the girls hate men and think they're only around to do the Sisters' bidding.

Brown pounds away on Venis to start but stops to walk around, allowing Venis to clothesline him down. A spinebuster puts D'Lo down again and it's off to Godfather for some chops. Another clothesline drops Brown and a hook kick to the shoulder (called the chest by Cole) has almost no effect. Off to Henry who powerslams Godfather down and chokes him on the mat. Back to Venis who tries a German suplex and gets elbowed in the face for his efforts.

A splash in the corner drops Venis and it's back to Brown who gets two off the Sky High. The Low Down (frog splash) only hits mat though and a double tag brings in Henry and Godfather. Everything breaks down and a double suplex takes Henry over. The two sets of girls get in an argument on the floor and Jackie comes in to pull Val's trunks down. Henry runs Venis over and splashes him for the pin at 5:54.

Rating: D+. This had its moments but the ending wasn't the best. It made things feel like a comedy match which usually only works if the popular team wins. Terri and Jacqueline would go on annoying people for months while not really accomplishing anything. Not terrible here but Brown vs. Venis would have been a better choice.

We see a clip from Heat where Mankind attacked Rock, injuring the champion's ribs in the process.

Rock says he'll wrestle tonight no matter what because if he doesn't, Mankind is the champion.

Headbangers vs. Oddities

The Oddities are a group of guys who have some sort of deformity. In this case it's Kurrgan, a giant said to be insane, and Golga, who allegedly has ridges and bumps on his head, necessitating a mask. He also carries a doll from some new show called South Park. They're accompanied by the abnormally large Giant Silva and Luna who is just strange in general. Luna is the reason the match is happening after the Headbangers cut her hair recently. Kurrgan throws Mosh into the corner to start but Mosh snaps his throat across the top rope to get a breather.

A sidewalk slam puts Mosh right back down but he avoids a big boot to bring in Thrasher. Another sidewalk slam puts Thrasher down this time and both Headbangers are sent into the corner for a big splash from the 400lb+ Golga. A legdrop gets two for Golga on Thrasher and it's back to Kurrgan who misses a middle rope splash.

Both Headbangers come in again for a double suplex and work on Kurrgan's back a bit. The giant finally gets tired of the beating and shrugs them off, allowing the hot tag off to Golga. The monster cleans house and powerslams Mosh down but Thrasher springboards in with a crossbody for the pin out of nowhere at 6:29.

Rating: D. This was really dull and didn't do much to pick up the bored crowd. The Headbangers wouldn't be around much longer and the Oddities would only be around a few more months as well. I can't say it fails though as Kurrgan and his stupid dancing are guilty pleasures for me.

Pat Patterson offers to take care of something for Vince.

Owen Hart vs. Steve Blackman

The idea is that a superhero named the Blue Blazer has been running around lately. Blazer was Owen Hart's old gimmick and everyone accused the then retired (due to injuring Dan Severn's neck) Owen of using it to get back in the ring. This led to a months long attempt to prove Owen is the Blazer but no one has been able to pull it off yet. The fans LOVE Owen here and he takes over quickly with a snap suplex and a legdrop.

Owen comes back with some shots to the chest and a kick to the face for good measure. Hart bails to the floor for a walk up the aisle but gets clotheslined from behind to put him down. Back in and Blackman puts on a surfboard which only lasts a few seconds. Owen comes back with an enziguri and a knee drop for two but stomps on Blackman's ribs instead of covering.

Owen goes to the middle rope but jumps into a boot to the chest and Steve takes over again. A loud US SUCKS chant starts up as Blackman drops an elbow for two. Hart starts to leave again but comes back and gets caught by a baseball slide. It doesn't seem to matter that much though as he comes back in and pounds away on Blackman and gets two off a spinwheel kick. A top rope elbow gets the same near fall for Owen and we hit the chinlock.

Blackman fights up but gets caught by an enziguri, allowing Owen to remove the buckle pad. Owen winds up going chest first into the steel and a Blackman kick to the back of the head puts him down. Steve's sleeper goes nowhere and Owen reverses into a dragon sleeper. Blackman escapes so Owen DDTs him down and goes up top, but his missile dropkick is countered into the Sharpshooter. Owen bails to the ropes for the escape and heads outside again where he finally gets away for a countout at 10:26.

Rating: C. Good match while it lasted but the ending hurt it a lot. Also the crushing of the fans continues with all three of the matches going to the heels so far. The match was good for the most part though with both guys looking good and Owen moving around well enough to make the boring Blackman bearable.

Vince is looking for Mankind for some reason. He goes up to the boiler room door which has a piece of paper taped on, reading "Mankind's Office." Vince is allowed inside and told to pull up a chair as Mankind is sitting inside.

Brood vs. J.O.B. Squad

The Brood is Gangrel, Edge and Christian while the J.O.B. Squash is Bob Holly, Scorpio and Al Snow, who have united together after getting sick of constantly losing to bigger stars. Edge pounds on Holly to start but walks into a powerslam and a falcon's arrow for two. A clothesline puts Holly down and it's off to Christian, who lost the Light Heavyweight Title to J.O.B. Squad member Duane Gill with help from Snow.

Scorpio comes in to kick Christian in the face and get a two count off a middle rope flipping legdrop. Off to the Squad's leader Al Snow for some headbutts to the chest but getting caught in a reverse DDT. Gangrel gets the tag and pounds away in the corner before clotheslining Snow down. They're not exactly getting out of first gear here. Snow comes back with a wheelbarrow suplex but Gangrel DDTs him down and brings in Edge. Off to a chinlock on Snow but he quickly fights up and a double clothesline drops both guys.

Scorpio and Christian come in to speed things up but everything quickly breaks down. Holly and Christian are left in the ring with Christian being dropped long enough to allow Snow to blast him with Head. Scorpio hits a moonsault legdrop for two as Edge makes the save. Edge follows that up by diving over the top to take out Holly and Snow before Christian hits what would become the Unprettier and then the Killswitch for the pin on Scorpio at 9:08.

Rating: D. This really didn't do much for me as it was a very dull match with a wild ending. Also, this makes the heels 0-4 on the show tonight which isn't the right way to get the crowd into things. The Brood would get better in the future while the J.O.B. Squad would never amount to anything, meaning they're living up to their name.

Vince and Mankind keep up their meeting.

Jeff Jarrett vs. Goldust

This is a striptease match where if Jarrett wins, Goldust has to strip but if Goldust wins, Jarrett's valet Debra has to strip. Therefore, Goldust is as over as he's ever been in his career. Jarrett is taken down twice in a row to start until Goldust grabs a headlock to send him to the mat again. Jeff fights up and elbows Goldust out to the floor but loses a quick slugout. Back in and Jeff scores with a swinging neckbreaker for two followed by a middle rope fist to the face. Even Lawler, a longtime Jarrett supporter, is cheering for Goldust here.

Goldust comes back with a suplex but walks into a dropkick for another near fall. Jarrett grabs a sleeper and the fans loudly cheer for Goldust. Back up and Debra sends in the guitar but the referee catches it, allowing Goldust to hit the Curtain Call but there's no one to count. Jarrett gets bulldogged down for a close two and gets loaded up for Shattered Dreams, only to have Debra come in and hit on Goldust. The distraction....doesn't work and Jarrett gets kicked anyway, only to have Debra sneak in with a guitar shot, giving Jarrett a chance to hit his front face legsweep (later named the Stroke) the cheap pin at 8:06.

Rating: D+. The match only worked because of the stipulations but their hopes have been dashed again, just like everything else tonight. Debra losing her clothes was teased for months if not years but in wrestling that's not something you can't exactly deliver on. Still though, not a great match but the fans carried it.

241

Post match here's new Commissioner Shawn Michaels to say that the guitar was a foreign object, meaning that's a DQ loss for Jarrett, meaning Debra has to strip. Debra is mad at first but gets into it as the clothes come off. She gets down to her underwear and goes for her bra (Shawn: "I LOVE MY JOB!") but here's the Blue Blazer to cover her with a blanket and get her to the back before anything immoral happens.

Vince leaves the boiler room, very pleased.

Tag Team Titles: New Age Outlaws vs. Big Boss Man/Ken Shamrock

The Outlaws are defending here of course and the fans are now reciting Road Dogg's opening speech with him in a pretty cool moment. Shawn has barred DX from ringside and comes to the ring with the challengers. The fans are all over Shamrock to start and Road Dogg is as well, pounding him into the corner. Shamrock comes back with a big clothesline and it's off to Boss Man to go after Road Dogg's ribs. The Dogg avoids a splash though and brings in Gunn to a big ovation.

Billy cranks on the arm for a bit before it's off to Dogg for an uppercut and a two count. Shamrock comes back in but misses a kick to the face, allowing Dogg to hit the Shake Rattle and Roll (series of punches) and the shaky knee drop for two. Back to Gunn for a Fameasser before Dogg comes in again, only to walk into a belly to belly suplex. Boss Man comes in to pound away on Road Dogg in the corner and shout trash talk to the crowd. Dogg fights out of a double arm front facelock but gets kneed in the ribs.

It's back to Shamrock for a jumping back elbow to the jaw for two as Gunn gets in a cheap shot on Boss Man on the floor. Shawn threatens to fire Billy as Shamrock kicks Dogg down and pounds away on him in the corner. Off to a front facelock on the Dogg as the beating continues. Boss Man comes back in to pound away and put on another front facelock. Shamrock kicks Road Dogg in his back to stop a comeback bid and we hit the front facelock again. Road Dogg finally drives him into the corner for the tag to Gunn but the referee was with Boss Man.

Billy and Shawn get in another argument but the threat of unemployment stops Gunn again. Road Dogg blocks a piledriver with a backdrop and sends Boss Man to the floor. He's too spent to follow up though and Shamrock gets to pound away even more. Ken runs into a boot in the corner to stagger him but Dogg can't get over to make a tag.

Gunn FINALLY gets the tag and cleans house, including countering a hurricanrana into a powerbomb for two on Ken. Shawn pulls the referee out of the ring, allowing Boss Man to hit Billy with the nightstick for two. Gunn tries a suplex but Shawn trips him up, only to have Gunn roll over and land on top of Shamrock for the pin to retain at 16:10.

Rating: D. Good night this was a long and dull match. The match runs over sixteen minutes and was mainly spent on the long beatdown segment on Road Dogg. That makes for a very boring match, especially when you consider how many front facelocks we had to sit through. DX vs. the Corporation would go on for a long time, with the Outlaws losing the titles to Boss Man and Shamrock in the rematch tomorrow night. That would make both of them double champions since Shamrock was Intercontinental Champion and Boss Man was Hardcore Champion (created only a few months ago).

We recap the WWF Title match. Rock and Vince pretended to feud until the tournament where it turned out Rock was in league with Vince all along and it was Mankind being strung along. We get a tournament recap showing how easy Rock had it until he won the title. Mankind is of course furious and tonight is the rematch.

Vince talks to Shane and Rock, saying "he" just wants witnesses and to have something whited out.

WWF Title: The Rock vs. Mankind

Rock is defending but has bad ribs. Mankind comes to the ring with a contract in hand. He thinks Vince can settle this affair like a gentleman but didn't bring a pen. Apparently he wants to get rid of the clause saying he gets the title if Rock can't wrestle, because he really wants to take Rock out himself. Mankind, calling Vince dad, says Vince knows Rock didn't make him give up at Survivor Series, and that Vince needs to get on his knees and admit it. Vince insists someone said I Quit so Mankind rips up the contract. Rock jumps Mankind and we're ready to go.

243

Mankind comes back with some right hands of his own and takes it into the floor, sending Rock into the steps. A whip into the barricade and clothesline drop the champion and Mankind sends him into the announcers' table for good measure. Vince grabs the mic and says if Mankind keeps it up, he's disqualified. Back inside and Rock clotheslines Mankind down to take over. He chokes in the corner and on the floor as well before punching Mankind in the jaw.

Back in and Rock charges into a big boot to the face and gets backdropped out to the floor again. A baseball slide sends Rock into the announcers' table but Shane grabs Mankind's leg before he can dive off the middle rope. Instead Rock slams him down to the floor and grabs the headset to do some mid-match commentary. Rock calls Mankind a piece of trash and Lawler asks for a high five. Rock: "How about I slap you in the face?" Mankind has water spat in his face so he dives over the announcers' table and pounds away on the champion who still has his headset on.

Mankind grabs a chair but Shane takes it away from him, allowing Rock to clothesline Mankind down for two inside. The People's Elbow gets two as they're rolling around on the ripped up contract. A swinging neckbreaker puts Rock back down and a discus lariat gets a near fall. Those clotheslines are popular again tonight. There's a legdrop for two more on Rock and another between Rock's legs so Vince calls for the bell. Mankind piledrives the referee and beats up the timekeeper before the bell can be rung, but Rock takes Mankind's head off with a chair shot.

There's the Rock Bottom back inside but there's no referee. Rock throws the referee to the side and calls for another referee as Shane gets inside with the belt. His shot hits Rock in the head as another referee comes out for a two count. Vince is on the verge of a heart attack as Rock hits the floatover DDT for two. Mankind hits a double arm DDT of his own for a near fall as the fans are WAY into this. There's the Claw with Socko and Rock goes out to give Mankind the title in a big surprise at 13:35.

Rating: C. This took time to get going but the ending with the second referee coming in had the fans going crazy. It's a good match and pretty easily the best thing tonight, but after we've had all the garbage so far tonight, that's not a major accomplishment. These two would keep fighting for months and this was just the beginning. Also notice something: Austin and Rock both won the title and were paired with Mick Foley for their first major feud. The same thing would be done in 2000 for HHH's first major title feud. Foley wasn't the best, but he could make anyone look as great as they ever could have.

Post match Vince says not so fast though, because he never heard Rock give up. Therefore, Mankind wins but since there was never an actual submission, Rock keeps the title. Mankind destroys everyone in sight until Boss Man and Shamrock come out to beat him down.

We recap Austin vs. Undertaker, because as usual, the person the show is named after doesn't main event the PPV. Anyway, Undertaker is mad at Austin because of the refereeing job at Judgment Day (recycling the storyline from the previous year) so he's tried to kill Austin several times now. He's promised to use his Ministry to destroy Austin and even crucified him on Raw. This was the beginning of Undertaker's demonic phase which would get WAY more intense. Tonight it's Buried Alive for a spot in the Royal Rumble.

Steve Austin vs. Undertaker

Bearer is with Undertaker. Austin charges at Undertaker to start and the fight begins in the aisle. Undertaker is choked over to the grave and sent into the barricade before kicking the lifted barricade into Austin's face. They fight around the dirt mound and over near the crowd before going inside the ring for the first time. The Thesz press takes Undertaker down and Austin drops the middle finger elbow on his face.

Undertaker's leg is wrapped around the post and Austin sends him into the steps, only to have Undertaker send him over the Spanish announcers' table. Back inside and Austin's arm is wrapped around the post before they fight up to the barricade. They head to the grave site with Steve ramming him with a piece of the barricade. Undertaker is sent into the grave but he comes back with a wreath shot to the face to knock Austin in as well.

Austin is choked against the dirt while still in the grave and they slug it out inside the hole. It's Austin out first but Undertaker puts him down again as they head to the other side of the arena.

That doesn't get them anywhere so they head back to the ring with Austin in control. Undertaker rams him into the barricade and grabs a chair to put Austin down again. After Steve is thrown into various other objects we head back inside and Austin kicks away, only to be chokeslammed down.

They head back up to the grave site with Austin being knocked into the grave for our first near ending. Undertaker starts to bury him but Austin gets out and sneaks behind him. Austin finds a gasoline can and whacks Undertaker in the face twice before a Stunner puts him in the grave. A wheelbarrow full of dirt mostly covers Undertaker but Austin goes after Bearer. He signals to start something but Undertaker gets out of the grave and grabs a shovel.

Undertaker hides while Austin comes back...but the grave explodes and Kane climbs out to beat on his brother. Austin is nowhere to be seen as Kane Tombstones Undertaker on the dirt. He rolls Undertaker into the grave as Austin drives a backhoe full of dirt into the arena. The dirt is dropped on Undertaker (after a LONG time) and Austin adds a few shovels full to finish the job at 21:33.

Rating: D. Long and pretty bad here with the ending taking way too long to get through. These matches are only as good as the brawling before the ending and that part here was only somewhat good. Kane popping out of the grave came off as stupid and the backhoe took WAY too long to drop the dirt.

Austin drinks a beer on the grave to end the show.

Overall Rating: F+. I know no one was going to watch this show, but that doesn't mean they need to completely waste our three hours like this. This show was terrible with nothing being advanced other than Austin getting a spot in the Rumble. Seriously, what else happened here? A bunch of worthless midcard matches, no title changes, and a screwy finish to the WWF Title shot. Horrible show here.

After that sluggish entry, things really started to crank up in the WWF. A few weeks later, Mankind still wanted a rematch with the Rock and went as far as kidnapping Shane McMahon to get one. On the Monday Night Raw airing on January 4, 1999, Mankind had gotten Shane away from everyone else and had him stretched out on the mat, threatening to injure him if he wasn't granted a title shot that night. Vince had no choice and the match was made.

That night, in one of the greatest feel good moments of all time, Mankind (with an assist from Steve Austin) beat the Rock to become the WWF WWF Champion for the first time ever. The ovation was through the roof and was later listed as the greatest crowd reaction in WWE history. Mankind was officially a main event star now and the fans loved him as a result.

However his title reign was short lived, as he lost the title to The Rock in an I Quit match at the Royal Rumble. The match was not without controversy though as the Rock had bashed Mankind's skull in so many times with a chair that Mankind was knocked out cold. Somehow Mankind still said he quit anyway, despite not moving at all. The next night on Raw, Mankind produced a tape of him on Sunday Night Heat before the pay per view saying the words I quit and the audio was clearly the same as his submission in the match. Something was afoot and the solution was another rematch.

The next match in the series took place on a special show called Halftime Heat which aired during halftime of the Super Bowl. The match was an Empty Arena match which is exactly what it sounds like. Mankind was able to put a forklift down on top of Rock's chest for the pin and the title, making him a two time champion. Rock of course wanted a rematch and would receive it on Valentine's Day in a Last Man Standing match.

The other major match at the Royal Rumble was of course the Royal Rumble itself, which saw Steve Austin enter first and Vince McMahon himself entering second. Austin of course destroyed Vince to start and chased him out of the ring (with neither being eliminated) and into the concourse. Once there, the Corporation attacked Austin and sent him to the hospital.

Vince, still in the match, came out to do commentary to brag about getting rid of Austin until an ambulance came back to the arena with Austin at the whee. Austin came back to the ring and cleaned house, until it was just Vince and Austin left. The Rock came out for a distraction though, allowing Vince to eliminate Austin and win the Royal Rumble, sending him to Wrestlemania.

Not being a wrestler, Vince said he was forfeiting his title shot, meaning Rock wouldn't have a title defense at Wrestlemania. This brought out the now good commissioner Shawn Michaels who said if the winner of the Rumble forfeited the title shot, the last person eliminated out of the Rumble would get the shot instead, meaning Austin was going to Wrestlemania after all. Austin used this as leverage to get what he really wanted: a match with Vince one on one. He offered to risk his title shot in exchange for a match with Vince at In Your House #27 inside of a steel cage, which the crazy McMahon accepted.

St. Valentine's Day Massacre: In Your House #27
Date: February 14, 1999
Location: The Pyramid, Memphis, Tennessee
Attendance: 19,028
Commentators: Michael Cole, Jerry Lawler

This is a bit different from the usual last stops before Wrestlemania as things are still up in the air. The WWF Title match at Wrestlemania was likely to be Rock vs. Austin, but at this point there was still a shadow of a doubt that it could be something else. That's one of the things that made this era so exciting for wrestling fans and it's holding up pretty well upon repeat viewings. Let's get to it.

The opening is set up like a movie from the early days of film, all in sepia with a perky song talking about driving someone crazy. The video itself covers Austin tormenting Vince into insanity and various other crazy people in the company around this time.

Goldust vs. Bluedust

This is another strange idea where comedy wrestler the Blue Meanie is trying to out-weird Goldust by imitating him while wearing all blue instead of gold. They've also been stealing Al Snow's Head from each other to keep things moving. Goldust jumps him to start and nearly knocks him out of the blue bathrobe. An uppercut to the jaw drops Bluedust and the robe comes off.

Bluedust tries to walk out but gets thrown back in without getting too far. He kicks away at Goldust's knee to take over and gyrates his overly large hips a bit. Goldust comes back by pulling up Bluedust's shorts and spanking him into the corner for

Shattered Dreams, only to charge into a boot to the jaw. Bluedust misses the moonsault and the Curtain Call is enough for the pin at 3:04.

Rating: D-. This was a comedy match minus the comedy but at least it was short. The problem here was the joke didn't quite work because there's nothing particularly funny about the Blue Meanie being a blue version of Goldust. That's one of the recurring problems in WWE history: comedy a lot of the time consists of "this exists, therefore it's funny." It doesn't quite work that way though.

Post match Goldust hits Shattered Dreams.

Earlier tonight on Heat, Austin was about to go after Vince but Commissioner Shawn Michaels made the save, allowing Vince to spit in Austin's face.

Hardcore Title: Al Snow vs. Bob Holly

The title is vacant coming in due to the champion Road Dogg being injured. The brawl is on to start with Snow scoring with a quick chair shot. They head into the crowd with Snow in control until he gets slammed down onto some steps. Holly blasts him in the face with a fire extinguisher and breaks a glass jaw over Snow's head, only to be sprayed down by the fire extinguisher as well.

They head backstage with both guys being thrown into doors until Snow pelts a trashcan at Holly. Bob comes back with a beer case and they fight outside where it's 40 degrees at most. Holly is rammed head first into the side of a truck and they head over to the fire lane with Holly breaking a no parking sign over Al's back. Snow seems to be laughing as Holly gets two. They head over to a wall and then a fence with Snow shouting at Holly for turning on him by leaving the J.O.B. Squad.

A stop sign to Snow's back knocks him onto the banks of the Mississippi River but Al knocks him into a wheelbarrow. They fight over to some trees and closer to the water with Holly hitting him in the head with something made of metal. Snow comes back with some kicks and choking on the dirt before Holly is thrown into the water to fire up the fans in the arena. Holly comes back by sending Snow into a tree before Snow comes

249

back with shots to the kidneys. They slug it out even more with Holly wrapping him up in some chain link fence for the pin and the title at 9:54.

Rating: D+. This is one where you individual taste may vary widely either way. The match was definitely more of a spectacle than a contest which is fine, but if that's not your thing then you were going to hate this. These two would have more and more of these insane fights which were very hit or miss. It wasn't bad but it was only for certain tastes.

Earlier today Undertaker gathered his Ministry (Faarooq, Bradshaw, Viscera (Mabel) and Mideon (Phineas Godwinn)) around a cauldron of fire to talk about how much evil they're going to unleash.

Mideon vs. Big Boss Man

This is Ministry vs. Corporation which has been going on for a good while now. Mideon has an eye in a jar (don't ask) and leaves it in Lawler and Cole's care during the match. Boss Man pounds away to start and knocks Mideon into the corner for some hard right hands. Mideon is sent to the floor but avoids a chair which hits the post instead.

Boss Man's hand is slammed into the steps but he comes back with a shot to the spine and a reverse chinlock in the ring. Mideon gets choked on the ropes and punched in the jaw as the fans rightly chant boring. A full nelson by Boss Man is countered into a kind of slam for two. Boss Man shrugs off some right hands but gets backdropped down to put both guys on the mat. They slug it out from their knees for a bit before the Boss Man Slam ends Mideon clean at 6:19.

Rating: D-. The only good thing here was how loud Boss Man's punches were. It was a bad contrast of styles which isn't something you want to see. It also doesn't help that neither guy was any good at this point and no one cared to see the C list guys from either group punch and choke each other for six minutes.

Post match the Ministry hits the ring and destroys Boss Man before taking him away.

D'Lo Brown and Mark Henry have found the solution to Debra in their new valet Ivory. If Debra tries to interfere, Ivory will rip Debra's clothes off.

<u>Tag Team Titles: Owen Hart/Jeff Jarrett vs. D'Lo Brown/Mark Henry</u>

Jarrett and Owen are defending, having won the titles from Boss Man and Shamrock back in January. Henry reads a Valentine's Day poem to Ivory and gives her a box of chocolates. Owen and Henry get us going with the power man throwing Hart into the corner and clotheslining him down before it's off to Brown to speed things up. Hart comes back with a bulldog into a facebuster and makes the tag off to Jarrett who walks into a powerslam for two.

Everything breaks down and Debra gets on the apron to do nothing at all. Things settle down with Jarrett grabbing a DDT on Brown's arm before it's back to Owen for a double clothesline to put D'Lo down. A spinebuster from Owen sets up a middle rope fist from Jarrett. Hart hits the enziguri as the match slows down again. A double back elbow from the champions sets up a chinlock by Jeff before Owen kicks Brown's head off to break up a comeback bid.

Brown finally scores with a quick Sky High to put Owen down, finally allowing for the tag off to Henry. Everything breaks down again and Brown catches Jarrett in a sitout spinebuster for a close two. D'Lo goes up for the Low Down but the girls get in a fight for a distraction. Henry gorilla presses Jarrett up but Owen hits him in the knee with a guitar. Jarrett puts on the Figure Four for a quick submission at 9:33.

Rating: D+. This wasn't horrible but the girls did nothing of note. I'm not quite sure how ripping Debra's clothes off was supposed to keep Brown and Henry more focused on the match. Jarrett and Hart were extended placeholders as champions and while they were solid in the ring, they didn't interest anyone for the most part.

Post match Ivory rips Debra's jacket off.

Mankind says Rock is going to have to do more than cheap shot his knee like he did earlier today to take the title from him.

We recap Shamrock vs. Venis for the Intercontinental Title. Val started a fling with Shamrock's sister and featured her in one of his movies. Ken's sister Ryan said she loved Val, sending Ken even further over the top. Billy Gunn offered to be guest referee because the referees refused to work with Shamrock and Billy can't stand either guy. Billy also recently exposed himself to Ryan just because he could. She didn't seem to complain.

Intercontinental Title: Ken Shamrock vs. Val Venis

Ken is defending. Lawler almost loses his mind over seeing Ryan in a short, strapless white dress. For the sake of clarity, I'll only refer to Ken as Shamrock here. Ken charges into the ring and the fight is on immediately. It's Val in early control though with some right hands and a clothesline to the back of the head to put Shamrock down. Shamrock sends him into the corner to take over and whips him across the ring into the other corner.

Ken pounds on Val on the mat and gets glared at by Billy to give Venis a breather. Back in and Val gets a quick suplex for two before firing off knees to the chest. A butterfly suplex puts Shamrock down again and Val bends him over his knee to work on the back. They head outside again where Val works on the back again before taking it inside for a camel clutch. Ken comes back with some right hands but gets caught in a double chickenwing rollup for two.

We hit the chinlock on the champion for a bit before Val hits a knee to the ribs for a VERY delayed two count. Shamrock grabs a DDT for a slightly faster two but Billy just stops before counting three. Val charges into an elbow in the corner and a powerslam gets two but Val kicks out before Billy can stop. Venis grabs a fisherman's suplex and Billy makes very sure to get a good angle before counting.

A Russian legsweep puts Ken down and it's time to grind a bit. Shamrock hits a quick hurricanrana and a belly to belly to set up the ankle lock but Ryan pulls Val's hands to the rope. Ryan slaps Ken in the face and Billy punches him for good measure. Back inside and Val grabs a quick small package for the fastest three count ever for the pin and the title at 15:53.

Rating: C-. This wasn't bad but it was much more about the angle than the match. That would be the case for the Intercontinental Title for months to come and the title would suffer as a result. It also didn't help that the stories never got a proper payoff because of some screwy changes in booking right before Wrestlemania.

Post match Billy comes back in and beats up Val post match.

We recap DX vs. the Corporation tag match. Chyna had turned her back on HHH and cost HHH a WWF Title shot recently and HHH wanted revenge. Kane and X-Pac are involved as well to avoid men on women violence.

HHH/X-Pac vs. Kane/Chyna

HHH is all fired up for this one and he takes off the DX shirt to reveal a Chyna shirt, which he rips to pieces. Shane McMahon comes out to do some commentary. HHH pounds away on Kane to start but is quickly clotheslined down. HHH comes back with a shot to the face and brings in X-Pac for some right hands, only to have Kane easily toss him into the corner to take over.

Chyna comes in with a forearm but misses a charge as this is the first man on woman match in WWF history. Chyna avoids the Bronco Buster and things slow down a bit until it's back to Kane. HHH comes back in with a top rope fist to the face but goes after Chyna instead, allowing Kane to come back with the top rope clothesline for no cover. Chyna gets the tag and escapes a quick suplex attempt to slam HHH down in a nice power display.

Back to X-Pac to crank on the arm and avoid a charge in the corner, setting up a double suplex by DX. Chyna tries to come in off the top but gets launched off the top rope at Kane to keep DX in control. Kane is clotheslined to the floor as everything breaks down. X-Pac dives at Shane before heading back inside to get slammed down by Kane for no cover. Chyna comes back in with a running powerslam before Kane gets the tag and pounds away as well.

HHH is watching a bit too intently, allowing Chyna to blast him in the face before clotheslining X-Pac down for two. Chyna hooks a sleeper hold on X-Pac but gets taken down by a belly to back suplex. A hot tag brings in HHH and everything breaks down again. HHH hits the knee to Chyna's face but Kane pulls him to the floor to prevent a Pedigree attempt. Chyna gets caught in the corner for the Bronco Buster but Shane sneaks in to jump X-Pac. X-Pac chases him to the back and HHH sends Kane into the steps. HHH loads up the Pedigree but Kane comes in with a chokeslam to give Chyna the easy pin at 14:46.

Rating: D+. The match was all built around the story but the question is which story. That was the problem with this whole thing: it was such a mess with all the twists and turns that people stopped caring. Eventually at Wrestlemania, Chyna would turn face again to rejoin HHH but then literally less than an hour later they would both turn heel to join the Corporation. Think that's enough twists and turns?

We recap Rock vs. Mankind, which started at Survivor Series with Mankind getting screwed, then continued at Rock Bottom where Mankind got screwed. Then after he won the title on Raw, Mankind was screwed at the Royal Rumble. Mankind has finally gotten the title with the help of some heavy machinery, so tonight is yet another chapter in their war. It has specifically been stated that there MUST be a winner tonight.

WWF Title: The Rock vs. Mankind

Mankind is defending and this is a Last Man Standing match, meaning there are no pins but the first person to not answer a ten count loses. Also remember Mankind has a bad knee coming in. Mankind turns his back on the Rock to intentionally allow him a cheap shot to start but Rock goes after the bad knee in a smart move. Mankind lets him do it again and Rock blasts him in the back of the head but this time Mankind blasts Rock in the face with the title belt for an eight count.

They fight up to the entrance with Mankind being whipped into a piece of the set. Mankind finds a table near the production arena and DDTs Rock through it for a nine count. Now we head over to some tarped off bleachers for nothing of note before Rock suplexes Mankind onto the exposed concrete. Back to ringside with Rock being whipped into the stairs for a five count before heading back inside. Mankind slams him down and loads up his own version of the People's Elbow but only hits mat.

Back to the floor again for another suplex on the floor, allowing Rock to go over to the announcers' table to offer Mankind a Rock

Burger with some Rock Sauce on the side. The champion dives across the table to take Rock out before laying him on the announcers' table and dropping him to the floor with an elbow from the apron. Mankind rips at Rock's face before throwing both Rock and the steps back inside.

Rock kicks them back into Mankind's face before bringing in a chair to fire away at Mankind's knee. Rock misses a big chair shot by hitting the ropes, knocking it back into his face instead. The Cactus Clothesline puts both guys on the floor again and Mankind drags him back to the announcers' table. He loads up a piledriver through the table but Rock backdrops him off the table and into the timekeeper's table to hurt the leg even worse. Just to further the damage, Rock goes inside and throws the steps over the top rope to land on Mankind again.

Somehow Mankind gets up again so Rock takes him back inside for the People's Elbow. Rock grabs the microphone to talk more trash and sing a little Smackdown Hotel. Mankind apparently doesn't like Elvis tributes and puts on the Mandible Claw but the referee is taken out. Mankind gets him back to the ring and helps start the count but Rock gets up at nine with a low blow.

Rock hits a DDT but Mankind is up at seven for a double arm DDT onto the chair for nine. The Mandible Claw is broken up by a knee to the ribs and the Rock Bottom puts both guys down. Both guys slowly get up and hit each other with chairs, knocking them both out for ten and a draw at 22:05. Remember that line about there must be a winner? Neither do I.

Rating: B-. Definitely the best match of the night so far but it's still not all that great. Mankind had definitely earned the right to leave a pay per view as champion so this was a nice treat for him. The ending doesn't work though as such an emphasis had been put on the match needing a winner.

Post match the fans are MAD as both guys are being taken out on a stretcher.

We recap Austin vs. McMahon. If you don't know the story by this point, you're not going to get it now. Basically Vince has spent about ten months tormenting Austin due to Austin rebelling against authority and has now cost him the WWF Title twice. Vince won the Royal Rumble but Austin was awarded the title shot, so he's putting it on the line tonight to get his hands on Vince inside a steel cage.

The cage is assembled as the announcers talk about the main event.

Vince McMahon vs. Steve Austin

This had to headline a pay per view at some point. Inside a cage with pinfall, submission or escape to win. Austin gets in the cage first so Vince makes him wait a bit longer. Steve gets tired of waiting and chases Vince around the cage but the boss gets inside to hide. The bell hasn't rung yet. Austin tries to climb up the cage but Vince punches from his high ground. Steve slips off the side of the cage and seems to have twisted his knee. Like an idiot, Vince comes out to check on it and gets clotheslined by a healthy Austin.

McMahon is sent into the side of the cage and choked with a cord. They fight into the crowd with Austin in complete control. Austin hits him in the head with the bell, making it ring the hard way. The match still hasn't actually started yet. Back to ringside with Vince being sent into the steps and running into the crowd to try to get away. The beating continues until Austin knocks Vince back to ringside. Vince tries to climb into the cage where there's less to cause him pain.

Austin won't let that happen though and rams Vince face first into the cage over and over. Vince tries to climb again but this time Austin follows him up and slams Vince's head into the top of the cage, sending him flying off the cage and onto the Spanish announcers' table. McMahon's head bounces off a monitor, knocking him out cold for a bit in a scary landing. Everything stops as Vince is taken away by medics and Austin chills in the cage.

The Fink is about to announce Austin as the winner but Austin isn't cool with that. He guaranteed to take Vince apart tonight, and since the bell never rang that's not good enough for him. Austin asks the doctor if Vince is still breathing, because if he is the fight isn't done yet. Vince is pulled off the stretcher and hit in the back with a backboard before finally being thrown into the cage for the opening bell.

Austin hits a quick clothesline and a middle rope elbow before going to leave, but Vince makes the eternal mistake of flipping Austin off. Steve climbs back inside and stomps a mudhole in the corner. Somehow Vince fights out with a low blow to get himself a breather before climbing up the cage. Austin pulls Vince down off the cage and leaves him in a heap. The boss is busted open and Lawler is losing his mind.

Steve can't help but smile and climb the cage but Vince looks up at him and flips him off AGAIN, bringing Austin back to the ring. Austin stomps on him even more, leaving Vince crumpled down in the corner. There's the Stunner but as Austin talks trash, a monster called Paul Wight breaks through the ring and throws Austin into the cage before helping Vince to his feet. Wight throws Austin against the cage but the wall breaks, allowing Austin to drop down for the win at 7:56.

Rating: C. This is a hard one to grade because it was again a story rather than a match. The ending was very smart though as Wight got to debut but also look strong with Austin winning due to Wight's strength. Austin got to give Vince the beating he needed to and win a the same time, but Vince gets to continue the feud with his new monster. In case you didn't recognize the name, Wight would soon be called The Big Show Paul Wight.

Vince is furious to end the show.

Overall Rating: D. This is a horribly bad show and a good example of what happens when the stories take the place of the wrestling. Everything moves so fast paced that it's almost impossible to care about anything. On top of that, nothing really changed here other than Wight debuting and the Intercontinental Title. Mankind is still champion and Austin still has his title shot, but things would change soon enough.

Things changed again the following night with Rock defeating Mankind for the WWF Title in a ladder match with an assist from Wight. This would be the final title change until Wrestlemania where the main event was Austin challenging Rock for the title. Rock wasn't quite ready to face Austin at this level but he was the best option (other than anyone named McMahon) that they had.

Austin won the title back at Wrestlemania to the shock of almost no one. His first title match would be against the Rock at In Your House #28. Other than that, the main story would become the Undertaker and his Ministry, which would continue its feud with the Corporation who was also at war with Austin. Undertaker would become more and more demonic every week and would face Ken Shamrock at the final In Your House.

Backlash: In Your House #28
Date: April 25, 1999
Location: Providence Civic Center, Providence, Rhode Island
Attendance: 10,939
Commentators: Jim Ross, Jerry Lawler

It's the final show and not a lot has changed. We're getting a few Wrestlemania rematches here as Austin is defending against the Rock again while Mankind is facing Big Show in a Boiler Room Brawl. Other than that we have the fully heel HHH facing X-Pac in a match for revenge. For once, the name of the show fits the theme perfectly. Let's get to it.

The opening video talks about Austin and Rock being the two biggest stars in the universe but only one can burn brighter than everyone else.

Shane McMahon has made the main event no holds barred and Austin loses the title if he touches the referee. The referee for the main event: Shane McMahon.

Brood vs. Ministry of Darkness

The Brood used to be part of the Ministry but got kicked out after Christian accidentally gave up the location of Stephanie McMahon, Vince's daughter who had been kidnapped by Undertaker. It's Mideon and the Acolytes (Faarooq and Bradshaw) for the Ministry here. Christian and Mideon get things going with Mideon pounding Christian some heavy right hands, only to be taken down by a spinwheel kick to the jaw. Gangrel comes back in to crank on the arm until Mideon tags in Bradshaw.

The big man kicks Gangrel's head off but charges into a boot in the corner, allowing Gangrel to hit a middle rope elbow to the jaw. The Brood starts double teaming to take Bradshaw down with Gangrel and Edge double suplexing him down. Bradshaw stumbles over to the corner for a tag to Faarooq who is dropkicked into a crucifix for two. Edge spinwheel kicks Faarooq down for no cover before walking into a spinebuster to change the momentum.

Back to Mideon who gets two off a suplex before Bradshaw comes in to pound away. Gangrel tries to come in for a save but Bradshaw goes after the entire Brood, allowing Faarooq to pound away on Gangrel behind the referee's back. Faarooq hooks the chinlock for a bit before it's back to Faarooq for a headbutt to the ribs. Edge fights back on the legal Mideon before hitting a middle rope spear, allowing for the hot tag off to Christian for the house cleaning.

Things speed up quite a bit with Christian and Gangrel backdropping Mideon as everything breaks down. Christian's Impaler DDT gets two on Bradshaw and he pounds away in the corner, only to have the tar powerbombed out of him for two. Edge's missile dropkick puts Bradshaw down for two but Viscera sneaks in to crush Christian, setting up Bradshaw's big clothesline for the pin at 11:38.

Rating: C. This was fine though cutting out a minute or so would have helped it. The Brood would get a lot better once they dropped Gangrel and became a goofy tag team, which wound up being the solution the entire time. This was a fun match though and the ending worked well. Take out the Viscera interference and the match is even better.

Rock arrives.

We recap Hardcore (Bob) Holly vs. Al Snow. There isn't much to say here as they're pretty much just picking up their feud from the last In Your House and ignoring Billy Gunn as Hardcore Champion in between.

Hardcore Title: Al Snow vs. Hardcore Holly

Holly is defending. They're on the floor almost immediately with Snow being sent into the steps. That's close enough to actual wrestling so they head into the crowd for the real meat of the match. Back to ringside with Snow getting two off a moonsault from the apron. Snow finds a hockey stick under the ring and breaks it apart to blast Holly in the back. Snow got busted open somewhere in there.

Holly gets beaten on with the stick for a few moments until Snow brings in a table. He takes too long setting it up though and Holly gets in a shot with the hockey stick. They head to the aisle where Holly gets two off a suplex. The fight goes into the back with Snow being rammed into various metal objects. Holly finds a well placed kitchen sink which is destroyed against a wall instead of Snow's head.

They go out to the parking lot with Holly setting off a car alarm when he's rammed into a hood. Snow finds a broom to break over Holly's back and walks him over to some steps back into the arena. Holly throws him over the ledge into a dumpster and follows in with a splash for two. They head back to more cars before fighting into the production truck with Snow throwing him out the door and onto the top of a car for two.

Snow accidentally kicks the window so Holly can punch him back into the arena. Holly whips him into a metal sheet and they head back into the arena where Snow hits him with a frying pan for tow. Hardcore avoids going through the table with a frying pan shot of his own before superplexing Snow through the table. The referee counts to nine until Holly drapes an arm over Snow for two. Snow crawls over to the corner and grabs Head so he can knock Holly unconscious for the pin and the title at 15:27.

Rating: D+. Lawler sums up the match as soon as it's over: "After all that, the Head did it?" That's the problem with something like this. After all the carnage and weapon shots, including frying pans and that great table spot, it was a mannequin head that got the pin? That's a bit of a stretch to put it mildly. Also way too long here as this was nearly sixteen minutes.

Austin has arrived.

Undertaker praises the Ministry for winning but says they have to prepare for the arrival of the greater power. The destruction and tragedy may now begin.

Intercontinental Title: Godfather vs. Goldust

No real story here and Godfather is defending. Goldust has Blue Meanie while Godfather has his ladies. Godfather won't even offer Goldust the girls as he usually does. The champion takes over with some clotheslines to start and faceplants Goldust down onto the mat. Goldust bails to the floor for a meeting with Meanie and tries to bail up the aisle.

Back in and Godfather gets two off a slam and a legdrop but Meanie's distraction lets Goldust take over. Another Meanie distraction lets Goldust load up some powder to throw in Godfather's eyes but Godfather kicks it into Goldust's eyes. The blinded Goldust beats up Meanie and gives him Shattered Dreams by mistake. Meanie accidentally hits Goldust low, allowing Godfather to hit the Death Valley Driver to retain at 5:12.

Rating: D+. This was just a quick comedy match and there's nothing wrong with that. Godfather was a very fun and laid back character which is exactly what a wrestling company needs at times. There's no pressure, no emotional burden and nothing you have to focus on. It's just having a good time with a wrestling character and giving the fans a breather.

Snow and Head argue over who won the title match.

New Age Outlaws vs. Jeff Jarrett/Owen Hart

The winners get a title shot against Kane and X-Pac at some point in the future. Debra is in a bikini with a jacket over it, sending Lawler through the roof. Road Dogg tries to convince Debra to show us her, ahem, puppies, but Jeff objects. Billy tries to drop his trunks but gets jumped to start the match instead. Owen and Billy get things going with Hart in control until Gunn comes back with a running dropkick to take over.

It's off to Dogg to work on the arm before putting on a headlock, only to be taken down by a neckbreaker. The fans start a SHOW

YOUR PUPPIES chant as the Dogg pounds away on Jeff's jaw but Owen tries to sneak in. Road Dogg is too smart for that and sends Jeff and Owen into each other, only to have Owen come back with a quick enziguri for two. Jeff stomps on Dogg in the corner as the chant starts up again. An atomic drop has Jeff in trouble but he sends Dogg to the floor to take over.

Jarrett misses a charge and hits the ropes by mistake but brings in Owen before Dogg can follow up. Dogg's backslide isn't seen as Jarrett has the referee, allowing Owen to spinwheel kick Dogg down for two. Back to Jarrett who collides with Road Dogg to put both guys down but Owen gets in again before Dogg can make a tag. Hart puts on a sleeper but gets reversed into one of his own until another collision puts both guys down.

Billy finally gets the hot tag to clean house and scores with dropkicks on both heels. A powerslam gets two on Jarrett as everything breaks down. Gunn Cactus Clotheslines Jarrett to the floor but Dogg hits on Debra instead of following up. Owen tries a cheap shot but gets caught in a pumphandle slam for two. Jeff makes the save and Owen gets the Sharpshooter on Dogg, only to have Gunn hit a Fameasser out of nowhere for the pin at 10:27.

Rating: C+. This is one of the best in ring performances by the Outlaws I've ever seen. They were working quite well together out there and the match had a nice flow to it. Dogg and Gunn never were a great in ring pairing but it's almost impossible to have a bad match with Jarrett and Hart. Nice stuff here.

Shane doesn't guarantee things like his dad but gives his word on his grandfather's grave that he'll count the pin for Austin tonight if Austin can get it. Shane insists that Vince is just a man and not his father.

Vince, sitting next to his daughter Stephanie, says he doesn't care for what Shane said and doesn't like Shane using his grandfather's name to swear by.

Big Show vs. Mankind

These two fought at Wrestlemania for the right to be the referee in the main event and Big Show also cost Mankind the WWF Title back in February. This is a Boiler Room Brawl and the only way to win is to escape the room. Mankind jumps him from behind to start and slams Big Show into an electrical closet. Big Show fights out and sends Mankind over a table before hitting him with the table itself. Mankind avoids a punch that hits a refrigerator instead before hitting Big Show with some Sheetrock.

Big Show kicks a trashcan into Mankind's face before wheeling him into a big metal folding board. The board falls onto Mankind and Big Show goes for the door but Mankind breaks a plane of glass over his head. Mankind climbs a ladder but gets shoved down through a table in a big crash.

Big Show is badly cut from the glass but he sends Mankind through a bunch of boxes. Mankind's hand is cut open as well. Big Show pounds on him a bit more but gets blasted by some steam from a pipe. Some stick shots put Big Show down and Mankind crawls away, leaving bloody hand prints along the way until he gets through the door for the win at 7:50.

Rating: C-. This is a hard one to rate because it was just a bunch of brawling but the blood helped a lot. Mankind did what he could in there but it wasn't nearly as intense as the original version with Undertaker. Still good brawling though with Mankind getting a big win and some revenge back.

Post match Big Boss Man and Test try to attack Mankind but Big Show makes the save.

Chyna says X-Pac needs to know the pecking order around here. HHH says he made X-Pac and tonight he's going to break him.

Big Show gets medical treatment.

Mankind says he doesn't want to fight Big Show anymore and looks at the carnage from the fight.

HHH vs. X-Pac

This is all about revenge after HHH turned heel to join the Corporation at Wrestlemania, costing X-Pac his European Title match with Shane McMahon at the same time. HHH has a new rock song as his theme music here which didn't last long. He gets in a cheap shot to start but X-Pac takes him down with right hands and chops. A kick to the face puts HHH down again and they fight to the floor with the fans all over X-Pac, who is the good guy here.

Back in and HHH sends X-Pac flying over the top to the floor but a Chyna distraction accidentally lets X-Pac get in a shot to HHH's ribs. X-Pac scores with some kicks in the corner but can't hit the Bronco Buster. Things slow down a bit until HHH realizes X-Pac's chronically bad neck is hurting again. HHH goes on a stomping spree before getting two off a neckbreaker. We hit a front facelock for a few moments before HHH drops some knees on X-Pac's neck for two.

HHH hooks a dragon sleeper to stay on the neck before a reverse DDT and the facebuster get two. X-Pac rolls to the floor and gets dropped face first onto the barricade by Chyna. Some elbows to the neck keep HHH in control before it's back to the front facelock. Now it's a sleeper hold to keep the match at a slow pace until X-Pac fights up and grabs a sleeper of his own. HHH rams him into the buckle to escape but X-Pac comes back with a belly to back suplex. A pair of spinwheel kicks put HHH down but X-Pac can't follow up on a flipping clothesline.

X-Pac pulls off a tornado DDT for a near fall as Chyna gets up on the apron. The distraction lets X-Pac get two more off a low blow and they head outside. HHH is whipped into the steps but the referee is bumped. Back inside and the X-Factor puts HHH out but Chyna hits X-Pac low. This brings out Kane to chokeslam both HHH and Chyna and put them both in position for Bronco Busters. X-Pac busts both of them but HHH is able to get up and Pedigree him for the pin at 19:19.

Rating: B. Solid match here with a nice story throughout the whole thing. The interference makes sense and fit the story well but didn't overshadow the match. That's the biggest problem with this era most of the time, which is a shame given the talent the company had at this point. Rather good stuff.

Ken Shamrock vs. Undertaker

Corporation vs. Ministry, but the version people might care about this time. Shamrock jumps him to start but runs into a hard clothesline for two. Old School connects as Undertaker is definitely in slow mode tonight. A big jumping clothesline gets two on Ken but he avoids a running boot in the corner.

264

Shamrock fires off kicks to the hamstring but Undertaker grabs a choke in the corner followed by a belly to back suplex to take over. Shamrock comes right back with a knee bar as the match slows down again.

Undertaker fights out with some legs to the face and gets back up. Shamrock grabs another rolling leglock, though this time on a different leg. Undertaker makes the rope for the break so they head outside with Shamrock pounding away at the head. He crushes Undertaker's ankle against the steps before taking it back inside to pound away on Undertaker's head. They trade drop toeholds until Shamrock takes him down by the arm.

Another rope break saves Undertaker and he bails to the floor where he's able to snap Shamrock's throat across the top rope for another break. Ken dives off the apron but gets rammed into the post for his efforts as Undertaker is taking over again. Back in and Undertaker pounds on Shamrock's back with forearms followed by a backbreaker. Shamrock's back is bent over Undertaker's knee for a bit, good for a two count.

It's off to a bow and arrow hold by Undertaker but Shamrock makes the ropes as well. Shamrock grabs another knee bar but Undertake uses the free leg to kick Ken in the face and grab a half crab. Back up and Ken slugs away but runs into a forearm to the face for two. Shamrock comes back with some shots to the jaw of his own but runs into a big boot for two more.

Ken hooks his standing hurricanrana but the ankle lock is quickly escaped. Undertaker can't hit the Tombstone and gets caught in the ankle lock. This brings out Bradshaw with a ball bat for a distraction but Ken still counters a chokeslam into an armbar. Ropes are quickly grabbed again so Shamrock belly to bellies Undertaker down, only to stand him up again and get Tombstoned to give Undertaker the pin at 18:53.

Rating: D. This was WAY too long and got dull with about ten minutes to go. Shamrock wasn't terrible but at this point undertaker was almost all character and nothing whatsoever in the ring. He needed someone to help him to a good match and this version of the Undertaker certainly wasn't it.

Post match Bradshaw comes in to destroy Shamrock just a bit more, including choking him out with the ball bat.

We recap the main event and again there isn't much to this one. Austin won the title at Wrestlemania but then decided he needed a new championship belt. He introduced the Smoking Skull belt which was personalized for him, but Rock stole it and threw it (and Austin) into a river, only to reveal he still had it the next week. Austin retaliated by destroying the Titantron and running over Rock's Lincoln Continental with a monster truck.

Vince has Stephanie wait in the limo until after the match.

WWF Title: The Rock vs. Steve Austin

Austin is defending and this is no holds barred with Shane McMahon as referee and Austin loses the title if he touches Shane. Rock, still in possession of the Smoking Skull belt, gets a big pop of his own but of course it pales in comparison to Austin's. Austin pounds away in the corner to start as the fans are immediately into this. Rock comes back with right hands of his own as the Smoking Skull belt is taken to the back. Austin hits the Thesz press and the middle finger elbow for one.

The champion gets sent to the floor and clotheslined down before they head up to the entrance. Austin tries a comeback but gets whipped through a fence, knocking part of the set over in the process. Rock's suplex is countered into one of his own to give Austin the advantage again. Now it's Rock being sent into the pile of the set and clotheslined down on top of it. Rock is whipped through a barricade and gets rammed in the head by a rolling anvil case for good measure.

Rock comes back by sending Austin into a camera and clotheslining him down. We shift momentum again with Austin slamming rock down on the concrete and whipping him into the steps back at ringside. Back inside and Austin stomps away in the corner, only to be reprimanded by Shane. The distraction lets Rock charge at Austin, who backdrops him to the floor in a big crash. Austin loads up a piledriver through the Spanish announcers' table but gets countered into a Rock Bottom.

Both guys are down with Shane telling Rock how excellent that was. Rock gets on Spanish commentary and calls Austin trash (in English) as Shane throws him a chair. Austin kicks him in the ribs to block the shot and they head back into the crowd for another clothesline to the champion. A low blow keeps Austin in trouble and Rock lays him across the announcers' table before taking over a camera for more comedy. Rock looks out at the crowd but pans back to Austin flipping him off and hitting a Stunner through the announcers' table. Nice idea there.

Both guys are down at ringside as we get a replay of the Stunner, this time entirely from Rock's perspective. Back inside and Austin tries another Stunner but Rock shoves him into Shane. There's the Rock Bottom for a close two after Shane put Rock's hand on Austin's chest. Shane grabs the belt (the regular one, not the Smoking Skull) but accidentally hits Rock. Austin covers for two but Shane flips Austin off at two. Shane starts bailing up the aisle but here are Vince and another referee. Vince knocks Shane out with the Smoking Skull belt and Austin hits a Stunner and belt shot to Rock's head to retain the title.

Rating: B+. This was a solid Attitude Era style brawl and the match that should have happened at Wrestlemania. The ending is more shades of gray than I prefer with Vince helping his mortal enemy to take out his new enemy. That's just not something Vince would do, especially with what's coming in the near future.

We cut to the parking lot with Stephanie in the limo. The Ministry comes towards her so security says go but the privacy screen drops and it's Undertaker driving. Vince is in the arena watching Austin drink to end the show.

Overall Rating: B-. This is a show where the stuff that's good is quite good but the stuff that's bad is quite bad. In other words, it's a perfect representation of the series as a whole. The Austin vs. Rock match was great but it would be left in the dust by what they would do a few years later. Still though, it's a very solid match and the rest of the card isn't terrible save for the Undertaker match. Good show overall but it's not a masterpiece.

Things would get even more insane soon enough, with the Shane-led Corporation joining with the Ministry just four days later to feud with the new Super Best Guys Who Tolerate Each Other But Aren't Friends Austin and Rock. Vince would be revealed as behind the entire Ministry in a grand plan to take the title off of Austin which he eventually would do again in May. That brought about even more insanity but we'll get to that another time.

Home Away From The Big Shows

That's a wrap for In Your House. To say the series evolved over the years is a huge understatement. The early shows range anywhere from tolerable to downright horrid with some of the worst matches and wastes of time I can ever remember sitting through. That being said, when the shows got good they got REALLY good with a string of masterpieces running throughout the series.

While the main pay per views from WWF had the most important action, it was the In Your House shows that allowed for a lot of the backbone of the company's storytelling. You had so many great moments with Bret Hart and Undertaker and Shawn Michaels and ultimately Steve Austin on here that the era as a whole wouldn't have worked without In Your House.

What you have to remember here is that the shows weren't originally meant to replace the major pay per views but rather to supplement them. There was no reason to believe that the short form versions of In Your House were anything more than than somewhere in between the major pay per views and Monday Night Raw. Most of the matches were just there because something needed to be on the card along with a big main event. That didn't make for the most important shows, but things would get better over time.

The shows finally started to feel like something that mattered once they expanded to the normal three hour time slot, things got a lot better, though it did take some time to change things up. Those early three hour shows are a little rough, but once the rather good 1997 storytelling took over, the shows took off and became just another pay per view entry on the calendar.

The series was at first an interesting idea as a gift to the fans with the reduced prices, which made the shows more accessible to the masses. Eventually they had to become regular shows to keep up the pace but at least they gave bigger and more important main events to make up for the changes. The latter ones are better overall, but the company was in a much better place by then.

Of all the entries, Canadian Stampede is by far the strongest. It has nothing bad on the entire card, some unexpected gems and the blowoff to one of the best done angles in company history. There's nothing wrong with it at all and the

268

show is required viewing for any wrestling fan, even for the main event entrances alone. The idea that a show that good was only $20 is mind blowing.

On the other end the worst show almost has to be Great White North which featured a best match that was ok at best. That was one of the worst times ever for the WWF and the product backs that up. It's closely followed by Rock Bottom, which was from a much better time in the company from a financial standpoint but a much weaker one from an in ring perspective. Both shows are absolutely dreadful and have almost no redeeming value.

You could go back and forth on who the best performer in the series was, though Mick Foley has to be a candidate. He had some excellent matches over the show's history, with his matches at Mind Games, Revenge of the Taker, Canadian Stampede and Over the Edge all ranging from gem to classics. At the same time you have the usual suspects like Steve Austin, Shawn Michaels and Bret Hart, who could be the best performers on any other given series of shows due to pure talent alone.

In Your House was a very interesting idea and something that could be brought back again in the future. With pay per views now far higher in price, dropping a show down $15-$20 could bring a lot more fans into the fold. That being said, the lesson to be learned from some of these shows, Great White North in particular, is that if the product is bad, not only will no one care, but more importantly not many people are going to pay. The series is good but the quality varies severely due to how strong the company was or wasn't as a whole. Still though, it's worth checking out if you haven't given it a look before.

Let's Talk About Me

Thomas Hall was born in 1988 and has been watching wrestling ever since. He's seen over 50,000 wrestling matches and odds are he's watching wrestling as you're reading this. His parents Brenda and Tony aren't sure what to make of him and often wonder where they went wrong. Thomas lives in Lexington, Kentucky with his wife Becca, who is not only way out of his league but far more patient than the average beautiful wife.

You can see his material and reviews at his website: kbwrestlingreviews.com

Made in the USA
San Bernardino, CA
01 June 2019